Long-Billed
Curlew

illet

Hudsonian
Curlew

Oyster-
catcher

Upland
Plover

rnstone
Killdeer

Wilson's
Plover

Black-Bellied
Plover

Northern
Phalarope

Ringed
Plover

MERICAN SHORE BIRDS

A Gathering of

by Henry Marion Hall

The Devin-Adair Company   New York

Shore Birds

edited and with additions by Roland C. Clement
Illustrated by John Henry Dick

ACKNOWLEDGMENTS

Avocet Chick

To Arthur Cleveland Bent's two classic volumes on the *Life Histories of North American Shore Birds,* all those who write on these birds in America owe an obvious debt. And the long list of references cited is only a small part of the literature from which we drew orientation and ideas, if not actual quotations; to all those writers of short notes and technical articles in ornithological journals, we therefore express appreciation. To a handful of other compilers, also, we owe particular thanks for shortening our own task. Among these are Richard H. Pough for his *Audubon Bird Guides,* Roger Tory Peterson and his *Field Guides,* Van Tyne and Berger's recent text, *Fundamentals of Ornithology,* Hellmayr and Conover's *Catalogue of Birds of the Americas,* and Goodall, Johnson, and Philippi's *Las Aves de Chile.*

To Dr. Ralph S. Palmer, editor of the forthcoming *Handbook of North American Birds* to be published under the auspices of the American Ornithologists' Union and the New York State Museum and Science Service, the editor owes a special debt for assistance with the literature.

The editor, also, is particularly appreciative of the patience and helpfulness of the Misses Amy Clampitt and R. Michel, librarians of the National Audubon Society.

Some of the material in this book has previously appeared in *Audubon Magazine.* Author, editor and publisher are grateful for permission to reproduce it here.

H. M. H., R. C. C.

CONTENTS

Publisher's Preface **xi**

An Introduction to the Shore Birds, *by Roland C. Clement* **1**

The Shore Bird Families 17

The North American Shore Birds:

Jacanas
 1 JACANA *Jacana spinosa* 24

Oystercatchers
 2 AMERICAN OYSTERCATCHER *Haematopus palliatus* 28
 3 BLACK OYSTERCATCHER *Haematopus bachmani* 32

Plovers
 4 RINGED PLOVER *Charadrius hiaticula* 38
 5 SEMIPALMATED PLOVER *Charadrius semipalmatus* 39
 6 PIPING PLOVER *Charadrius melodus* 42
 7 SNOWY PLOVER *Charadrius alexandrinus* 46
 8 MONGOLIAN PLOVER *Charadrius mongolus* 49
 9 WILSON'S PLOVER *Charadrius wilsonia* 50
 10 KILLDEER *Charadrius vociferus* 52
 11 MOUNTAIN PLOVER *Eupoda montana* 56
 12 DOTTEREL *Eudromias morinellus* 59
 13 AMERICAN GOLDEN PLOVER *Pluvialis dominica* 60
 14 BLACK-BELLIED PLOVER *Squatarola squatarola* 66
 15 SURFBIRD (R.C.C.) *Aphriza virgata* 72
 16 RUDDY TURNSTONE *Arenaria interpres* 75
 17 BLACK TURNSTONE *Arenaria melanocephala* 79

Sandpipers
 18 AMERICAN WOODCOCK *Philohela minor* 83
 19 COMMON SNIPE *Capella gallinago* 87

20 LONG-BILLED CURLEW *Numenius americanus* 92

21 WHIMBREL *Numenius phaeopus* 96

22 BRISTLE-THIGHED CURLEW *Numenius tahitiensis* 100

23 ESKIMO CURLEW *Numenius borealis* 103

24 UPLAND PLOVER *Bartramia longicauda* 108

25 SPOTTED SANDPIPER *Actitis macularia* 112

26 SOLITARY SANDPIPER (R.C.C.) *Tringa solitaria* 116

27 WANDERING TATTLER *Heteroscelus incanus* 119

28 WILLET *Catoptrophorus semipalmatus* 122

29 GREATER YELLOWLEGS *Totanus melanoleucus* 126

30 LESSER YELLOWLEGS *Totanus flavipes* 130

31 KNOT *Calidris canutus* 133

32 PURPLE SANDPIPER *Erolia maritima* 136

33 ROCK SANDPIPER *Erolia ptilocnemis* 140

34 PECTORAL SANDPIPER *Erolia melanotos* 143

35 WHITE-RUMPED SANDPIPER (R.C.C.) *Erolia fuscicollis* 147

36 BAIRD'S SANDPIPER (R.C.C.) *Erolia bairdii* 150

37 LEAST SANDPIPER *Erolia minutilla* 154

38 RUFOUS-NECKED SANDPIPER *Erolia ruficollis* 157

39 CURLEW SANDPIPER *Erolia ferruginea* 159

40 DUNLIN *Erolia alpina* 162

41 SHORT-BILLED DOWITCHER *Limnodromus griseus* 166

42 LONG-BILLED DOWITCHER (R.C.C.) *Limnodromus scolopaceus* 170

43 STILT SANDPIPER (R.C.C.) *Micropalama himantopus* 174

44 SEMIPALMATED SANDPIPER *Ereunetes pusillus* 176

45 WESTERN SANDPIPER (R.C.C.) *Ereunetes mauri* 179

46 BUFF-BREASTED SANDPIPER (R.C.C.) *Tryngites subruficollis* 182

47 MARBLED GODWIT *Limosa fedoa* 187

48 BAR-TAILED GODWIT *Limosa lapponica* 189

49 HUDSONIAN GODWIT *Limosa haemastica* 191

50 RUFF *Philomachus pugnax* 195

51 SANDERLING *Crocethia alba* 198

Avocets

52 AMERICAN AVOCET *Recurvirostra americana* 202

53 BLACK-NECKED STILT *Himantopus mexicanus* 205

Phalaropes

54 RED PHALAROPE *Phalaropus fulicarius* 211

55 WILSON'S PHALAROPE *Steganopus tricolor* 215

56 NORTHERN PHALAROPE *Lobipes lobatus* 217

Thick-knees
57 TWO-STRIPED THICK-KNEE *Burhinus bistriatus* 221

THE SOUTH AMERICAN SHORE BIRDS 223

THE WANDERERS 227
 American Shore Birds in Europe 229
 European Shore Birds in America 231
 Siberian Shore Birds in America 233

BIBLIOGRAPHY 235

INDEX 239

PUBLISHER'S PREFACE

To ATTEMPT TO BRIDGE THE GAP between a scientific monograph and a popular presentation of a suborder of birds, is to ask for trouble. Nevertheless, that is what has been tried here in the case of the American shore birds. Not since Bent's "Life Histories" appeared in 1927 and 1929 has a serious study of this spectacular family been attempted and the need for it is generally acknowledged.

Dr. Henry Marion Hall initially got his first-hand information about these birds while he was shooting them in the days of their plenty at the turn of the century. But as he observed their decline in numbers he became an arch conservationist and has since used binoculars instead of a gun. For more than half a century he has studied their flights along our coasts and inland waterways and, fortunately for all of us, has seen them come back from the danger point of near extinction to something like their former numbers. His beautifully written accounts of a number of species have been enjoyed for years by readers of *Audubon Magazine*.

In order to make the book more useful, the services of the editor were enlisted; and because of Mr. Clement's very valuable additions, we are able to present brief accounts of all the fifty-seven species which have been known to occur on the North American continent north of the Panama Canal. This definition of North America we hope is here to stay; stopping at the Mexican border seems old-fashioned and unrealistic at this late date.

In treating the individual species, races have been suppressed and except in rare instances have all been lumped. The ranges given cover the entire species.

Wherever a species is common to both Great Britain and North America and the popular name differs, we have added the British counterpart in parentheses. In some other cases where the A.O.U. committee on nomenclature has recently changed the popular American designation the older name appears also in parentheses. The Spanish names have been taken from C. C. Orlog, *Las Aves Argentinas* (Tucuman, 1959).

The drawings are designed to enhance the text. They are not intended to show field characters or plumage variations, especially those evidenced seasonally by so many species. Although the artist has interpreted the birds in typical attitudes, his effort has been primarily artistic. For plumage variations the colored drawings of Roger Peterson and Don Eckleberry in our two widely-used series of field guides can hardly be improved upon. The drawings which accompany the species write-ups are not to scale because of the great disparity in size within the shore bird family. Mr. Dick has attempted to show these relative sizes in his end-paper drawings. Fortunately, the shore bird family lends itself well to pen-and-ink treatment, color in most species being relatively unimportant. We believe the artist has succeeded in capturing the spirit of each bird remarkably well in his chosen medium.

Author, editor, artist and publisher join in hoping that *A Gathering of Shore Birds* will fulfill its dual purpose of proving useful and providing enjoyment.

DEVIN A. GARRITY

Oystercatchers

CHAPTER 1

AN INTRODUCTION
TO THE
SHORE BIRDS

by ROLAND C. CLEMENT

American Woodcock

"After all, to our human judgment, the outstanding feature of bird life is its marvelous diversity."
—Wm. Leon Dawson.

ABOUT 75 MILES NORTH of the Arctic Circle, near the very center of the continental mainland which faces the Canadian archipelago and the arctic sea, is Queen Maud Gulf. Into it, from the south, flows the Perry River, one of many streams—most of them unnamed— draining a shallow basin which lies along the gulf. The Perry River post of the Hudson's Bay Company is located near the mouth of the river. The latitude is 67°48′ North, the longitude 102°10′ West. It is in the heart of the arctic tundra of North America.

Angus Gavin,[22] * who spent four years as manager of this post, describes the summer thus: "At this season the hills are ablaze with red, yellow, orange, and gray-green lichens and white, yellow, and purple heather. In the valleys are acres of white arctic cotton; but red arctic poppies, purple dryas, and a blue flower like a forget-me-not, make glorious patches of color. Foot-high grass grows abundantly in the marshy

* Note: Postscript numerals refer to the Bibliography at the end of the book.

places of the valleys, and the tundra is green with mosses upon which the caribou feed. The prostrate arctic willow is common on the hills and in the valleys. August is the most colorful month."

The Kogmuit Eskimos who live here call it "The place of the swans." Their own name, indeed, derives from it, for Kogmuit means "people who live at the place of the swans." It is a country of innumerable small and large lakes, marshes, streams, outwash fans, and small islands. Here nest myriads of water birds—loons, swans, geese, ducks, cranes, and shore birds.

In North America the arctic zone includes that part of the Canadian archipelago which is not ice-covered or barren rock, and all the treeless country on the adjacent continental land mass which lies north of the great circumboreal forest of spruce, fir and larch. This is the region we often call the barren grounds, which the Eurasians call tundra, from the Finnish word "tundren" for a treeless rolling plain.

Depending upon available moisture, soil, and other conditions—all of it is cold—the tundra zone may be broad or narrow. On the west it begins near the Yukon delta and includes a strip sometimes 200 miles wide along the Bering Sea, includes the north slope of the Brooks Range, and then nearly pinches out at Aklavik, where the forest pushes down the Mackenzie basin almost to the sea. Timberline then swings eastward and inland almost to Great Slave Lake, cuts southeastward across Keewatin to the Churchill region on Hudson Bay, and ends near Cape Henrietta Maria on James Bay. East of Hudson Bay, the tundra line starts at Richmond Gulf, cuts inland across the base of the Ungava Peninsula, extends but a short distance inland along the edge of Ungava Bay, then cuts inland again along the Torngat plateau of Newfoundland Labrador, and goes down that coast to pinch out in a pseudo-arctic strip near the mouth of Lake Melville below Goose Bay.

As elsewhere on the tundra, summer comes late to the Perry River coast. May is well along before the hills begin to show through the thinning snow, and ice does not leave the rivers until mid-June. Ice persists even longer on the lakes, and sea ice is present off the shore throughout July, sometimes into August. Indeed, ice barely relaxes its grip at all; only the surface of the ground thaws a few inches in summer. Beneath the mud and slush of spring is permafrost, the permanently frozen ground of the arctic; in late summer it may be dry as a desert.

As soon as the snow melts, however, and the dark ground is exposed to the warming sun, vegetation burgeons forth. Then great swarms of

insects—mosquitoes, midges, craneflies, and caddisflies—bestir themselves in the mud of the innumerable shallow pools created by the melting snow on the disrupted drainage pattern which is typical of a region
of frozen subsoil.

And then come the birds. Though they people the tundra in thousands, they make no great show of arrival, as migrants often do farther
south. Instead they spread out quickly to occupy all suitable sites, each
to its own, for the tundra is a great mosaic of differing habitats. Yesterday there were no birds; today they are everywhere, some already paired
and launched on the business of maintaining the race. Chief among
these—for anyone who can see birds smaller than a duck—are the shore
birds, from ten to twenty species of them in favorable areas, half a dozen
of them common species, the others thinly scattered.

These long-legged sprites have a particular charm for a surprising
number of us who count them their favorite bird group. It isn't easy to
account for such preferences, but whether you call them shore birds, or
waders as the British do, there is no mistaking their characteristics.
Graceful of form and movement, wild enough to require some care to
approach (only propinquity reveals the charm of birds), they are the
very embodiment of unfettered freedom, denizens of wide horizons, and
almost all accomplished travelers. And they are difficult enough in their
varied summer and winter dress, their divergent groupings, to pose a
challenge to our powers of discrimination. And, finally, so many of them
connote the arctic, the last physical frontier, that an aura of romance
mantles their long wings.

I recall a wartime incident at Goose Bay, Labrador, which has often
seemed to me analogous to the problem birds face in arriving in the
arctic. A flight of B-17 Flying Fortresses had arrived from the States in a
blinding snow storm, too low on fuel to turn back, buffeted by wind,
their pilots harried by the uncertainty of an unexpected and unfamiliar
situation. They had to be "stacked up" to 18,000 feet, spaced at one
thousand foot intervals of altitude to prevent collisions, and "talked
down," one by one, to make landing runs on a runway lit by rows of
rocket flares. Once down, their crews were fed and rested briefly, the
planes refueled, and off they all went again.

In the arctic almost all birds are "weather migrants," pushing
north as soon as territory is relinquished by winter. The shore birds
arrive on the tundra while snow still covers two-thirds of the ground.
In places, or years, where the season is very late, this forces them to nest

in loose colonies on the only available ground. And even after the eggs are laid, late snowstorms may cover the sitting birds and lead to nest abandonment. The arctic environment is harsh, extremely variable from one year to the next, and a ruthless test of adaptability for living things who would occupy its vast expanses.

But most of us, nurtured in a steam-heated environment, exaggerate the discomforts of life in the open, even in the arctic. To a small bird settled on a nest among the low plants and pebbles of the tundra, wind and cold have little sting. On a sunny day the temperature in the black moss of the tundra may be 40°F. higher than the air temperature three feet above ground. It is such microclimatic contrasts that make life for plant and bird possible in these high latitudes. Generations of selection for survival in the arctic's rigorous situations have produced especially adapted species. The margins of the sea and other habitats occupied by non-arctic species require special adaptations also, and even the prairie, with its summer heat, shares many habitat characteristics with the tundra.

More than half of the shore birds are dwellers of the tundra, whether high or low arctic, or alpine. And, although most of the shore birds visit the seashore in their migrations, only a very few nest in its sandy wastes. The same is true of the prairie, as the following tabulation shows.

The major obstacle to life in the far north is the brevity of the summer season. A few mammals have become almost independent of this seasonal factor, but for most plants, birds, and insects, the answer has been found in compressing the reproductive season. Like the almost explosive blooming of the flowering plants, and the hurried swarming of the insects, the shore birds have been forced to abbreviate and synchronize courtship and nesting behavior.

Most species therefore arrive on the breeding grounds already paired, and engage in such a brief courtship that many visitors to their breeding grounds miss this entirely. A variety of wing-tilting displays have become ritualized in the pairing and mating of the smaller sandpipers, and most species engage in some song-flight display, an adaptation to the problem of maintaining territorial dominance in a wide and windy landscape. Being almost all birds of the open—whether tundra, shore or grassland—where they cannot rely on cover to protect them from enemies, the shore birds have perfected a wider range of attack and distraction displays than any other bird group. Distraction displays,

NESTING DISTRIBUTION OF SHORE BIRDS

Arctic and Alpine [1]	Coniferous Forest [2]	Prairie
Ringed Plover	Common Snipe	Long-billed Curlew
Semipalmated Plover	Solitary Sandpiper	Upland Plover
Mongolian Plover	Greater Yellowlegs	Marbled Godwit
Dotterel	Lesser Yellowlegs	
Golden Plover	Least Sandpiper	
Black-bellied Plover	Short-billed Dowitcher	
Surfbird		
Ruddy Turnstone		
Black Turnstone		
Whimbrel (Hudsonian)		
Bristle-thighed Curlew		
Eskimo Curlew		
Wandering Tatler	Sea Shore	Miscellaneous [3]
Knot	Am. Oystercatcher	Jacana
Purple Sandpiper	Black Oystercatcher	Killdeer
Rock Sandpiper	Piping Plover	Snowy Plover
Pectoral Sandpiper	Wilson's Plover	Mountain Plover
White-rumped Sandpiper		Woodcock
Dunlin		Spotted Sandpiper
Long-billed Dowitcher		Avocet
Stilt Sandpiper		Black-necked Stilt
Semipalmated Sandpiper		Willet
Western Sandpiper		Wilson's Phalarope
Buff-breasted Sandpiper		
Bar-tailed Godwit		
Hudsonian Godwit		
Sanderling		
Red Phalarope		
Northern Phalarope		

which are confined to birds with eggs or young, serve to deflect the hunting instincts of predators away from the nest area, thus enhancing survival. The "injury feigning" activities of the Killdeer, or the wonderfully deceptive "rodent run" performance (see under Purple Sandpiper) which appears to be characteristic behavior in so many of the smaller northern shore birds, are typical though perhaps elaborate examples.

1 Because some species are high arctic, others low arctic, some panarctic, it is difficult to provide a simple classification. In this list only the alpine species are segregated by indention. Even so, some of these, though principally alpine, occur on the lowland tundra farther north.

2 The first and the last two species of this list are sedge bog dwellers; the others occur about ponds in the coniferous forest region.

3 This assemblage includes forms not otherwise easily grouped (see text for details).

It is important to realize that these are ritualized responses to emotional situations which recur in the lives of these birds, and not examples of ingenuity in handling survival problems. This is not to say that birds are unintelligent, but, rather, that they have specialized in stereotyped, "instinctive" responses to certain environmental stimuli and thus relegated intelligence to a subordinate role in their lives. Solving life's problems in this way has many advantages, but Katharine Scherman, who looked over Josselyn Van Tyne's and William Drury's shoulders on the Bylot Island Expedition of 1954, made the following interesting comments about birds in her popular *Spring on an Arctic Island:* "We humans, in comparison, are sloppy, imperfect creatures. Nothing of us works quite right. Our instincts, though strong, are few, misty and vague, and our physical structure leaves a great deal to be desired. The human brain, developed to a remarkable extent, has apparently grown at the expense of other functions, which have been retarded and in some cases have deteriorated. This dulling of instinct, however, has resulted in an extraordinary freedom of action and thought, exclusively human. We cannot envy the birds the set and narrow paths of their uncompromisingly efficient lives." But perhaps there is tragedy in that so few of us ever use our higher gift.

The systematic study of the displays of shore birds has only just begun, and these are so important that it is probable that the true relationship of many species of plovers and sandpipers will not be known until a critical comparison of the behavior of these birds has been added to our existing stock of knowledge about them. It has become literally true that the way a sandpiper scratches itself may be a truer indication of relationship to some other species which scratches the same way than the bones of the skull or the presence of a hind toe on which we relied so much in the past.

The young of plovers and sandpipers are all precocial, and able, with a little help, to begin coping with the temporarily benign environment of summer the same hour they hatch from the large eggs. The usual clutch of four seems to be the maximum number these birds can cover successfully.

Young and old alike are so protectively colored that they are difficult to see when quiet. Abbott and Gerald Thayer,[57] who studied this problem at the turn of the century, felt that "Obliterative shading, pure and simple, is the rule among the shore birds. Littoral flats, whether of sand or shingle, are for the most part characterized by great monotony

(*upper*) Plover exposed and against natural background to show
disruptive pattern.
(*lower*) Sandpiper exposed and blending with sand or mud.

and blankness . . . and almost wholly wanting the complex element
of vegetable life. Since the birds that inhabit these beaches are almost
all great wanderers, making long semi-annual migrations, one would
expect to find their patterns not only simple but highly generalized, and
varying little among the species. A comparison of the more strictly
littoral among the smaller shore birds will show that this is actually
the case.

"Good examples of the pure beach type are the winter costumes of
the Knot, the Sanderling, the Semipalmated Sandpiper, and the (other)
stints. Most of the birds of this family wear a more grass-like pattern
in summer than in winter, a fact which is in perfect keeping with their
habits, for during the nesting they tend to forsake the beaches and to
live among the weeds and grasses. Some, like the Pectoral Sandpiper,
stick to grassy swamps throughout the year, and their pattern tells the
tale."

Almost all the northern shore birds are primarily insect predators and feed chiefly on the swarms of aquatic midges (chironomids), crane-flies and their larvae, and the abundant small spiders, caddisflies, mosquitoes, and beetles of the tundra. The hatching of millions of chicks is apparently synchronized with the peak of the insect cycle, though studies of the food economy of the tundra are still so scant that we can only surmise these relationships at present.

This problem of a sufficiency of food to maintain the extra demands of a seasonal peak in the bird population always enters into the discussion of why these birds, like so many others, defend a definite territory during the breeding season. Song is used to advertise their attachment to a particular area, isolated from but usually contiguous with similar areas held by other birds of their own kind. A high degree of intolerance to intrusion by birds of either sex is characteristic of such territorial males. At present, one school of thought argues that territory is largely a function of sexual needs, a view summed up by Edward A. Armstrong's statement[4] that "Territory is a psychological construction before it is geographical." Others argue that under certain conditions, even if these conditions be given only occasionally, territory may mean the difference between success and failure in providing adequate food to ensure the survival of the young, and that its defense is thus primarily ecological rather than behavioristic. Frank A. Pitelka,[38] who holds this view, insists that this emphasis on the manner in which a population partitions the available habitat through the exclusive use of territories points to the true significance of territory, and that "the special antics of the birds and the crowds of people studying them (have) warped the emphasis too much too long."

Dr. Pitelka's conclusions may have been strongly influenced by his studies of the unusually specialized Pectoral Sandpiper. Not only is there great disparity in size and behavior between the sexes in this species, but the males leave the tundra as soon as their role as sex partners has been concluded. Dr. Pitelka considers this an adaptive trait designed to contract population size, and thus reduce competition for food just as the young are about to place added demands on the available supply. Be this as it may, the tyro should view these differences of opinion not as mere academic dissension, but as evidence that despite an abundant literature on birds and their behavior, almost everything is still in need of fresh insights and careful reappraisal. Books—whether popular like this one, or technical—are mere landmarks in the quest for understanding, not canons to be taken on faith.

The male Pectoral Sandpipers are exceptional in leaving the nesting grounds before their young are hatched, but all adult shore birds leave the tundra as soon as the young begin to fly, but before they can follow their parents. It is this early dissolution of family ties that accounts for the double peak of migrants experienced farther south. The last of the northbound shore birds have barely left the New Jersey flats when the first return movement begins in early July. By mid-July the migration is well under way and soon reaches a peak comprised largely of adults; and a second peak occurs early in September when the young shore birds follow the migratory lanes their parents pursued a month earlier. The occasional very early return of small numbers of adults is probably correlated with the abandonment of nesting in unusually severe seasons on the tundra. It is, actually, often difficult to determine the onset or termination of migration in middle latitudes because of birds which summer along the way, or winter beyond the "normal" range of the species. We have grown increasingly aware of this year-round scattering of shore birds along the shores of the continents in recent years, but it is nothing new.

The long over-water hops of many of the larger shore birds have always stirred our imaginations, and the perfecting of direct routes across open water (see Golden Plover) is a fascinating illustration of the continuing exploration of all possibilities that goes on in nature. The elliptical migration routes of birds like the Golden Plover and the Lesser Yellowlegs, passing up the interior of North America in spring, and along its eastern rim in the fall, are admirable adaptations. The interior of continental land masses warms up sooner than the seashore in spring, and thus allows occupancy earlier in the season for species that feed largely on insects. Most impressive, however, is the feat performed by young shore birds in following their parents to wintering grounds they have never seen. Left to shift for themselves on the arctic tundra, they have no experience of winter's grip on this land, no one to start them off ahead of danger, nor show them where to go. And yet they do leave in good time, follow the ancestral pathways and rejoin their kind, now all strangers, at the other end of the Earth. How much of these amazing journeys up and down the continents is based on "tradition," how much on stellar or other navigational skills, is currently the subject of much investigation. Unfortunately, despite the fact that their migrations are such outstanding feats, the shore birds themselves are not good experimental subjects.

CONSERVATION

The decline of hunting opportunity which has resulted from the increase of human populations is causing more than one wild-life administrator to cast covetous eyes at modern shore bird numbers and suggest that they could again stand hunting. This must be opposed firmly because shore bird habits make them particularly vulnerable to hunting pressure. The small egg clutch, and the inability to renest in the north's short summer, result in an annual reproductive success of only 25% instead of the 50% which is usual with gallinaceous game birds. The shore bird migrations are so long and hazardous that they place special stress on the population; and the fact that these birds do not resort to cover, often fly in flocks, are easy to decoy, and concentrate on now much reduced feeding areas during their migrations, all combine to make it unthinkable that they should again be subjected to gunning pressure within our borders. For there is no doubt that shooting was the cause of the nearly catastrophic decline of shore bird numbers at the turn of the century, and that stopping this shooting—whether for commerce or for sport—has allowed them to recover to their present status. All, that is, except the Eskimo Curlew, which we hope still clings to life as a species in a few surviving individuals.

There is, of course, another source of pressure on these open country birds in the "development" of the countryside, at first for agriculture and more recently for residential and other man-directed activities of all sorts that tend to drain and fill so many of the marshlands these birds once used. The Marbled Godwit, the Long-billed Curlew, and the Upland Plover all have their fortunes tied to changing agricultural land use patterns. And though the northern breeding grounds of the majority of shore birds remain almost untouched, their wintering grounds are being usurped by agriculture and human population growth in all the Americas. Unfortunately, also, they are still being shot in most of the Latin-American countries.

We could easily confuse cause and effect here. The remaking of North America's temperate zone eliminated a handful of bird species dependent on mature plant communities or already in precarious bal-

Dead Eskimo Curlew

ance. Conversely, these changes made it possible for several other species to increase greatly. We lost the Passenger Pigeon, but the Mourning Dove, a bird of field borders and open woodland, is certainly more abundant today than it has ever been during our occupancy of the continent.

But of all the shore birds, only the Killdeer could be said to have benefited from our manipulations of the landscape. The Upland Plover did too, for a while, but has since lost these gains. All the others have suffered a decline in numbers, and this trend may be expected to continue so long as human numbers increase. The decline induced by hunting was fortunately temporary, subject to correction, but the increase which came with protection from the gun is also likely to be temporary.

If and when we decide that we want the other creatures to continue sharing the Earth with us, we will have to leave room for them. Not least among these reservations will be marshes and grasslands for the shore birds. It is a happy coincidence that these habitats are necessary to the survival of the ducks and geese, in which a sizable human population segment feels a vested interest; but this won't be enough because the ducks, too, are threatened.

Charles Urner,[62] who combined the acuity of the old bayman with the insights of the modern ornithologist, commented on some of the results of hunting shore birds on the New Jersey coast. By 1905 their numbers were so sadly reduced that gunners who persisted in shooting at all were killing Tree Swallows in August and September for want of fairer game, along, of course, with the smaller peep which gunners of a prior generation would have rightly considered beneath them. The migratory bird treaty with Canada at last put an end to spring shooting in 1918; but because fall shooting was legalized, the decimation continued and soon only yellowlegs, turnstones, and Black-bellied Plovers were seen regularly in migration. A completely closed season (except for woodcock and snipe) in 1927 came in the nick of time. How close we came to losing several more species forever may be seen in the writings of the most competent students of the 1920's, men like E. H. Forbush, W. L. McAtee, and Alexander Wetmore, all of whom were very pessimistic about the future of many of these birds. But recover they did, and as soon as the guns were stilled. Within ten years they were all increasing rapidly, so that today we need feel special concern only for a few species like the Buff-breasted Sandpiper and Hudsonian Godwit. Woodcock and snipe, because they nest over a much broader range and are difficult birds to hunt, have been able to withstand continued hunting pressure. But many fear that the combination of diminishing habitat and the new hazards of chemical poisoning from widespread insecticide spraying programs may be threats even these adaptable species will not survive.

The migratory bird treaties with Canada (1916) and Mexico (1937) halted the decline of the North American waterfowl and benefited the shore birds greatly. In view of continually diminishing habitat in both hemispheres, what is now needed is an extension of these treaties to the Caribbean and South American nations.

WATCHING SHORE BIRDS

It is to be expected that the pre-protection era should have provided the greatest accumulation of records of rarities, especially of such difficult-to-identify species as the European Woodcock. This might be called Phase I in the field study of these birds, a period when all identifications were made, or at least confirmed, in the hand. It came to a close in the 1920's, when protection and a new interest in living birds occasioned by well-illustrated bird books and good binoculars shifted the emphasis.

Phase II was the era of modern binocular birding. For shore birds it may be called the Urner-Griscom-Peterson era because these men perfected the techniques of field identification and channeled the interest already awakened by the fine State books of Eaton in New York and Forbush in Massachusetts. Roger Tory Peterson's new *Field Guide* approach created a revolution in bird identification. Armed with a *Field Guide,* a good binocular or a spotting telescope, and a knowledge of the fact that shore birds concentrate on certain bars or spits at high tide, the bird watcher can quickly become familiar with most of the regular coastwise migrants. A little extra work in other favored spots will round out his list in a few seasons, and if he has done his homework as well as his field work, he will acquire a surer familiarity with even the difficult species in much less time than the collector of old. The latter had certain advantages, however, including the opportunity of double-checking his field identifications.

The one disadvantage of popularizing field identification by making it easy lay in the false sense of certainty it generated in people who failed to realize that there is much more to birds, and their identification, than can be encompassed in a pocket guide. Since this phase of bird study happily coincided with the increase of shore birds, more expert observation began once again to accumulate records of extra-limital occurrence during the 1940's and 1950's, but without the substantiation of specimens this time. During the 1950's a growing awareness of the weakness of sight identifications as records of rare birds led to the increasing use of the camera and the telephoto lens or telescope as a tool for recording rarities. Unless these photographic records are published, however, they are not likely to last as long as museum specimens.

There has been enough controversy over the relative merits of sight records during the past twenty years. It is time the amateur learned not to expect his reports of first occurrences or difficult identifications to appear in scientific works; but the professional must also recognize that specimens already anointed with alum and arsenic, where they represent accidental occurrences unlikely of repetition, have no more value than the sight records he rejects. The proper attitude seems to me to have been given excellent expression by William H. Drury, Jr.,[65] in reporting his disagreement with an arctic expedition colleague when it came time to publish their results. Dr. Drury wrote that he was "more impressed with the reliability of our Eskimos' observations" than his colleague had been, and that he believed they should "report as much as we could learn (from them), indicating our judgment of reliability, but allowing others the opportunity to make use of hints which may mean more in the future than they do to us now."

Phase III in our study of birds is on the horizon but has hardly excited popular interest in this country as yet. It is the true bird watching (in contrast to bird listing or "birding"), the study of individual and group behavior that has been opened to amateurs by the development of the subscience of ethology. This work began in Europe and is slowly being taken up in America. Its chief reward lies in learning for oneself how little is really known about anything, and in helping, little by little, to unravel the mysteries of life. The binocular and the camera have taught us how unnecessary it is to destroy life in order to satisfy our love of the hunt. Bird watching can teach us to add intellectual and aesthetic content to our avocation.

CLASSIFICATION

In America, the age of exploration as regards arctic shore birds began in the early 1880's when Lucien M. Turner, Edward Nelson, and John Murdock worked the coasts of northwest Alaska, and it is only now drawing to a close. As early as 1888, Henry Seebohm of England compiled a remarkably useful monograph on *The Geographical Distribution of the Family Charadriidae,* but much as we have learned since, we are by no means ready to turn out a monograph on the Order in modern terms.

The hope of every taxonomist in carrying out his function as a classifier of living forms is that he will discover sufficiently variable, yet conservative, characteristics to allow him to discern basic relationships.

These may be the arrangement of the bones of the skull, or a muscle formula, but he has learned from painful experience that nature is not easily pigeonholed, and that many traps lie in wait for the unwary. He has learned, for example, that ecological adaptation may make for convergence in the structure of the parts he studies, so that two birds that seem at first rather alike may be of quite different origins. By the same token, birds of common origin may come to look very different because of the way of life they have pursued. The puzzle is that of the hen and the egg. And because it has by no means been solved as yet, we may expect several rearrangements in the check-list of North American shore birds in the not distant future.

Among the more intriguing recent discoveries in the field of bird anatomy is that many birds have salt glands lying on the front of the skull, between the eyes. These are larger glands in marine birds but much reduced in fresh-water birds, since their function is to de-salt the bird's diet. This is of importance to the taxonomist because it is now apparent that the size of such organs may affect bone development. Large glands press on the underlying bone sufficiently to prevent its growth, whereas smaller glands allow fuller ossification, with sometimes strikingly different skull configurations. In a series of anatomical studies published between 1914 and 1933, R. P. Lowe of Great Britain suggested radical revisions in the classification of the shore birds; but, since many of his conclusions were based on the form of the bony structure above the eye, just that portion of the skull most affected by the salt glands and therefore subject to wide variation as a result of the birds' feeding habits, Dr. Lowe's proposals must now, in their turn, be completely reappraised. Walter J. Bock (in *A Generic Review of the Plovers*, 1958) has undertaken part of this task, and in giving a list of the South American shore birds, we here follow his proposed reclassification of the plovers. For North America,* however, the *A.O.U. Check-list* is followed.

This book, which grew out of a series of deft word sketches of shore birds in their haunts by Henry Marion Hall who knows how to capture the play of light and wind on the saltings of the coast, and of some lively and attractive line drawings of these lovely birds by John Henry Dick,

---

* For the purposes of this book, North America extends south to the Panama Canal. Readers should also be aware that in birds of such variable length of leg and bill, the Length measurement given applies to total length (from tip of bill to tip of toes in a supine specimen) and is thus only a clue to relative size.

is therefore neither the long-awaited monograph nor a handbook of the
North American shore birds. What we have tried to do, is to bring Dr.
Hall's essays up to date in a series of comments on recent changes of
status which have occurred, and to interpolate some of the more read-
able scientific commentaries gleaned from a perusal of an extensive
literature in order to introduce the non-professional reader to a particularly attractive group of birds.

Nesting Snowy Plover

CHAPTER 2

Woodcock Chick

THE SHORE BIRD FAMILIES

THE WORLD'S 8600 or so species of birds are, of course, too large and varied an assemblage of entities for anyone to master or even study conveniently. They have therefore been subdivided into 28 Orders and 168 Families, the latter again subdivided into Genera into which are grouped anywhere from one to a score or more species. Though they are obviously convenient groupings, the higher categories (Orders, Families and Genera) are necessarily arbitrary, because the origins of many groups are lost in antiquity and our knowledge of both fossil and living forms is still incomplete. For this reason, various authorities rearrange them according to their particular views of evolutionary history, sometimes, one almost feels, to their own taste.

In nature, the individuals comprising an interbreeding population —the species—are the real entities. Here there is increasing agreement among taxonomists, aided by ethologists and by the amateur naturalists who still collect many of the important data professionals need to fill in the great mosaic of a continuing creation, evolution.

The *Charadriiformes,* the Order which includes the shore birds and their relatives, contains 314 species. These are subdivided into three sub-Orders, the *Alcae* with 22 species in one Family of marine divers (the alcids); the *Lari* with 89 species in three Families of gull-like

Jacana

Painted Snipe

Oystercatcher

Plover

Sandpiper

Avocet

THE TWELVE SHORE BIRD FAMILY TYPES
(Not to scale, and captions refer to family rather than species)

Phalarope

Crabplover

Thick-knee

Pratincole

Seedsnipe

Sheathbill

birds (jaegers, gulls and terns, skimmers); and the *Charadrii* with 203 species of more or less typical shore birds often classified in twelve Families, as listed below. The jacanas are transitional, to an outside order, rails and cranes, at one end of the lineage, and pratincoles and sheathbills are transitional to an inside (*Charadriiformes*) sub-order, the gulls at the other.

Jacanidae (Jacana family)   7 species in the world, of which one breeds in both North and South America. (British ornithologist P. R. Lowe, who has studied shore birds closely, believes that Jacanas should be given Ordinal rank rather than Family status within the *Charadriiformes*.) SPANISH: Gallitos de Agua.

Rostratulidae (Painted Snipe family)   2 species in the world, of which one is indigenous to South America. SPANISH: Becasinas Falsas o Agachonas.

Haematopodidae (Oystercatcher family)   6 species, of which 2 are indigenous to North America, 2 others to South America. SPANISH: Ostreros.

Charadriidae (Plover family)   63 species of which 9 occur in North America, 10 in South America. SPANISH: Teros y Ciertos Chorlos; Avefrías.

Scolopacidae (Sandpiper family)   82 species, of which 34 occur in North America, 6 in South America, the latter being 3 typical snipe (Capella) and 3 snipe relatives (Chubbia). SPANISH: Chorlos o Gordillos, Becasinas y Chorlitos; Agachadizas.

Recurvirostridae (Avocet family)   7 species, of which one stilt and one avocet occur throughout the Americas, with a second avocet in South America, often considered conspecific. SPANISH: Teros Reales; Zancos.

Phalaropodidae (Phalarope family)   3 species, all 3 of which breed in North America (2 circumboreal); none breeds in South America. SPANISH: Chorlos Palmados, Falarópodos.

Dromadidae (Crabplover family)   one species occurring around the Indian Ocean (not in the Americas).

Burhinidae (Thick-knee family, the Stone Curlews)   9 species, of which 2 are South American, one of these occurring north to Costa Rica. SPANISH: Alcaraván o Rodillón.

Glareolidae (Pratincole family)   17 species on all continents but the Americas.

Thinocoridae (Seedsnipe family)   4 species restricted to South America. (German ornithologist Erwin Stresemann considers these somewhat dove-like birds deserving of Ordinal rank apart from the *Charadriiformes*). SPANISH: Chorlos Aperdizados.

Chionididae (Sheathbill family)   2 species of subantarctic coasts, one of them breeding in southernmost South America. SPANISH: Palomas Antarticas.

PART 1

THE NORTH AMERICAN
SHORE BIRDS

Northern Phalaropes—Winter

Bristle-thighed Curlew Nest and Eggs

CHAPTER 3

THE JACANAS

THESE SMALL rail-like, largely nonmigratory waders of tropical and subtropical regions are sufficiently characterized by the species account given herewith.

The largest of the seven species found throughout the world is the Pheasant-tailed Jacana of southeast Asia with tail feathers reaching 20 inches in length; the smallest is the Lesser Jacana of tropical Africa. There are none in Europe.

1

JACANA

Jacana spinosa

MOST of the North American shore birds (excepting only the Woodcock and the Purple Sandpiper) reach at least the latitude of Mexico during their winter sojourn, and most of them go deep into South America; but of the several South American species, only the Jacana and the Thick-knee extend north of Panama except as vagrants.

The Jacanas are small, gaily-colored gallinule-like birds of tropical "lettuce" lakes, so unlike in form to most waders that some authorities would set them apart in an Order all their own.

The slender, greenish legs of all Jacanas terminate in a most extraordinary pair of feet, the toes and nails of which are incredibly long and spreading. Many ages spent running across floating vegetation must have been required to develop such remarkably adapted appendages. I can think of no bird more highly specialized for a particular way of life, though all birds are indeed marvelously adapted. Glancing at a Jacana you might think that such a bird couldn't swim, but you would be wrong. It can and does swim and dive as slickly as a grebe on occasion. Jacanas wounded by shot have been known to plunge and then vanish for good, perhaps holding to bottom vegetation as some ducks do. And newly hatched chicks, when surprised, will roll into the water and swim out of sight in the dimly-lit pools.

The Jacana is in every respect a creature of shallow, cypress-shaded ponds, tule swamps, or other plant-choked fresh waters of tropical lands. It spends its life dashing over floating bonnets, feeds on the swarming insect life there, and even nests on the floating vegetation of the black waters. Its nest is a mere saucer in the wet weeds or at most a handful of materials, barely enough to hold the eggs which, however, seem to suffer little from being wet a good part of the time. Completely covered with black scrawls and scratchings, they are protectively colored and look like integral parts of the bog. They are worth noting—glossy, buff-colored, short- or rounded-ovate and covered with swamp hieroglyphics.

The usual clutch is four, and, following the pattern which we increasingly recognize as typical of many shore birds, the male incubates the eggs and cares for the young until they have achieved independence. The female, phalarope-like, sports showier adornments and takes the lead in courtship.

Unlike their relatives, the marsh-haunting rails, who have dusky mites of chicks, Jacanas have handsome young who quickly sprout the lemon-yellow wing feathers of their parents but are white-cheeked and white-bellied, a contrasting plumage they retain for nearly a year, well into the following spring.

Adults are handsomely plumaged indeed, with deep chestnut body and glossy black head and neck, strikingly yellow frontal shields, and pale yellow-green secondaries. Not in the least secretive, they strut about and often raise their wings high over the back, holding them there in garish advertisement for a moment, much as stilts will do. When flushed, a flock of Jacanas flutter away like yellow-winged butterflies, cackling like coots, and pitching back to the bog in awkward exhaustion. In alighting, they are as likely as not to dive and swim under the margins of the weeds. They are as much the authentic geniuses of the places they inhabit as a school of turtles cascading off a log.

Jacana spinosa (Linnaeus). Named in 1758 from a Panama specimen.
LOCAL NAMES: Pond coot, river chink, poule d'eau. SPANISH: Gallito de agua.
FIELD CHARACTERS: Smaller and more slender than gallinule which it superficially

resembles. Our race has head, neck and upper back blackish, body chestnut, but secondary flight feathers strikingly greenish-yellow. Bend of wing with a long, sharp spur. Bill plover-like but somewhat longer; legs green, long, with extremely long toes and claws. *Adults* have a striking yellow frontal shield. *Females* brighter and larger. Immature lacks frontal shield (or has much reduced one) and is brownish above, darker on crown and hindneck, buffy white below, with same greenish legs and wing patches. Length 8½″.

Habitually raises and opens rounded wings, revealing the conspicuous yellow patches. Voice is a noisy cackle, mostly given in flight.

RANGE: A number of well-marked races breed from Tamaulipas across to Sinaloa in Mexico, and most of Caribbean Islands, south to Buenos Aires in suitable areas. Occasional summer visitor (mostly as immatures) to coast of southwest Texas; accidental in Florida.

CHAPTER 4

THE OYSTERCATCHERS

Stout, foot-high, blackish or black and white waders with long bright red, laterally compressed bills, and pinkish legs. Strong-flying, noisy and excitable but social birds of temperate and tropical shores around the world, occurring on inland waters in Eurasia. Somewhat migratory. Sexes alike. Eggs, in our two species, 3, laid in a hollow in the ground and more or less lined with flaky materials or grass. Both sexes incubate and care for the young.

There are six species: two North American, two South American, the European Oystercatcher and the Sooty Oystercatcher of Australia. Some ornithologists consider the three Northern species to be one, with racial differences in plumage.

2

AMERICAN OYSTERCATCHER

Haematopus palliatus

LANDING on the northern tip of Wreck Island, Virginia, early one May, I found a large colony of Black Skimmers nesting on the sand within a rod of high water mark. Their white eggs, marbled with lilac and brown, lay everywhere, so close together that it was necessary to move with care for fear of stepping on them. The long-winged skimmers circled around, screaming and scolding.

As I watched their aerial gymnastics a shrill *Weep! Weep! Weep!* sounded overhead, and a pair of oystercatchers spun by on swiftly vibrating pinions. Theirs is a style of flight rather unlike that of other large shore birds. Curlews, for example, occasionally lurch as if trying to shrug their sandy shoulders in mid air, and then glide. These oystercatchers flew more like ducks, the white of their under parts, lower backs, and primaries flashing in the sun.

When they settled on the beach a few rods west, I crept up behind a hillock to watch them. They stood in the open, their color patterns showing strongly against the glittering background of sand and sea.

Their heads, necks, and upper breasts were black with a faint, bluish-green lustre. Taking the binoculars to bring them closer, I noted that their eyes were orange yellow, circled with red lids, and that their short legs were between lead and flesh color.

Their beaks were very striking, quite four inches long, broad, flattened laterally like knives, and bright red. Oystercatchers, particularly the big females, measure as much as twenty-one inches and have a wing-spread of three feet. Of all American shore birds the sickle-bill curlew alone is larger and has longer wings.

After preening a moment, they ran a few steps, rather more nimbly than one would expect from such bulky birds. Presently one plunged its bill into the wet sand as if groping for something and twitched out a small clam. In similar fashion they seize blood-worms, shrimp, and juicy sand-fleas.

Molluscs are their favorite food, although they also take sea-urchins, crabs, and small starfish. Their stout beaks make mince-meat of all such creatures, but are equal to much harder work. They chip barnacles and mussels off shoreside rocks, and readily split open razor clams and other small shellfish.

"Raccoon" or "coon" oysters are a staple food on the Atlantic coast south of Chesapeake Bay. These grow close together in sharp-edged clusters, are stunted in size because of crowding, and usually point upward, all this in contrast to "single" oysters which have more room for growth and are therefore larger and more often lie on their sides. Some years ago Ivan R. Tomkins [59] of Savannah published an interesting account of the oyster-eating habits of this species and showed how the oystercatcher depends on oyster ecology.

Oysters, Tomkins pointed out, prosper only where they are covered by salt water for a major part of each day; but oystercatchers cannot feed on them unless they are sufficiently exposed each day to allow the birds to wade out and find them open. For both the oyster and the oystercatcher, then, the tidal range must be sufficient to ensure that the beds will not be covered by storm tides for days at a time. Though adult oystercatchers might find alternate food sources to live out protracted storms, the young would probably starve unless fed regularly from the abundant oyster beds. And although, as Dawson said of the situation in California, "oysters are not much given to sprinting," the oystercatcher's art is no simple one. The slightest touch or jar will usually cause every oyster within reach to snap shut, so the oystercatcher must stalk the beds when the oysters are feeding most actively, their valves parted about one eighth of an inch as they sift the changing tide for its microscopic plankton. The birds probe their "oyster-knife" mandibles into such a feeding oyster, press down, tip the head from side to side while the bill is held almost straight up and down, and in this way cut the adductor muscle that closes the valves tightly when tensed. This provides free access to the meat of the oyster.

The great reentrant of the Atlantic coast which sweeps from Cape Hatteras to Florida provides a mean tidal range of nearly seven feet in the central area, which usually means that the intertidal oyster beds are exposed daily, and in this region the oystercatcher population reaches its peak. In the Cape Romain region, where oysters have remained plentiful, there were some 300 breeding pairs, and winter flocks of a thousand or more birds in the 1940's, conditions reminiscent of the throngs of European Oystercatchers that pipe and kleep at the tops of their voices in the estuary of the River Clyde and elsewhere in northern Britain.

In the days of Audubon and Wilson oystercatchers were apparently regular as far north as Nova Scotia and Labrador. They are now rare on the Atlantic coast north of the Virginia Capes, though a few have reinvaded New Jersey in recent years and in 1960 there was a Long Island breeding record. Elsewhere, they are common again only in the Aransas Pass region of Texas.

This wild and wary bird was never gunned to any extent, but though it is almost impossible to stalk on the open shores it frequents, guns on outlying points probably took their toll over the years. Oystercatchers have always bred very locally throughout their vast range, laying their eggs, two or three in a set, on mounds between the ocean shore and the first low dune. Sometimes they decorate their roomy, bowl-shaped nests with bits of clam shells or scallops. The eggs are large, heavily spotted, ovate, and vary but slightly. The base color varies from drab to white, but their protective markings make them difficult to spot on the pebbly shingle.

These big shore birds swim and dive well. And unlike willets, they do not betray the whereabouts of a nest by anguished cries or "demented" actions. They flush and fly far away from any intruder and do not circle back as plovers do. Long may they grace the barrier beaches.

Haematopus palliatus Temminck. Described in 1820 from a Venezuela specimen. SPANISH: Ostrero commun.

FIELD CHARACTERS: A crow-sized, black and white wader of bright, sandy shores. Its bright red, flattened bill; its shyness, and swift flight, all combine to make it unique and unmistakable. Length 17–21″, bill 2¾–4″, female larger.

RANGE: The eastern race, *H. p. palliatus,* breeds at scattered localities from New Jersey (formerly the St. Lawrence) to Yucatan and Caribbean coasts to Brazil; also, on Pacific side, from Isthmus of Tehuantepec to Colombia. *H. p. frazari* is resident on the Pacific coast and islands of Baja California from Todos Santos southward through the Gulf of California and south along the Mexican coast to the Tres Marietas Islands, Colima and Guerrero. Other races extend the species range to Chiloe Island, central Chile, out to the Galápagos Islands (where Darwin failed to see it); and, on the east coast, south to Chubut Provence, Argentina. The racial status of several of these populations is in need of review.

3

BLACK
OYSTERCATCHER

Haematopus bachmani

*Prosy hedgerows and quiet duck-ponds for such
as like them: but roaring reefs and a pounding
sea for the Black Oystercatcher! . . . he is the
self-constituted guardian of all the sea-girt rocks.*
—Wm. Leon Dawson.

THE world's oystercatchers are all very alike though they
come in two types: black and white and all black. Our Pacific coast
species, named after his friend Bachman by Audubon, is one of the
black type. Slightly smaller than its cousin the American Oystercatcher,
it has the same long, red screwdriver mandibles, strong enough to cut
the adductor muscles of oyster or mussel. Both have a yellow iris ringed
in red, dark backs, and pinkish legs and feet. The feet of the black species are equipped with caulk-like pectinations which prevent the bird
from slipping on rocks. The head, throat, and breast of both species are
something between jet black and green. But this black carries through
all the under parts in this species whereas in the eastern bird these are a
gleaming white.

The rather short-legged Black Oystercatcher inches slowly over the reefs at low tide, cutting off a barnacle here, hammering open a mussel there. It is less flighty than its eastern relative, and prone to squat and hide among the rocks when an intruder draws near. Flitting by alternate bursts of flapping and sailing from one point to another, they seem to consider flight a matter of convenience only, and alight on half-way rocks at every opportunity. But let not this deliberateness deceive you; they can be spry, and can swim and dive deftly when the occasion demands.

Watching a Black Oystercatcher striding slowly along, nodding its head at every step, and never seeming in a hurry, one would hardly suspect how lively it is during courtship. Although the famous piping ceremony of the European Oystercatcher has not yet been worked out in detail for American species, it is plain from the observations of Webster [67] and others that the Black Oystercatcher does engage in this territorial ceremony which is a type of formalized fighting in which the pugnacity or the thwarted emotions of territorialism and sex are channeled into nondestructive activity. R. B. Perry (in Armstrong) [4] has given such a colorful description of this ceremony in the European Oystercatcher that it is worth quoting here:

"With heads stiffly down-stretched and hackles raised, with half-open, vibrant mandibles straightly pointing the ground like scarlet clothes-pegs, and broad tails depressed, two birds run side by side at a third bird, piping hard the while: their motion like nothing so much as two old rams charging, hell for leather. Beginning with plangent *peek* or *pic*, the cheery piping swiftly gathers way into a prolonged diminuendo: *kervee-kervee-kervee-kervee-kervee*, etc., etc., which dies away and crescends into a beautiful rippling. The precision with which the piping pair charge and turn together with lightning swiftness is as astounding as that of small waders in simultaneous flight. They do not attempt to drive away the 'pipee' by physical force, but persist only with this automatous running and turning together when short of, or alongside, the intruder: to and fro, to and fro. I am strongly reminded of the haphazard rushes of the displaying ruff, who is as likely to bow to a clod of turf as to a reeve. But this 'ram-piping' of the oystercatcher serves its purpose, and, ninety-nine times out of one hundred, the 'pipee' soon takes to flight, although I have known a pair to pipe at a third bird for fifteen minutes without a break, before achieving the desired end."

From April through August the pairs defend territories on promontories and off-shore islands along this humid coast, warding off the attacks of ravens who prowl for eggs, and, later, of gulls and eagles who would scoop up the downy young. The nests are placed well out of reach of flying spray on some rocky outcrop and may vary from a mere hollow scraped in gravel to a bowl so well lined with grass and moss that it could pass for a gull's nest. Full clutches of two or three (rarely four) eggs are laid between May 9 and July 10 on the southern Alaska coast. These birds apparently mate for life and are most devoted parents. Both sexes incubate, changing places at twelve-hour intervals at each low tide; and when the chicks hatch out, after 27 days of incubation, the parents again take turns at guarding them, "baby-sitting" for twelve hours, then feeding and standing guard for the next twelve.

The newly-hatched nestlings are brooded continuously for the first thirty-six hours of life, during which time their grayish pepper and salt down dries out. After this start they are typically precocial young, growing darker after the third week, and attaining full juvenal plumage by the sixth week or so, when they resemble winter adults.

But the rocky, surf-pounded rocks which are their homes must be explored cautiously and it may be five weeks before they have developed enough sureness of foot to clamber down to the low-tide flats and there forage with their parents. And the feeding tactics of oystercatchers are such a specialized art that it takes the young three or four months to learn to open mussels and barnacles deftly, or to chip chitons and limpets from the rocks. Like all young, they have avid appetites and consume the equivalent of 120 large mussels per day during the period of rapid growth.

These creatures of the dark coastal reefs and ledges, like the Black Turnstones, Surfbirds, and Wandering Tatlers that share this marine habitat with them, are fortunate that the great equalizing influence of the seas that wash this shore has provided nearly uniform littoral conditions for four thousand miles of coast line. In this productive environment they find ample supplies of Ribbed Limpets and Common Mussels which, together, comprise half of the Black Oystercatcher's food. The Pacific Goose Barnacle, California Mussel, and Shield Limpet make up the bulk of the balance, and chitons, Dunce Cap Limpets, and marine worms (*Nereis*) help diversify the diet. Come the high tide, they seek a lee shore and squat in the sun, crying a sudden alarm, *Wick! Wick! Wick!* if disturbed. The winter flocks are social aggregations and only the tides move them about.

Haematopus bachmani Audubon. Described in 1838. SPANISH: Ostrero negro.

FIELD CHARACTERS: A large (18″) black shore bird with 3 inches of bright red bill, and pink legs. Unmistakable. The Black Turnstone, which shares its rocky habitat in winter, is much smaller, shows considerable white in flight.

RANGE: Pacific coast of North America from Kiska in the Aleutian Islands east and south to Abreojos Point and Natividad Island on the central coast of Lower California. Winter flocks seldom wander more than thirty miles from the nesting place.

Black Oystercatcher

CHAPTER 5

THE PLOVERS

Plovers are small to medium-sized shore birds rather well characterized by a chunky body, short neck, and round head; with a short, stout, somewhat "swollen" bill. The sexes are nearly alike but can be distinguished in some species. Eggs number 2 to 5 (usually 3–4), are laid on the ground in a scrape or a flimsy nest, and cared for by both parents. Most plovers are migratory and as such have long, tapered wings (except lapwing). All are good runners, and some prefer upland areas to the shore.

There are two large sub-groups and a small assemblage of uncertain relationship, as follows:

Lapwings: medium to large, noisy plovers with broad rounded wings; the primary feathers are black and often show a broad, contrasting white stripe. The tail is usually white, with a broad, black, subterminal band. Several species have crests, wattles on the face, spurs on the bend of the wing. They are all fresh-water birds, world-wide in occurrence except for North America, where they are accidental visitors.

Typical plovers:
  (a) small plovers with a conspicuous breast band or "ring" and striking head patterns. The Semipalmated Plover is typical. The breast band is reduced in some (sand plovers, which are also paler), may be absent, or double in others. World-wide.

    (b) medium-sized plovers, dark-bellied in spring. The Golden Plovers, Black-bellied Plover, etc. Arctic and (1) New Zealand.

    (c) medium-sized plovers with gray-speckled back and a chestnut breast. The Dotterels. Circumboreal and extreme southern tip of South America.

    (d) medium-sized plovers, gray above and with a gray breast band. Bill somewhat flattened. The Magellanic Plover. Southern South America.

The so-called Short-winged Sandpiper of South America, and the closely-related Surfbird and Turnstones of northern regions are of uncertain affinities.

Ringed Plover with Chicks

4

RINGED PLOVER

Charadrius hiaticula

THIS is the north Atlantic representative of a series of small ringed plovers whose populations ring the arctic. Only more detailed field studies will decide whether this form and our Semipalmated Plover should be considered separate species, or whether they had better be combined as geographical races—European and American—of a single species. Some discussion of this problem is given under the Semipalmated Sandpiper.

In addition to the ground displays quoted from Sutton under the Semipalmated Plover account, these birds, so alike in much of their behavior, perform flight displays of the butterfly type, in which the fully-extended wings are beat softly and slowly.

Charadrius hiaticula. Linnaeus. Described in 1758 from a Swedish specimen.
   SPANISH: Chorlo semipalmado.
FIELD CHARACTERS: Slightly larger than the Semipalmated Sandpiper of North America, with (usually) a conspicuously broader breast band. In the hand, the absence of a toe web will distinguish it.
RANGE: Breeds from arctic Baffin Island, southern Greenland, Iceland, Britain, Scandinavia (the nominate race); another race (*C.h.tundrae*) breeds in the Eurasian arctic.

5

SEMIPALMATED PLOVER

Charadrius semipalmatus

WHENEVER the summer tide starts to ebb in Province-town Harbor on Cape Cod a sweet, plaintive call, *Chee-wee!* or *Tee-lee!* is heard while a flurry of beautiful Semipalmated Plovers drop down to the first foot or so of sand left bare.

As the water slides back and back, leaving more and more sand exposed, more of these birds arrive as if thoroughly familiar with the calendar of the tides. Many other kinds of "peep" flock with them, and by the time the tide is half way out, throngs of shore birds are busy feeding.

The Semipalmated Plover is always known Down East as "ring-neck," and I shall so term it. Although half an inch longer than the Piping Plover, the ring-neck closely resembles it. But it is much darker above and wears a broader, blacker collar. It is the color of wet sand while the Piping Plover is that of dry sand. Although as strongly marked as the Killdeer, it is readily told by its smaller size, much shorter tail, and its single rather than double neck band.

While on the flats from which the tide is still straining, the pattern of the ring-neck completely conceals it. The dark bands break up its outline while the light under parts blend with the water in which it wades. Only when it runs does motion betray it. Sometimes when you spot two or three and walk close to them, several dozen will whirl away, whistling, *Tee-lee! Tee-a-lee!*

Ring-necks trot forward a few steps, stop, and then go on again, never rushing around with beaks submerged like feeding Sanderlings, but moving with a set purpose. Presently you will see one grab a long, wriggling bloodworm. The motions of the plover remind one of robins hunting earthworms on a lawn. Worms are quick to vanish in the wet sand but not fast enough to evade a hungry ring-neck. Any plover who catches one has to swallow it instantly because he may be pursued by another less lucky bird. But although they are ever ready to snatch food from another of their own kind, I have never seen one interfere with the sandpipers with which they consort.

Take off your shoes and wade in the shoal water. A glance or two will show you that the harbor flats have plenty of food for the shore birds. You will note tiny crabs and a myriad of other crustaceans, sticklebacks (translucent, insect-like fish known to small boys as "tickle-fish" because they tickle the soles of their feet), the eggs of horseshoe crabs, minute mussels, and much other sea spoil. On all this food ring-necks grow incredibly fat. But though they gain much weight they can fly swiftly and to any required distances. They can also swim whenever they like, but I have happened to see them do so only in shoal water where they were splashing themselves.

Although they frequent the ocean beaches, they are much more numerous and conspicuous on the tidal flats and inshore bars. Many hundreds pass in April and May, but towards the first of June all but the comparatively few summering birds take off for northern breeding grounds. These extend from Alaska all the way around, along the shingle beaches of the arctic coast, to Newfoundland and Nova Scotia.

At Clyde Inlet, in northeastern Baffin Island, Professor Wynne-Edwards [71] found that the American Ring-neck and the European Ring-neck now overlap their ranges. Although ours is a smaller bird and of course has the toe webbing which gives it its name, the two are otherwise not easily distinguished. But the birds have no difficulty in recognizing their racial differences and apparently do not attempt to interbreed. Since reproductive isolation is the best test of a species, American ornithologists take this evidence as proof that the two birds are now distinct species, but the conservative British consider them merely races of the same species. Wynne-Edwards shares the latter view and points to this instance of overlap without interbreeding as the result of a recent invasion of territory newly exposed by the receding ice of the glacial epoch by the terminal populations (links) of a chain of races that interbreed at their other contacts.

Another versatile professor, artist George Miksch Sutton,[53] has described the courtship of these little birds on Southampton Island at the head of Hudson Bay in these words: "The courtship of this round-bodied, serious-faced little bird was performed with such vigor and such violent tempestuousness that I was sometimes impelled to laugh aloud at them. A performing bird would fly about wildly for minutes at a time, crying loudly, beating his wings stiffly, circling back and forth, zigzagging down the beach, racing out to the end of a promontory, then coming back again, repeating over and over this energetic little song, which usually began definitely enough with a few clear syllables, but wound up in a harsh blur of slurred notes, which sounded as much like a threat or burst of anger, as an expression of joy. The courtship flights were varied with odd battles, sparrings, and pursuits, during which the birds puffed out their throats and chests, ran at each other as if intent upon a killing, or flattened themselves out comically as they waddled along the sand. By the middle of June these noisy exhibitions were for the most part over, and the mated pairs near the Post settled down to the task of rearing their young."

The high arctic rigors of the Southampton Island beaches are so harsh that even the precocity this group of waders is noted for is not enough to ensure survival. The helpless young would not live long without constant brooding during their first few days. Even so, driven by racial instincts, they often leave the shallow scoop that passes for a nest and stumble away as soon as they are dry. Exhausted by their first run, they pause and the mother comes to brood them again because the warmth of the July sun is uncertain in the arctic.

Charadrius semipalmatus Bonaparte. Described in 1825. SPANISH: Chorlo semi-palmado.

FIELD CHARACTERS: A small, *dark* brown ringed plover with orange-yellow legs and a short yellow, black-tipped bill. A deliberate feeder on sandy mud flats. l. 7½″, b. ½″.

RANGE: High and low arctic coasts from Alaska around to Newfoundland, and inland along cold rivers and lakes to Great Slave Lake and James Bay, and south to northwestern British Columbia and the North Shore of the St. Lawrence and Nova Scotia and Sable Island, and occasionally on Grand Manaan Island. Migrates along both coasts and through the interior of North America to winter from central California and New Jersey south to Patagonia.

6

PIPING PLOVER

Charadrius melodus

WHEN the beach birds ride north to us on the wings of spring most of them linger only for a breathing spell before taking off for the "Land of Little Sticks," the tundra, or the barren shores of the Arctic Ocean. Driven by some mysterious urge, strong as that which moves the Gulf Stream, they summer under the Northern Lights but winter below the Southern Cross. In this drive the migratory impulse is paramount, and mating just one significant detail.

Shore birds seem mere exhalations of the sea and reflect its eternal restlessness, somewhat as do the sands over which they scamper. Subject to every whim of the waves, the beaches never emerge from the ocean quite the same, though they repeat patterns dating back to creation. The fore-shore is somewhat more stable; yet anybody who has seen it smoking in a gale must realize that it forms but an ephemeral basis for the nests of birds. Nevertheless, several species brave the perils here and brood their eggs between storms.

Of these the Piping Plover, or pale ring-neck, is pre-eminently the Cape Cod representative, a typical denizen of the barrier beaches of the northeast. It deposits its eggs in the sand, sometimes barely out of reach of the tide, but more frequently over the first range of hillocks facing the strand. They are about the size and shape of those laid by bobwhite

quail, with ground color cream or buff, and practically identical with
their surroundings.

Look closely at a handful of beach sand and notice that many parti-
cles are nearly black. The evenly distributed speckles on the Piping
Plover egg closely match the gray and sable of the grit. It takes a keen
eye to spot them because of this protective coloration and because the
mother bird prudently runs from her nest in time to mislead inter-
lopers.

Her incessant, quavering whistle is the sole suggestion of the proximity of the precious eggs. The nest is a slight hollow prettily lined with
pebbles and bits of shell, either for decoration or to prevent it from
blowing away. On windy days one may flush these dove-like plover from
bare depressions holding no eggs. These are places where beach birds
have been crouching to avoid the blast of the wind and the sand.

Here in May an observer may readily discover a dozen sets of eggs
laid within half a furlong, either inland from the dunes or in breaks
where the gales have swept corridors leading to the outer shore. Coast
Guardsmen often drive stakes beside nests to protect them from injury
by people walking on the beach.

On some shores one may count half a dozen such sticks within a few
hundred paces, some of them also marking the homes of Least Terns. In
these sandy stretches the sad, sweet note of the plover seems a perfect
expression of the gentle, trusting nature of these little birds—not afraid
to brood their eggs on the shifting sands of old Monomoy Point, which
every storm destroys and remakes.

Sandy depressions inshore from the dunes of Jones Beach, High
Hill Beach, Fire Island and many others farther south are also favorite
nesting areas. On these barrier islands one notes plover sitting on eggs
one week, but finds them a few days later running along the strand with
their newly hatched chicks trailing behind. Plaintive pipings sound
everywhere, with the bass rumble of surf as accompaniment. The Norse-
men, landing on our coast centuries before Columbus came, probably
heard and saw these fascinating waifs, for the ways of this order don't
change.

Although Piping Plovers shun an intruder by stealing away from
unhatched eggs, they never do so after the chicks pip the shell. Then
they feign helplessness, wriggling along the strand or trailing a wing to
distract attention from their young. I have held fluffy chicks in the palm

of my hand and seen their indomitable souls looking out of their black and limpid eyes—eyes indescribably guileless and beautiful.

These young are so tiny, that when one slips from my fingers and scurries away, it sometimes stumbles over a blade of grass and falls down, peeping and fluttering its infinitesimal wings.

What of the abandoned home? The first blow erases the hollow, sweeps the empty shells into the sea, and "the place thereof shall know it no more." The top-shaped eggs, notably large for so small a mother, have special significance. The chicks are extremely precocial, able to run and feed almost from birth. You will never see the female bring home food, although she broods them for many nights on the wind-swept strand.

What a contrast these mites make with the blind and naked off-spring of our perching birds. Between two tides young plovers gain more strength and confidence than callow robins do in as many weeks. Their down turns to plumage so rapidly as to suggest the unfolding of flowers—feathered blooms not anchored by roots like purple beach-peas, but equally littoral. They feast on minute crustaceans, molluscs, hoppers, shore-bred insects and their eggs.

So many species of shore birds nest far north that the pre-maturity of the fledglings, and the almost incredible swiftness with which they learn to fly and fend for themselves, have sometimes been explained as due to the brevity of boreal summer, and the necessity of becoming fledged in time to flit south before cold weather.

There is plausibility in this view, but it is not wholly satisfactory. Oystercatchers and willets, for example, breed in the South, yet their large eggs and the liveliness of their young are as notable as those of birds nesting in the extreme North. The same is true of Wilson's Plover, Mountain Plover, Spotted Sandpiper, Upland Plover, and other kinds which nest in our middle latitudes. Since higher forms of life seem less precocious than others lower in the scale of evolution, the whole matter of shore bird precocity is probably more closely connected with their place in the biological chain than with the geography of their nesting areas.

Piping Plovers are as sandy as their eggs. Ashy above and mainly white below, with a pale black collar and just a touch of this color above their foreheads, they are practically indistinguishable from the beach itself. If they remained still few people would notice them, and even their movements are inconspicuous.

When they run they suggest mere ripples in the sand and when they fly it is as if a pinch of sand had taken wing. Alighting a few rods ahead of you they vanish into the background. You will usually hear a dozen whistling to every pair you actually spot. On Cape Cod their seaside music fades late in August when most of them drift south. Their lives with us seem like pleasant summer weather, early to arrive, transient as blossoms, and blown away like sand by the first gales in the fall.

Charadrius melodus Ord. Described in 1824 from a New Jersey specimen.

LOCAL NAMES: Pale ring-neck, beach plover, butter-bird, clam-bird, mourning-bird, yee-o, feeble, peep-lo, etc.

FIELD CHARACTERS: A small sand-colored plover with a more or less complete black ring around the neck, black forehead, and orange-yellow legs, eye-ring, and base of bill. Fall birds show only a vestige of the ring around the neck, may have no black at all on the forehead. Call a plaintive, ventriloquial *peep-lo* or *peep-loay*, suggesting the drawn-out call of the Wood Pewee (Saunders). l. 7″, b. ½″.

RANGE: One race breeds on the Atlantic coast and its reentrants, from Newfoundland to Virginia, and winters from South Carolina to Florida. An interior race breeds from central Alberta to southern Ontario, south to central Nebraska and the southern shores of the Great Lakes, and winters on the Gulf Coast and, to some extent, in the Caribbean.

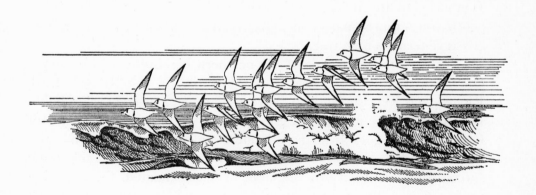

7

SNOWY PLOVER (*Kentish Plover*)

Charadrius alexandrinus

SMALL ringed plovers dot the beaches of the world, adding touches of life and beauty to stretches otherwise most desolate. Their gentle voices repeat marine melodies as ancient as Creation but as modern as yesterday's high tide.

Take those of our side of the northern hemisphere, for example. On the eastern slope of the north Atlantic are the Ringed, Little Ringed, and Kentish (Snowy) Plovers. The first of these strikes boldly west from Europe in the spring to span the stormy seas to Iceland and Greenland and goes as far as Ellesmere and Baffin Islands, migrating back in the fall. Farther west, and south, on the American side come, successively, the American ring-neck or Semipalmated, the pale ring-neck or Piping Plover, the Wilson's Plover; and far down on the Caribbean coasts, the Snowy Plover, the latter the widest ranging of them all.

The Snowy Plover often feeds along the margins of shallow, alkaline lakes, but the sandy margins of the world are its true home. It spends most of its life on the long benches of sand just inshore from the ocean beach but raised a few feet above tidewater. Such stretches, often many miles in length, border the shore line of both our oceans excepting in the extreme north, where rocks and reefs take over. On these sandy belts the Snowy Plover is often only a disembodied voice, plaintive, and strangely ethereal. It suggests those "airy tongues that syllable men's names on sands, and shores, and desert wildernesses."

Sometimes an observer almost stumbles on a Snowy Plover brooding two or three chicks. An odd scene ensues, the mother bird scuffling away, belly to the sand, fluttering her wings as if broken, peeping piteously in an effort to draw the intruder away from her precious young. The chicks resemble pinches of down blown before the wind as their match-stick legs bear them to safety. Hiding in the shelter of any chance bit of flotsam, the tiny creatures vanish like puffs of smoke.

Unless it moves the Snowy Plover is almost invisible on a sunny beach. Its back is even lighter in hue than that of the Piping Plover and practically identical with the sand. The pale neck ring familiar on the Piping Plover gives way to an inconspicuous mark on either shoulder and a dusky dab on the forehead. You can sometimes spot the Snowy Plover when it scuttles along the shore ahead of you, but if it pauses you might think it had evaporated. It reminds one of Banquo's words, "The earth hath bubbles as the water hath and these are of them. Whither are they vanished?" to which Macbeth replies, "Into the air: and what seem'd corporal melted as breath into the wind."

The Piping Plover sometimes scrapes out several nesting hollows not far apart on a sandy level, but lays eggs in only one. The extra depressions are sometimes termed "cock nests." They remind an observer of the round extra nests woven by the Long-billed Marsh Wren. I have seen a plover crouch in such a hollow on a windy day as if to avoid rumpling her plumage.

The Snowy Plover also digs a number of superfluous hollows, and lines the one in which she deposits her eggs with bits of pink and white shell. On Cobb's and Wreck Islands, Virginia, I have known Least Terns to do the same thing, but without making any superfluous depressions.

Whereas the Piping Plover lays three or four eggs, the Snowy lays no more than three, and occasionally only two. These are lustreless, clay-colored, and short and top-shaped. They are so evenly dotted with black as to be perfectly camouflaged in the sand. And the downy chicks of the Snowy Plover are buffy above, liberally and evenly dotted with dusky, whereas the young Piping Plover is sandy above, peppered with brown, and wears a faint brown V on its crown.

Snowy Plovers do little migrating. They merely shift about a bit from time to time, particularly at the northern limit of their range, in southern Washington, and interior birds move to the coast in winter. Here they feed on the ocean beaches, dodging the surf, and chasing it down the slope at the reflex to seize the hoppers which kick themselves free of the spume by myriads. They devour flies, crabs, beetles, minute mussels, sea-worms and the like marine provender. On inland creeks and inlets they pluck bloodworms from the muddy banks, or an occasional small fiddler-crab. On this diet they grow round and fat, like so many of their sandpiper neighbors.

Snowy Plovers are almost the smallest of their family, being only six and one-half inches long. But they possess vigor out of all proportion to their size. They fly swiftly, veering and twisting, and showing power and grace in every movement.

Charadrius alexandrinus Linnaeus. Named in 1758 (for Alexandria, since the first specimen came from Egypt); our race, *nivosus* (Cassin) in 1858.

LOCAL NAMES: Nowhere more than in the case of this world citizen do racial names stand out as provincial and, in the end, foolish. We have called our Gulf Coast bird the Cuban Snowy Plover, the British call their race the Kentish Plover, yet they are the same bird.

FIELD CHARACTERS: A small, sandy-colored "broken ring" plover with a black or blackish patch on the sides of the breast only instead of a continuous or nearly-continuous dark ring around the breast as in Piping and Ringed Plovers. Paler than Piping Plover even, but with *dark* legs, bill, and dark eye-ring instead of yellow-orange markings in these areas. A rather quiet bird, but with occasional guttural trilling notes, or "a series of 3 rather low, mellow whistled notes, the second louder than the others" (Pough). l. 6", b. ⅝".

RANGE: Almost throughout the world south of 50° North latitude, except for eastern coasts of the U.S. and South America. The bird that breeds on our Gulf Coast (from Louisiana to Pensacola, Florida) is local throughout the West Indies, winters from the breeding area south to Venezuela. Another race breeds on our Pacific coast, from southern Washington to southern Baja California, east nearly to the 100th parallel, and winters throughout this region except in the interior. Another race occupies the coast of Peru and Chile.

8

MONGOLIAN PLOVER

Charadrius mongolus

THE nesting of this small Asiatic plover in Alaska would appear to be fortuitous so far, but it is probably a good example of how species become established in new territory. Though a half dozen or so individuals have been taken there since 1849, Alfred M. Bailey first took a female in breeding condition at Lopp Lagoon near Cape Prince of Wales on June 11, 1922, after strong winds from Asia. This at least suggested the possibility of nesting. The first nest was discovered on June 10, 1933, when D. Bernard Bull, collecting for the U. S. National Museum, found a nest with three eggs and took the male of this pair.

Charadrius mongolus Pallas. Described in 1776 from a Siberian specimen.

FIELD CHARACTERS: A small black-legged plover with cinnamon breast and nape. The typical head markings lose their blackness in winter, becoming grayish-brown, and the cinnamon turns to a gray wash. l. 7″.

RANGE: Breeds in alpine and low arctic areas, from the Chukchi Peninsula and the Commander Islands of the Bering Sea region, south across the uplands of Manchuria and Mongolia to the Himalayas, where it nests up to the 15,000 foot level. Winters from Japan south to Australia and New Zealand, and is casual in western Alaska below its presumed breeding area on the Seward Peninsula.

9

WILSON'S PLOVER (Thick-billed Plover)

Charadrius wilsonia

ONE morning late in June I overtook a pair of Wilson's Plovers leading three chicks on the seaward beach of Cobb Island off the Virginia shore. They let me approach rather close but then manifested those paroxysms of anxiety which almost all the shore birds exhibit when their eggs or young are threatened. The young, like the eggs they came from, were heavily peppered with brown and black and melted into the sand whenever they stopped running.

Being only a few paces away I readily noted all the field marks which distinguish this southern ring-neck. I missed first the orange-yellow eye-ring of its cousins, the Piping and Semipalmated Plovers, and noticed it had a faint white one instead. The back color was somewhere between those of the other two, and I saw that the broad black collar of the male did not encircle the neck but merged with the brown of the shoulders. The female sported a brown collar instead. Had I not been so close these differences could not have been checked with the naked eye. But the bill was different enough to have served at a much greater distance. The bills of the smaller ring-necks are short, yellow at the base, and black-tipped; but Wilson's Plover has longer, much stouter mandibles which are entirely black. The legs are grayish-buff, not yellow.

Ivan R. Tompkins [59] of Savannah, who has studied these birds closely, stresses that this is pre-eminently a running bird, preferring to run away from danger than fly, and that for that reason, it stays away from rocks or plants that might obstruct its vision. Its preferred habitats are the open areas of sand at the mouths of rivers, and the edges of the dunes. Here it stands and surveys its domain until food is sighted, and then runs directly to it. Fiddler crabs, various land crabs, shrimp, crawfish, beetles, spiders, and other "bugs" are eaten, depending on local conditions. Some of this diversity in food items may result from the fact that the bird often feeds along the edge of the water, where waves cast a variety of organisms onto the sand.

The courtship includes a posturing, with puffing out of the throat so that the feathers bearing the dark collar stand out like a ruff; even the breast feathers then stand out almost like a skirt. This may be done either while standing erect, or in a running crouch, when it is adapted either to courtship or to threaten another male who invades the territory.

Scrape-making is part of courtship and, once the birds are paired, precedes nest-selection. "The male approaches the female, picks a suitable nest site, and settles into it as though preparing a nest hollow. He picks up bits of shell or small sticks and arranges them. If the female is uninterested and moves away, he follows and again picks a spot near her for more scrape-making. After the pair is formed and territory is established, a similar performance takes place in locating the nest. At that stage the female has accepted the male and goes to him when he settles in a possible nest site and calls." Nesting territories are circles seldom less than 200 feet in diameter. When eggs are in the nest, and before the young have become independent, the adult birds perform a distraction-display, with injury-feigning, which is much like that of the Killdeer and other small plovers.

Charadrius wilsonia Ord. Described in 1814 in Alexander Wilson's *American Ornithology,* from a Cape May, N. J. specimen. A western race, *C. w. beldingi,* was recognized by Robert Ridgeway in 1919.

LOCAL NAMES: Thick-billed plover, ring-neck, stuttering plover.

FIELD CHARACTERS: Given in text. The usual voice is a clear, whistled *peet,* sometimes doubled or in sequence. l. 8", b. ı".

RANGE: From southern New Jersey, along the Atlantic, Gulf, and Caribbean coasts, to British Guiana on the east; from Baja California and central Sonora south to Peru on the west coast, the latter population distinguished as *C. w. beldingi.* Casual north to New England and Nova Scotia, mostly after hurricanes, in the east; also to San Diego County, California (western race).

10

KILLDEER

Charadrius vociferus

ALTHOUGH an observer must journey north at least as far
as Churchill, on Hudson Bay in early June, in order to study the breeding habits of most of our beach birds, nearly a dozen species nest in
middle latitudes and are thus more accessible to most of us.

The killdeer plover is one of the most familiar because it breeds
almost throughout the United States and lower Canada. Its distribution
is somewhat sporadic, so that farmers may be ignorant of its existence in
one county while those in some neighboring region know it well.

I hear its cheery call, *Kill-dee! Kill-dee!* from Maine to Florida,
sometimes on the coast, but more often in the grass of some inland pasture, in freshly cultivated fields or in rocky fallows. In such places the
mellow notes of the Killdeer, and its hovering pinions, are as native and
pastoral as the bleating of sheep. These calls herald the arrival of spring.
It is a seasonal voice, heard with the warble of bluebirds and the long
laugh of the golden-shafted flicker. Casting my first fly for trout on the
Spruce Run in central New Jersey, I often flush a pair in the green

world of the stream valley. Away they flutter, crying loudly. They never fly far but settle in the meadow or on a side-hill where a farmer is plowing the red earth.

The Killdeer is unmistakable. A long-tailed, long-winged slender bird of open places, its orange rump is pure reflected sunlight. The sexes being alike, both birds wear a double collar of broad black bands about their snowy necks. Sir Julian Huxley has suggested that, since such neck bands play a ruptive role, breaking up the bird's patterns and thus rendering them less conspicuous, the Killdeer has two because of its large size. The smaller plovers have but one ring, but if the width of this collar increased as the bird's size increases, it would become conspicuous instead of ruptive. The necessity of adapting has thus led to the development of two bands of more or less equal size.

As a typical open-country bird, the Killdeer has several other defenses against would-be predators. The nest is particularly easy to overlook among the pebbles of some eroded patch in the pasture. The four large eggs fit snugly together with the pointed ends downward, enabling a medium-sized bird to brood them all efficiently. It is notable that if an investigator changes their position, the brooding bird will promptly shuffle them back again. The Killdeer will readily leave her treasures, but since their blotchings are thickest at the large, upper end of the eggs, they are rendered almost indistinguishable from the surrounding shingle.

Almost everyone who has met the Killdeer on its home grounds has witnessed its "broken-wing" behavior, a highly-developed form of distraction display. These displays are varied so to suit the circumstances that they must almost certainly involve experience and intelligence in addition to innate behavior. Like the Mountain Plover and the Surfbird, two species of similarly open country, the Killdeer sits tight on the approach of a non-predatory animal, whether horse or cow or caribou, and explodes into its face at the last possible moment, thus diverting its path enough to save the nest from being trampled. But when men or canines approach, the bird "knows" that such a threat will come too late to distract attention from the eggs or young. Whether by design or the slow process of selection by trial and error methods, the Killdeer has learned to shift the danger inherent in invaders from its eggs to itself by a series of wild alarm calls and frantic posturings.

C. Douglas Deane [16] has distinguished three phases of this distraction behavior varying with the nature and intensity of the threat: (I)

"When I opened the gate of a field in which Killdeers were breeding, the brooding bird ran off the nest almost immediately, although I was still at least fifty yards away. Crouching, running silently and fast, the bird made for the opposite corner of the field. If I stopped or kept away from the nest no action was taken beyond agitated alarm calls and constant flights around the territory by both birds. When I approached the nest, one of the birds, presumably the one that was brooding, would alight about twenty feet away and run toward me, crouching with wings half open but the primaries not extended, uttering a piercing alarm call." Or, "if I moved too fast towards the nest, the bird ran toward me with wings held high over the body and the tail spread but not depressed. If I stopped or moved away, the display ceased but the bird continued its wild alarm calls."

When the threat to the nest or young became imminent, (II) "the Killdeer suddenly turned around so that its tail was toward me and the yellow threat-color was shown. The bird now exhibited the true broken-wing behavior. Calling all the while, it crouched on the full length of the tarso-metatarsus with the wings drooping, exposing the brilliant ochraceous color of the rump and tail. The tail was depressed with the feathers cutting the soil, one wing was beating violently on the ground and the other wing was half open, twisted against the back, and waved excitedly in the air. The bird eyed me for a sign that I was interested; I was and so followed it. The Killdeer immediately rose and ran rapidly for some six feet with its wings hanging loosely, the tail still spread, and the bird leaning to one side. It crouched again and performed the same trick, sometimes with variations, beating both wings on the ground or waving them above the back."

By a repetition of this procedure, the enemy is normally lured away from the eggs. Even when tense with the excitement of full display, Mr. Deane noticed that the birds always tried to interpose some cover between them and their "victim," be it a plant or a stone, no matter how small. Once the threat has been removed a sufficient distance from the nest, the bird ceases displaying and merely calls its alarm for a while.

A final phase (III), probably representing excitement of very high intensity, is one in which the bird, instead of slipping off the nest in time, stands in front of the nest with wings spread on the ground in an arc and tail spread wide, and calls excitedly. These displays are characteristic of the nesting period and are continued until the young are about ten days old.

Charadrius vociferus Linnaeus. 1758, based on Mark Catesby's Chattering Plover
in the *Natural History of Carolina, Florida and the Bahama Islands* (1731–
1743), the first truly important work on American natural history.

LOCAL NAMES: Kildee, killdeer plover.

FIELD CHARACTERS: A good-sized plover with *two* breast bands, orange rump, and
loud plaintive calls. These calls may be a (1) *dee dee dee dee-ee kildee dee-ee,*
(A. A. Saunders) given especially by birds disturbed by intrusion; (2) a drawn-
out *t-rrrrrrrrrr* given in fighting, distraction, or fear; and (3) the familiar
kildeeah, kildeeeah, kildeeah, given with a downward slurring (instead of upward as in 1) by birds in flight, and often heard on moonlight nights. Fresh
water birds except in winter, when they also frequent the seashore to feed on
flies in the kelp wrack. l. 10″, b. ¾″.

RANGE: Breeds in suitably open areas almost everywhere south of the sub-arctic
forest across the continent, south to south-central Mexico and central Florida.
Winters from southern British Columbia, Colorado, Ohio Valley, southern
New England south to Venezuela, Colombia and Peru. Two other races
occur, one in the West Indies, the other from Peru to northern Chile.

11

MOUNTAIN PLOVER

Eupoda montana

THIS species takes its name from the immense Rocky Mountain region, but might be called more appropriately the "plains plover." It haunts the high, semi-arid lands from northern Montana and western Nebraska south to Colorado, Kansas, New Mexico, and northern Texas. It seems equally at home on desert sands, buffalo-grass prairies, and the fields of new homesteads. It breeds throughout this section of the West.

The Mountain Plover is rather a plain little bird, an inch longer than eastern ring-necks, grayish brown above and pale buff to whitish below, with no dark ring. Its only striking marks are a black cap and a dark stripe from the base of the mandibles to the eye. It is as graceful and trimly modeled as all of its kind, and lends a welcome touch of life to the arid wilderness.

Although anatomically a true shore bird, the Mountain Plover shuns lakes, sloughs, ponds or streams, being almost as much a desert species as the Road-runner. It is a thoroughgoing westerner, never appearing in the East except as an extremely rare straggler. It flies as lightly as a swallow, and easily crosses a thousand miles of peaks towards the Pacific. Reaching California, it avoids the booming shores of the ocean and pitches on level land at some distance from the sound of surf.

Driving west across the high, sweltering plains, the motorist complains loudly of the fat green grasshoppers—as big as eastern katydids—locusts, and other pests which infest the plains. These insects splash against windshields, sometimes forcing a driver to stop his car and wipe them off. Shields specially designed to prevent the scum from blocking up radiators, are sold at most gasoline service stations on his route. These hoppers form the favorite food of the Mountain Plover much of the year, but I doubt whether the birds can even thin them out. Like so many of their Order these birds were formerly gunned under the name of "Upland Plover" and were regarded as game throughout thousands of square miles of open range. Under present-day protective laws and influences they are gaining in numbers, but probably have never been extremely numerous anywhere.

They whistle dreamily on the uplands, or utter a low, sweet medley of calls during the nesting season. Although hatched on the hottest, driest levels in North America, the chicks run about and feed there unaffected by the searing sun. Where agriculture springs up Mountain Plovers soon appear and make themselves at home, just as Killdeers do on farms in the Middle West and in the East.

The nests, eggs, and young of the species, found almost invariably on open, exposed terrain, have been endangered time out of mind by the hoofs of antelope, bison, and in later years, of horses and cattle, and the lumbering treads of farm machinery. Mountain Plover seem absolutely fearless. They have been known to stick to their nests while a herd of dogies was driven towards them and to start up at the last second and explode into the faces of the leading beasts. This frightens the herd, forcing them to split ranks and to pass on either side.

Mr. Lewis Wayne Walker, who has witnessed this bit of strategy, writes in *Audubon Magazine* (1955) that it is not casual but customary. He shows also that these birds show versatility enough to try very different ruses when approached by human beings. They do not attempt to scare them, as they do range cattle, but scuffle away from the intruder, dragging a wing as if it were broken. The Killdeer makes similar responses to these two major threats to its eggs.

Early in the fall Mountain Plovers indulge in many practice flights, usually in flocks of two or three dozen, and then suddenly disappear southward. In winter they drift down to the border and far over into Old Mexico. There, precisely as in the North, they shun the sea-coast and live contentedly on the highest, driest plains until the migratory urge starts them northward again in the spring.

Eupoda montana (Townsend). Described in 1837 from a specimen taken near the Sweetwater River, Wyoming.

LOCAL NAMES: Upland plover.

FIELD CHARACTERS: Almost as large as the Killdeer, which it resembles in general form and coloration, but the crown is black, with a conspicuous broad white forehead and eye-stripe. The breast is washed with a sandy-buff tone, and the otherwise uniformly colored tail is sub-terminally black and tipped with a narrow white band. In flight, the strikingly white wing linings against an otherwise nondescript tone are helpful. And, unlike the Killdeer, this plover crouches when disturbed, and flies off low over the ground with a soft croaking note. l. 9″, b. 7⁄8″.

RANGE: Breeds in semi-arid and arid uplands east of the Rocky Mountains, from n. Montana south to w. Texas. Winters from central and coastal Texas and adjacent Mexico, westward to central California and s. Baja California.

12

DOTTEREL

Eudromias morinellus

THIS attractive plover's right to a place on the North American list of breeding birds is even more tenuous than that of the Mongolian Plover, but is included because the female of a pair taken by Charles D. Brower [6] at Point Barrow on June 14 and 16, 1930, was carrying a fully-formed egg. Only a few others have been taken since, but it seems likely that the species will gradually establish itself between Point Barrow and the Seward Peninsula.

This bird is tame to the point of being called "foolish," though this is always more a reflection on the behavior of humans than on the bird itself. The role of the sexes is reversed, also, the female doing most of the pre-mating displays.

Eudromias morinellus (Linnaeus). Described in 1758 from a Swedish specimen.

FIELD CHARACTERS: A medium-sized, stocky plover with black crown, conspicuous white eye line, white throat and cheeks, blue-gray breast separated from chestnut belly by a white line. Black belly patch in breeding season. Grayer in winter, when cinnamon turns to gray, but white breast line still diagnostic. Orange legs. Length 9″. Call trisyllabic.

RANGE: Alpine tundra and low arctic of Eurasia, overflowing to Alaska at Bering Straits. Winters mostly in southern Europe, the middle East, and north Africa. Casual in western Alaska, Japan, the Canary Islands. Accidental in western Washington.

13

AMERICAN GOLDEN PLOVER

Pluvialis dominica

I HAVE ample reasons for remembering the flats of Goose Creek, between Far Rockaway and Jamaica Bay. With a crony I arrived there soon after the pike had been completed alongshore, and when millions of tons of sand had been pumped on the flats to reinforce the highway. It had settled, and the metal pipes which had discharged it lay rusting nearby.

We constructed a blind and set out some folding tin pocket decoys in hopes of whistling in a few shore birds. It was a bluebird day and very few migrants were flying even on the rising tide. Two or three Golden Plover circled past, far up under the clouds, whistling a merry, *Ter-eee-lee! Ter-e-leeee!* but most of the birds were drowsing in the meadows waiting for the tide to ebb.

Not until the water receded did we sight any sizable flocks, but about a dozen alighted far out on the artificial bar. Watching these plovers through binoculars I noted that they never ran round nervously with beaks down, as hungry Sanderlings do. They scattered widely and walked slowly from place to place with heads high, whistling dreamily every so often. Occasionally one would seize a bit of food—usually a long bloodworm, too big to be swallowed at one gulp.

It would have been better for us if we had limited our efforts to observing those migrants. Unfortunately a handsome flock suddenly planed in from the sea and decoyed to those feeding on the bar. Tempted by the sight we rose and stepped a few yards nearer. Then the sand, being so newly poured and being undermined by salt water, waved under our feet like thin ice and next thing we knew my companion had slumped through up to his armpits.

Seizing a driftwood plank I tried to pull him out, but presently broke in myself, and we were soon engulfed to our chins. C. L. was large and heavy, and had a weak heart, so that matters appeared desperate. Only by gripping our well-oiled guns could we keep from sinking deeper in that unholy quicksand. It took us half an hour to crawl out on our bellies, panting and exhausted.

What had become of the plover meanwhile is anybody's guess. We felt thankful that we had not been sucked down twenty or more feet in that awful place. We had been punished for molesting shore birds, and soon afterwards relinquished that sport for conservation, something which had been in our minds for months.   (*H.M.H.*)

We have been well lectured on the tragedy of the Eskimo Curlew's fatal decline, but the decline of the Golden Plover's legions is equally dramatic, although the final chapter is happier because this bird has made a remarkable recovery.

The flights of Eskimo Curlew were impressive because these birds moved up and down the continent along narrow pathways, an ancestral habit which made them the most vulnerable species of all. But the Golden Plover moved right across the land, so vast were its numbers. It was as much a manifestation of a fabulous continent's accumulated wealth as the bison and the Passenger Pigeon were. Like these two other products of America's early overflowing, the plovers arrived in great migratory waves in spring, "in large compact, marshaled flocks, strong of wing and direct in action when in passage" that led the early settlers to mark these as "plover days," just as the most callous of them could not help but be impressed by "pigeon days."

But these great flights aroused the cupidity of the market gunner, and stirred that strange desire to emulate for "sport" the nasty work of the trafficker in wild game. All that was now needed to spell disaster to the plover legions was the westward march of an acquisitive people.

The plains once breached, the end was as sure as it was for the bison and the pigeon.

It is on record that in 1890 two Boston wholesalers of game received from the West in one shipment forty barrels of birds. These were crammed with ten thousand Golden Plovers and four thousand Eskimo Curlews, the interstices being stuffed with the bodies of Upland Plovers. The merchants had a standard formula: 25 dozen Eskimo Curlew or 60 dozen Golden Plover to the barrel. This traffic got underway soon after 1880 when the abrupt decline of the Passenger Pigeon forced the market gunners to shift their attention to the still abundant shore birds, but so great was the drain on the continent's "inexhaustible" resource that it petered out quickly after 1891, after a decade of gluttony.

Indeed, the last great flight along the Massachusetts shore was in the fall of 1863, when for a last time, the birds, driven from the sea by storm, swarmed over every acre of open farmland in the eastern part of the colony, only to be beset by every man and boy who could abandon his chores and shoulder gun or club and wade into the fray. Even so, goodly numbers continued to visit the New England coast until 1886, but after that the combined decimations of sport along the coast, and the methodical commercial slaughter in the interior of the continent proved too much even for a bountiful Nature.

As always, there were professional optimists who denied any serious decline, who insisted that the birds had simply shifted their routes a bit. George H. Mackay,[30] who hunted plovers on Nantucket, but who had, also, the disciplined ethics of a sportsman-naturalist, was one of the first to deplore the trend. He foresaw the end in an ironic comment: "While we may not be able to answer the question: are they fewer than formerly, we shall be ably fitted to do so in a few years."

Almost unlimited and undisturbed breeding grounds, the good fortune of having an off-shore fall migration route, and the habit of long flights in spring which caused them to "touch down" briefly only here and there as they went north up the broad interior of the continent—all these helped the Golden Plover to avoid extermination. In 1913 and 1918 laws at last gave them surcease from the gun. This was, and will remain, essential to them, because although fast on the wing Golden Plover were never adapted to serve as game birds. Much tamer than the still numerous Black-bellied Plover, they came too readily to decoys. Being fired into, the flocks would scatter; but they could be whistled back three or four times in succession.

For the first twenty-five years of our century it remained a rare bird, especially on the Atlantic coast. Slowly, then, but with gathering momentum—and despite the fact that it continues even to this day to be shot on its South American wintering grounds—it reoccupied empty niches. It is once again seen in flocks of a thousand or more in the interior, and not only is it again a regular fall migrant east of the high plains, but northbound spring migrants are now almost regular, if few in numbers, on the east coast. This attests to a healthy overflowing of population. However, though the species now seems safely recovered, not again are we likely to see such "plover days" as gladdened the skies annually until a century ago.

Long migrations always have an aura of romance about them, and because they are easier to visualize than are numerical fluctuations, we long ago accorded the Golden Plover a well-deserved reputation as one of the most adventurous of our feathered travelers. In this it is of course not alone, certainly not unique.

The origin of these long migration lanes is a great challenge to men's minds and has therefore been the source of intriguing speculations. Wells W. Cooke,[11] who reported on these things at the turn of the century, had an amazing insight into them. Despite the accumulations of knowledge since his day, no one has improved on the migration pattern he suggested for the Golden Plover in 1911.

It was Cooke's conviction that birds don't strike out blindly across the continents when they set out for the antipodes, nor do they commonly blunder into new routes. We know of course that birds may be blown off course and that their innate navigational skills may fail them on occasion. But by and large their instinct serves them well, and it seems plain that today's migration lanes have evolved on a trial and error basis.

For example, the direct transgulf route from Yucatan to Texas is very probably the result of consecutive shortenings of an arc that began by going entirely around the Gulf of Mexico. The present transoceanic route from Nova Scotia to Brazil is likewise the perfected shortening of a route that may at first have been coastal, then shortened to pass from Cape Cod to Cuba via Bermuda; and, finally, became the audacious but shorter and more efficient oceanic route most Golden Plovers now follow southward.

The Pacific race of this plover has an even more amazingly complex history behind it, if we accept Cooke's speculative but logical reconstructions. This bird is primarily a member of the Siberian tundra community, and as such has long migrated north and south across Asia, as it does today, wintering in southeast Asia but overflowing southeastward to all the beaches of Australia and Oceania as far east as the Low Archipelago. A summer range which spans some 5,000 miles of latitude is abandoned for a wintering range 10,000 miles wide and 8800 miles to the southward!

This breeding population has—in what are probably comparatively recent times—overflowed eastward and colonized the west-facing coast of Alaska. Now, in all probability, these Alaskan birds at first migrated westward to Siberia, whence their parents came, and then moved south along the China coast in the company of Siberian birds. Later, some birds ventured a shorter route down the Kamchatka Peninsula, to Japan, and eastward into the oceanic islands that compose Micronesia, spreading then into Polynesia. Northbound birds especially, probably pioneered more direct routes which cut off the big west-east loop and took them directly to the Aleutian Islands from points in the Leeward group of islands. It is only about 2200 miles from Midway to the nearest of the Aleutians, not 10,000 as the roundabout route was.

Even so, these are amazing and wonderful journeys. We believe today that these birds can probably navigate by the stars. We know that they are probably capable of "shifting into high gear" on these long flights (*see under Dunlin*). What we need to remember is that these long flights are not necessarily all done by stellar navigation, and that the oceans they cross are not the featureless expanses portrayed in our school geographies. F. W. Preston [42] has pointed out that some of the most spectacular "sign posts" of the planet are the cloud belts that lie over the seas like white quilts. In July such a cloud belt extends westward from San Francisco for 800 miles, with broken cumulus clouds extending even farther toward Hawaii, marking the contrasting border of a major ocean current. Another feature of oceanic horizons lies in the towering turrets of great cumulus masses that shoot upward on the windward slopes of volcanic peaks like those of the Hawaiian Islands, some of the latter attaining nearly 14,000. These are visible nearly 300 miles away to birds flying at 10,000 feet elevation. The level at which birds migrate is still disputed, but it seems obvious that creatures so sensitive to the currents of the ocean of air they ply will adapt to conditions, flying now low over the waves, now high in the clear air, since they know much better than we what will hasten their long trek.

(R.C.C.)

Pluvialis dominica (Muller). Described in 1776.

LOCAL NAMES: Black-breast, field-bird, green-back, green-head, frost-bird, pale-belly, and many others.

FIELD CHARACTERS: A medium-sized plover, darker, slimmer and more shapely than the Black-bellied Plover, with a smaller head and bill, and decidedly more brown in the "gray" phase of winter. Flying away from an observer, the uniform tone is distinctive (Black-belly has white tail); axillars gray (black in Black-belly and white in European Golden Plover). Prefers short grass areas to tidal flats; bobs more than the Black-belly. Call note a rolling, chuckling "coodle, coodle, coodle" (Mackay), sometimes a harsh, whistled "quee" (Peterson). l. 10½", b. ⅞".

RANGE: Breeds on the arctic coasts of Siberia, east to North Devon Island and south to southwestern Alaska, central Mackenzie (Artillery L.); Churchill, Manitoba, and southwest Baffin Island (Nettilling L.). The American race (*P.d.dominica*) occupies the eastern half of this range, from the Bering Sea coast of Alaska, and migrates south across North America, chiefly off the Atlantic coast, to winter in southern South America. The Siberian race, the Lesser Golden Plover (*P.d.fulva*), overlaps the American race on the Bering Sea coast of Alaska and extends westward across arctic Siberia to the Yamal Peninsula, where it overlaps the range of the European Golden Plover (*P. apricaria*), and winters in southeast Asia and throughout Oceania. It is casual on the West Coast of the Americas, and in Europe and east Africa, one of the world's greatest wanderers.

14

BLACK-BELLIED PLOVER (Grey Plover)

Squatarola squatarola

THIS largest and most magnificent of American plovers is the king of all the birds which throng our beaches or wing it above the eternal surf. Ten and a half to well over thirteen inches in length, it has a wingspread of from twenty-two to twenty-five inches. It is very robust, with powerful pectoral muscles to drive its extremely long wings and carry it round the shores of the seven seas.

Black-bellied Plovers breed all the way from Point Barrow east to the frozen Melville Peninsula, to Greenland and the arctic coasts of Europe and Asia. On their southern migration they reach Brazil and Peru. From European shores they trek to South Africa and Madagascar. A Siberian variant, almost indistinguishable from the American bird, flies down to India, the Malay Peninsula, and Australia. In other words, Black-bellied Plovers fly north, south, east or west over most of the beaches of the world.

The loud, clear cry of *Toor-a-lee! Toor-a-leee!* floating from the clouds in early April, heralds the descent of these plovers on our beaches. They suddenly appear on the sands from New Jersey and Long Island to Martha's Vineyard, Nantucket, and Cape Cod. They linger until nearly the middle of June, when they depart for their nesting areas on the Arctic tundra and coastal islands in the polar seas.

In bridal plumage the Black-bellied Plover is very striking, its under plumage being jet black from chin to thigh, with faint metallic gloss. The forehead, sides of the large head, and tail-coverts are snowy white, very conspicuous even at considerable distances. The pattern of the back and shoulders is largely grayish with dusky markings, and much white shows on the upper wings in flight. The axillars are black and may be plainly seen whenever the plover flushes. The legs and feet are lead colored, and the front toes webbed at the base. The hind toe is rudimentary or missing. The sexes are alike excepting that light streaks show in the black bellies of some females. The winter plumage is plainer, being slightly paler everywhere, and the sable under parts largely replaced by white streaks.

The Black-bellied Plover is a creature of the tides. It rests in green saltings when the water is high but is always first at the feast when the tide bares vast expanses of sand or mud leaving behind countless millions of hoppers, sandworms, and minute crustaceans. Feeding there until chased out by the next flood tide, the plovers fly back into the meadows to rest, or start on another lap of their long migration.

Our eastern bays, estuaries, and marshes offer feeding grounds almost without limit. At Plymouth, Barnstable, Yarmouth, Rock Harbor, Wellfleet, Chatham, Monomoy, Nantucket, Martha's Vineyard and all the inlets and estuaries from Montauk to Fire Island, thousands upon thousands of acres of tidal flats spread marine tables for all our shore birds. And there are even larger areas of the sort from Sandy Hook to the Marshes of Glynn in Georgia, and from there to the southern tip of the great Florida peninsula.

On the white sands facing all these flats you will see the large, clear footprints of Black-bellied Plover, showing bigger and bolder than the tracks of Ruffed Grouse on drifted snow. They are far apart where the plovers have been racing one another and end where the birds have launched into the air.

It is noteworthy that whereas the market-gunners almost annihilated the main flocks of Golden Plover before legal protection rescued the remnants, our Black-bellied Plover were never greatly reduced in numbers. They were gunned, of course, but not to any dangerous extent. Having lived close to the beaches for fifty years, and having watched the shore birds come and go, I will explain why Black-bellied Plover never suffered such casualties as the beautiful golden species.

In the first place they are more wary, always keeping out of range of vagrant boys armed with inferior guns and without decoys. In the second place Black-bellied Plovers usually fly in smaller flocks. I must admit that they came readily to decoys, particularly the young of the year, and were readily whistled in. I have known a flock of these young plovers to decoy to duck stool, which sounds like a stupid performance. But it was not typical.

Mature Black-bellied Plovers more frequently drove past at almost incredible speed, barely dipping to the decoys, and out of reach in an instant. Even with deep pits, decoys, and plentiful ammunition, it took a crack shot to make high scores on these birds. All this required money, effort, and equipment beyond the means of mere pot-hunters.

Another thing helped Black-bellied Plovers to survive even in the days when they were considered legal game and were sold in city markets. In mild weather the biggest flights dawdled in the north and moved south rather late. Sometimes they did not arrive until sportsmen were too much preoccupied with wildfowl to take any interest in shore birds. Migration by night and a tendency to keep well off shore on the southern trek likewise saved any number of flocks from persecution. Their flights over salt water were comparable to those made by the golden species. And like those beautiful migrants their flesh in the fall was so thickly coated with fat that they could not be cooked without removing the layers. Presumably both species of plover burned up their fat by muscular exertions over immense distances.

Notes taken at one specific point are somewhat more suggestive than mere generalizations.

A funnel-shaped extension of Provincetown Harbor in Massachusetts extends more than a mile to the neck of the cape, here only thirty paces across from the tideway. Following the creek, migrating shore birds all pass this bottleneck, after which they fly towards Race Run, two miles northward, or take off for the lower cape across Cape Cod Bay.

A lagoon, or at half tide, its dry bed, lies directly under this flyway, and a pit dug there and screened by an armful of weeds, makes a strategic blind. Its precise location was my own secret for many years and I still use it occasionally for observing migrants at close range. A dozen snipe or plover decoys will generally toll down birds enough to satisfy anybody. It is an excellent spot to take motion pictures.

The last week in August and the first in September are golden days on the sea-meadows of the Atlantic coast. Sometimes the wind will blow cool and sweet, with the sun like a vast jewel in the sapphire sky, and the plover whistling across the broad expanse of green from the heaven. It would be difficult to say which is the more beautiful—the piping of the birds or their flight on down-curved pinions, itself music made visible.

Black-bellied Plover, or "beetle-heads" as they are termed locally, come winging steadily along as swiftly as wildfowl, in crescents consisting of anywhere between five and perhaps a score. When the breeze is strong they drive by at a terrific pace, quite as fast as Canvasback ducks. If they espy a patch where salt hay has recently been cut, they may be attracted to it, but most of them pass at a speed that makes you gasp.

They have been disturbed at breakfast on flats in Cape Cod Bay and generally reach you long before the first glint of water tells that the tide is following up the dry creek-bed. The flight often continues while the tongue of the advancing creek licks out over the sand beside the blind.

Sometimes the water comes no farther; but when the full moon and the sun are pulling together, particularly towards the Equinox, this entire district—sands, saltings, and creeks—is whelmed by the ocean. At such times if easterly storms have piled the Atlantic in on our shores, you may fancy that the sea will swallow the whole tip of Cape Cod.

Marvelous as bright days prove, the weather in which to witness a really large flight is usually foul. On one occasion it was my good fortune to see a press of plover which must have resembled those reported in olden times.

It had rained steadily for three days, with a northeast gale, and it was a "high course tide" in September. I foresaw that the tide would drown me out of my blind, yet I lingered until it had engulfed the meadows and converted the saltings into a swirling sea. In my immediate neighborhood only a hummock or two still projected from the racing water. My decoys kept tumbling over and drifting away, and finally the sea seeped into my dugout. I then crawled to the crest of a hillock and clung there.

All at once Black-bellied Plovers came hurtling up the creekways from the harbor. They appeared at first in dark flurries of a dozen or so, but then in bows numbering nearly a hundred, with flankers of robin-snipe and smaller varieties. Thicker and bigger came the bunches, one after another for the next twenty minutes.

Now and then came an interval when I thought the show was over, but more plovers followed, always helter-skelter like wind-blown leaves. They were certainly not local plover which had been dawdling on the Provincetown flats. The latter had passed some hours previously, as they always do. I was watching a large flight which had been driven in from the sea while passing to the east of Cape Cod.

In the days when gunning shore birds was still allowed, such a concentration furnished excellent shooting. Riding on a gale the plovers passed at incredible speed. It was necessary to take them quartering in from the left, or at right angles, or by following through after they had passed. If a gunner failed to lead the birds liberally, they never stopped. They traveled so fast that when one was hit it would thud several rods beyond the decoys, the momentum being extraordinary. Sometimes sizable flocks continued to go over until it looked as if the gunner might have to swim ashore.

I have watched other memorable flights of shore birds from that same dugout, but none comparable with the one just described. These large movements are seen only when weather conditions are just right. Moreover, most such migrations take place by night and so pass unobserved. The smaller species are always with us; but Black-bellied Plover, winter yellowlegs and dowitchers appear in greatest numbers only when blown ashore by adverse winds.

Squatarola squatarola (Linnaeus). Described in 1758.

LOCAL NAMES: Beetle-head, grey plover (Europe), bull-head (N.J.), black-breast, etc.

FIELD CHARACTERS: Large, chunky, big-headed, and erect plover. Spring plumage has white head but black face and belly (crissum white, so actually less black-bellied than Golden Plover; fall and winter plumage almost silvery gray (with just a wash of brown). In any plumage, best told by its wild, rather lonely behavior: head tucked in as though dejected, standing on one leg (more than any others); in flight, by the white tail (fine barring shows at close range only), and black axillary patch where the underwing joins the body. Its calls are rich, whistled notes, the characteristic one a strong, plaintive 3-note "*ple-u-wee*," the middle note low. l. 10½–13½", b. 1–¼", female larger.

RANGE: Arctic tundra from n.e. Siberia (Kanin Penin.) eastward to Devon Is. and s.w. Baffin Is. Non-breeders occur south to n. South America in summer; s. to British Isles in Old World. Winters on almost all coasts south of 45°N. lat. In America, migrates up both coasts, heading inland over New England, and through interior west of Hudson Bay. In fall, down same routes, but overflowing east to Newfoundland.

Five Black-bellied Plover and (r) two Golden Plover in flight

15

SURFBIRD

Aphriza virgata

WHETHER because ornithologists are not much given to mountain climbing, or because the 20,000-foot massif of Alaska's magnificent Mount McKinley seemed so unlikely a nesting ground for two shore birds of the surf-girt and fog-shrouded Pacific coast, the fact is that McKinley's alpine slopes long withheld knowledge that both the Surfbird and the Wandering Tatler nested there.

Three Alaskan waders, the Surfbird, the Wandering Tatler, and the Bristle-thighed Curlew, derive their first description from the work of Englishman John Latham, a foremost ornithologist of the 18th Century. Latham's *General Synopsis of Birds* (1785) formed the basis for many of Johann F. Gmelin's descriptions when he edited and expanded Linnaeus' classic catalogue of the world's known fauna and flora, *Systema Naturae*, a decade later. It is Gmelin's name, therefore, which is appended to the scientific name of these birds, as of many others, not because he was the first man to describe them, but the first to give them a binomial name in the Linnaean tradition.[2]

It is even more interesting that these three Alaskan birds, known to Latham before 1785, should all have kept the secret of their nesting until well along in the 20th Century, being among the very last North American species to yield to ornithological exploration. It was Olaus J.

Murie[32] who first consciously discovered, and reported, the breeding of the Surfbird above timberline on Mount McKinley's slopes in 1921. But Murie merely found a pair of adults with a downy young, and museum specialists were still ignorant of the nest and the eggs, so the search continued.

Five years later, California ornithologist Joseph Dixon[17] and his party succeeded in this quest and brought back the coveted evidence. Their account emphasizes that the Surfbird's summer haunts are as rocky and difficult to maneuver as the rugged reefs they inhabit in winter.

These McKinley slopes are Mountain Sheep country, a jumbled terrain of alpine ridges above timberline, where rock stripes and great frost polygons lace the slopes, and every stream basin is a bed of rubble. The Surfbird's nest, unlike that of the Wandering Tatler which nests in the brook basins, is a mere depression on the open tundra, incompletely lined with wisps of lichen and dead leaves, exposed to all the elements. Mr. Dixon's dedication to the search for an understanding of these birds, and the Surfbird's well-adapted behavior in this bleak environment, is interestingly told in Dixon's account of this trip: "When it began to rain the surfbird merely fluffed up and then spread out the feathers on his back so as completely to cover the nest. This proved an effective method, because the melting snow and the rain ran readily off the surfbird's back and was absorbed by the moss outside the nest. We were not so well protected and were soon shivering and wet to the skin.

"At 4 o'clock a female mountain sheep appeared, silently, like a ghost, out of the mist that came drifting over the mountain peaks in great white swirls. She did not see us at first, but when she was within 6 feet of and headed directly toward the surfbird's nest she became suddenly aware of our presence and took a step or two forward. When the ewe was about to step on the nest the surfbird suddenly "exploded" right in the astonished animal's face. This unexpected movement and the sudden noise and flash of white of the bird's spread wings and tail caused the mountain sheep to jump back quickly; then she whirled around and bounded off back up the trail. This sudden movement of the surfbird at the critical moment doubtless serves to prevent sheep and caribou from trampling upon its nest and eggs. We found through repeated experiments that this was the bird's regular reaction. When we approached, whether fast or slow, the bird would stay on the nest until the last minute, and then, instead of sneaking off low to the ground like most birds do, would fly directly up into our faces. Even after we knew that the bird would do this the psychological result on our part was the same. A person would involuntarily recoil when the bird "exploded" like a firecracker right in his face."   (R.C.C.)

Aphriza virgata (Gmelin). Named in 1789.

FIELD CHARACTERS: A chunky, short-legged gray bird slightly larger than the Black Turnstone it often associates with. Wings dark gray, with prominent white stripe; tail with a broad black band but upper tail and lower rump white. Head and neck streaked evenly with black, breast and belly strikingly spotted with brownish-black. Legs and base of lower mandible yellowish. A quiet bird as a rule, but calling a shrill *ke-week* when flushed. l. 10″, b. 1″.

RANGE: Breeds above timberline in the Mount McKinley Park region, perhaps west to Kotzebue Sound. Winters along Pacific coast from Petersburg in s.e. Alaska, south to the Straits of Magellan.

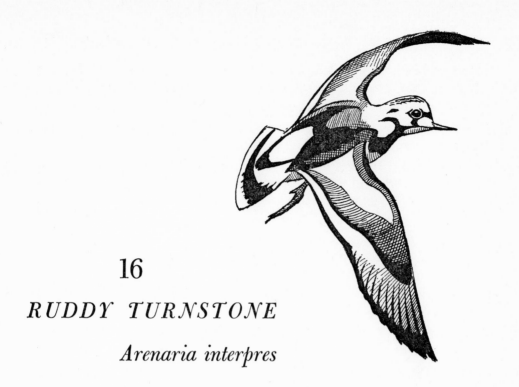

16

RUDDY TURNSTONE

Arenaria interpres

WALKING along the sea-wall at St. Augustine, Florida, one March 7th, I noticed that the retreating tide had bared beds of "coon oysters" incredibly dense and high. They banded the beach as far as I could see in every direction and incrusted the piles of every wharf.

I was wondering what value so many tons of these molluscs could have, when I noted a slight movement at the edge of the beds about twenty paces distant. It proved to be a flight of shore birds whose grayish backs blended so perfectly with the mud and shells as to be practically invisible until they moved. Looking more closely I saw that they were Ruddy Turnstones, birds slightly smaller than Knots, with short, orange-colored legs, and sharp mandibles, somewhat like those of woodpeckers, but slightly upturned at the point.

Whenever one watches such a flock he is likely to note some trifling item overlooked in earlier observations. In this case it was a faint tinkle made as the turnstones tripped along beside the shelly ridges. Every click, a sound so faint that any breath of wind would have rendered it inaudible, came from the turning over of an empty shell or other bit of flotsam.

These birds flicked over hundreds of empties to seize the eggs of horse-shoe crabs, worms, minute mussels—all sorts of marine provender

which lurks under such shelter. That is the way turnstones feed, for no
other bird has been more aptly named. Once in a while you may see one
probe the mud or rock-weed, but turning stones is a standard occupa-
tion between tides.

Recently I sat on the St. Augustine ocean beach, eating my lunch
and occasionally sharing it with these shore birds. Ring-billed Gulls also
crowded around, and soon about fifty birds were gathering crumbs.

We were all so much engrossed in this food that when a sharp cry
sounded near at hand and a big brown hawk whizzed by my head and
seized a shore bird—not one of my turnstones but an inconspicuous
sanderling—I jumped up with a yell and the predator dropper its victim.
It was unhurt and flew out over the surf. The incident shows that any
interference with birds, however amiable the intention, may endanger
them. These shore birds were thrown off their guard by my feeding
them.

The birds at St. Augustine were northward bound but not yet in
breeding plumage. Even so, the rich chestnut mottling on the shoulders
and wing-coverts of the males made a strong contrast with the white of
their under parts. With the black bands across their breasts, heads, and
faces it made a pattern so gay as to earn these birds such familiar appel-
lations as "calico backs" and "calico plover." Down East they are often
termed "chicken plover," an appropriate name. The plumage patterns
of the females, particularly in winter, are much grayer and more sub-
dued than those of the males.

Even the gayest turnstone colors are highly protective. I had
counted ten of this particular flock when some whim put a bird or two
to flight. Clusters jumped up everywhere along the beach until I had
noted twenty-seven, and there were many more a bit farther off. Most
of them had been completely camouflaged against the beds of dark
oysters. Taking wing they flashed into sight, the blacks and whites of
their primaries and three white streaks down their backs showing
vividly, and making the fugitives appear double their real size.

Turnstones have increased rapidly because of protective laws.
Every year the flights appear larger, and the species may soon become as
numerous as it ever was. Although we note plenty of turnstones all
along the Atlantic coast from March onward, they breed only in the
Arctic wastes where they spend the short summer.

Birula [40] depicts the summer habits of the Eurasian race in interesting terms: "Upon their arrival in the Siberian tundra the Turnstones

are paired and at once set about egg-laying. I never succeeded in finding a nest of this bird chiefly because at the first alarm-notes of its neighbors it leaves its nest and only returns to it when the tundra is once more at peace. One's appearance is always proclaimed by a cry of alarm from some Turnstone, *tiwu-tiwu-ti-ti, tiwu-tiwu-ti-ti-ti*. At once a pair of these birds follows you, flying from one stone or tuft to another, with importunate cries, until you have gone some distance from the nest. But no sooner have you left the territory of one pair, when a second pair circles about you so that during your entire excursion over the tundra you are pursued by the noisy cries of the Turnstone. One always finds both parent birds near the nest as well as tending the young and the two share equally in protecting their progeny, flying to attack any man or arctic fox that approaches the nest or young. The appearance of a jaeger in the neighborhood of the nest and especially near the place where the young are hiding is followed by such a furious attack on the part of the Turnstones that the enemy beats a hasty retreat even when attacked by only a single Turnstone. The uproar in the tundra reaches the highest pitch on the appearance of an arctic fox, and although all the birds of the tundra join in it, the loud notes of the Turnstones predominate."

Arenaria interpres (Linnaeus). Described in 1758 from a Swedish specimen; our race, *A.i.morinella* (L.) in 1766 from a Georgia bird described by Catesby.

LOCAL NAMES: Calico-back, chicken plover, rock plover, red-legged plover, sea-quail, bishop plover, and many others, all attesting to the conspicuousness and popularity of this bird. SPANISH: Playero Turca.

FIELD CHARACTERS: A chunky, orange-legged, plover-like bird of sandy shores, rubble and offshore rocks. A real harlequin, with bold black and white and rusty-red markings that fairly explode when the bird takes flight. The short stout bill is pointed and slightly upturned. Winter adults and immature birds are brownish above but retain a broad sooty stain on the breast, have duller but still orange legs. Call a chattery *kek-kek* or a shrill *kewk*. l. 8–10″, b. 1″, female larger.

RANGE: Circumpolar, and high arctic except for an extension into the islands of the Baltic Sea. Our race probably intergrades with the nominate race in the Canadian archipelago. Winters from c. Calif. and No. Carolina to coasts of central South America and from Gr. Britain, the Mediterranean and s. coast of Asia, south to Africa and throughout Oceania to New Zealand. Chief migration in America along the east coast, but regular in small numbers in interior and west coast.

17

BLACK TURNSTONE

Arenaria melanocephala

THE exuberant and lively Black Turnstone is one of the abundant and conspicuous birds of the southern Alaska coast, though it nests as far north as Bering Straits and occurs, in winter, as far as southernmost Baja California.

While resting on rocks along shore the chunky form and dark coloration of these birds make them look like so many projecting knobs. The head is dusky, with the exception of a small white patch at the lores and a light streak over the eyes. The chest, back, and throat show black but the belly is white. Squatting on a rock the bird is remarkably inconspicuous, but the instant it flies, white patches on scapulars, back, and rump flash into sight, much as on the Ruddy Turnstone which this bird replaces in large measure on the Pacific coast, though both occur.

These bold little shore birds consort freely with the equally adventurous Surfbirds and Rock Sandpipers, spending their days and nights on the flinty islets, reefs and ledges exposed to pounding seas. They all pluck mussels, snails, and various other small animals from the sounding ledges and from beds of floating weeds uprooted by the wintry sea.

Sometimes a few are engulfed by a wave but instantly burst from the seething surface, still peeping and squealing, as agile as phalaropes, sometimes marine as the very fish, it seems.

Dr. Gabrielson, in *Birds of Alaska,* reports the strange spectacle these birds produce at Petersburg almost any time outside the nesting season: "At high tide the floating drift boom logs, the docks, rails and the roofs of canneries and warehouses are decorated with thousands of shore birds. Black Turnstones are the most abundant but mixed with them are some Surfbirds and a greater number of Aleutian Sandpipers. Day after day they sit quietly and unafraid, leaving to feed on the great mud flats that are exposed in Wrangell Narrows with the fall of the tide, and returning again to their odd roosting places as the flats are again covered. Petersburg has one of the greatest wintering populations of water birds to be found in southeastern Alaska and this congregation of shore birds is one of the main attractions even in the superlative show that goes on continuously at this point. Like the gulls, the shore birds soon learn that they will not be harmed and hardly offer to get out of the way as one walks down the docks. Often they walk to the edge, take wing, make a short circle and land behind the intruder, repeating the performance as he returns." [21]

Arenaria melanocephala (Vigors). Described in 1828.
FIELD CHARACTERS: Plump, sooty-black, white-bellied birds usually seen in small
    groups on offshore ledges on the Pacific coast, and seldom feeding on sand as
    Ruddy Turnstones do. Bill black and legs dusky. With a conspicuous white
    spot before the eye in spring. In flight, strikingly black and white; the wing
    stripe is longer and broader than in the Ruddy Turnstone or the Surfbird.
    Back otherwise pied as in Ruddy Turnstone. l. 9″, b. 7/8″.
RANGE: Nests on coastal tundra of Alaska coast from Bering Strait south to Sitka.
    Winters from southeastern Alaska to central Sonora, Mexico. Casual inland
    on Pacific coast.

CHAPTER 6

THE SANDPIPERS

Tʜɪs ɪs a large, very diversified assemblage of brownish, protectively-colored waders with more tapered bodies and longer necks than plovers, and with slender bills of variable length and curvature. The sexes are usually alike but differ in size (more rarely in markings) in several species, the female being somewhat larger as a rule.

Most species migrate and tend to flock during migrations, and have colorful summer and plainer winter plumages.

Since most of them nest in the open, on the ground (a few species in old nests in trees), they have elaborated highly formalized "courtship" flights and distraction displays. The eggs are almost always four in number.

The British *Handbook* makes a very useful subdivision of the diversity of species into subfamilies, as follows:

Limosine types: the godwits with upturned bills, curlews with downturned bills, and the Upland Plover with straight bill, all of them tall, long-legged birds with many anatomical features held in common. The name is from the godwit genus *Limosa*.

Scolopacine types: the snipe-like species with flexible upper mandibles and the ear placed under the eye. These include the woodcock, which one student called a shore bird caricature, the snipe, and the dowitchers. Named after the European Woodcock genus *Scolopax*.

Calidrine (or Eroline) types: the smallish stint-like birds we call sandpipers in
America, birds with rather soft bills, in which the females often do most of
the courting and may or may not help incubate and care for the young.
Named after the genus *Calidris* applied to many of these small species in
Europe, but subdivided into two groups, *Calidris* and *Erolia,* in America.
Tringine types: the "true" sandpipers or tatlers, including yellowlegs (shanks in
Europe), the Spotted Sandpiper, and the Solitary Sandpiper.

Many students consider the Surfbird and the turnstones as another
sandpiper subfamily, though our Check-List currently includes them
among the plovers.

Least Sandpiper
Chick

18

AMERICAN WOODCOCK

Philohela minor

IN THE ruddy woods of Indian Summer your eye is caught by chalky splashes in a fence corner. You stoop to peer more closely under the ferns and note borings in the mud of a pool. As you straighten up, your Llewellyn setter freezes into a point a yard beyond the wet spot and under the tangled branches of a wild apple tree.

Whirrrr! Up whistles a prime woodcock, giving a glimpse of russet plumage, long bill, and a flirt of white in the tail feathers as it tops out and dodges away over the saplings. It is as if a handful of fallen leaves had been whirled up by the wind.

You have interrupted the siesta of the most nocturnal of all shore birds. That beak, those mottled feathers exactly the hue of the dusk through which it flitters, the stumpy tail—all betray one of the noblest of the Order. Your woodcock may be a descendant of ancestors who left the sounding shores to wander up this inland valley a million years ago and liked it well enough to call it home. Only a theory, of course, but rather a pleasing one. You glance round, marking the place well. You are a furlong uphill from a trout stream swirling through an alder run and long vistas of yellowing cattail swamp. On your right a stand of birch whitens a ridge from north to south. On your left fields of faded goldenrod slope towards the river. Every hundred paces or so runlets trickle down from bosky pockets.

This stream valley has been a flyway for woodcock from time immemorial. The birds feed in its fens by night and doze in its thickets by day. During a flight they drop into such nooks as that where you stand and may be flushed there year after year if you know the Open Sesame of the region.

The western heights are a jumble of knobs, just now (October 12th) an incredible blaze of color—carmine, crimson, gold and ruby-red —rolling away in wave after wave of incredible magnificence. Somewhere beneath the horizon haze the Grand Sachem of Indian Summer smokes the Pipe of Peace, stopping the hands on the clock of time and long postponing the fall of the leaf.

There are hundreds of similar valleys all the way from Nova Scotia to the Gulf of Mexico. Woodcock migrate down routes spread like the radiating ribs of a gigantic fan. One runs along the eastern coast, fed by every promontory from Maine to Florida. West of the Appalachians another carries birds from eastern Canada, the Great Lakes, New York and Pennsylvania down all the eastern affluents of the Mississippi.

The majority of the woodcock which breed in the eastern United States and southern Canada—a population of several million birds— winter in the Gulf States, mostly between Louisiana and South Carolina, with especially heavy concentrations in the wetlands of the Mississippi delta region.

Almost as soon as you flush the first woodcock of the season, it is time to look for your first woodcock nest. The birds arrive in the middle tier of States in March, and the female commences laying immediately after her arrival, when you may enjoy the fascinating aerial love-song of the male circling on hovering wings high over some brushy meadow at dusk or by moonlight, its chippering notes falling from the sky before the bird itself pitches back to a strutting ground. Recent studies of banded birds lured down by stuffed birds, and by netting in travel lanes, have revealed an heretofore unsuspected amount of interchange in the male population. It seems now that woodcock populations are loosely knit; both sexes maintain small territories and the males may visit several in turn, mating with more than one female, as the females also accept more than one male.

Many a trout fisherman, wading some brimming brook in early spring, passes within a few paces of the sitting woodcock on her leaf-lined nest without noticing her. The protective coloration of the bird is so perfect, the pattern of the back being practically identical with that of the withered leaves around her, that she will not move as a rule unless about to be touched, and so escapes detection. The three or four slightly ovate eggs, buff and marbled brown, are more polished than those of species whose eggs are laid in the sun.

In a marsh near Pelham Manor, N.Y., one morning late in May, I once flushed a pair of woodcock from a thicket. The mother bird rose close to my face, there clutching at the branches and apparently trying to induce me to snatch at her in mid-air. Failing in her ruse she tumbled away in the cover, followed by the male bird which had been watching her.

A mother woodcock sometimes carries her young across a stream one at a time, holding the precious burden between her feet and tarsi. Putting one down she flies back for another; nor will any chick move until she peeps a command.

The bill of the mature woodcock is admirably adapted to probing for worms. Two and one half to three inches long, it has developed a sort of hinge half way down the upper mandible by which it may be opened under the mud to grasp a worm. Unless the worm is a very large one, it can apparently be sucked up without lifting the bill. This may have led to the old popular name of "bog-sucker." Audubon it was who called attention to the fact that earthworms are almost always found intact in the bird's stomach, never broken as they might be by tweaking or pulling. Epicures once prized the swallowed worms as "trail." When it cannot find worms the woodcock consumes a variety of insects and grubs, many of them found by turning over the leaf litter on the forest floor. During a prolonged dry spell I once watched a pair of these birds half way up the Watchung Mountains in New Jersey turning up fallen leaves and devouring the flat, gray, many-legged "sow bugs."

The woodcock may be so nearly nocturnal because it lives largely on earthworms, which are more easily secured near the surface by night than by day. Its large, luminous eyes enable the bird to flit about after dark, seeking moist spots where worms are readily found.

These wonderful orbs are set well back and high in the head as if to guard against predators which otherwise might swoop on the bird while its mandibles are plunged in the mud. This position also keeps the eyes out of reach of the mud into which the bill bores so deeply. They remind us of those of the flounder.

Frank Forrester, one of the earliest sportsmen to write about woodcock, sometimes bagged as many as 125 in a single day's hunt. He and his cronies used to send out servants in a trap loaded with food, wine and spirits. They would then put down a brace of fine English setters and gun alders swarming with flight woodcock. After shooting all morning they would meet the trap at some rendezvous, lay out their forenoon bag of game, relax, and lunch under the greenwood trees, washing down the meal with brown October ale.

When at long last their eager dogs got them started again, they somehow never shot so accurately as during the forenoon. But though the afternoon bags were always smaller than the morning ones, they would be more than enough to land a man in jail these days. No wonder Forrester prophesied that the American woodcock would be quickly exterminated. In his day they were shot spring, summer, and fall, and were sold in the markets everywhere.

But Forrester was wrong. As soon as gunning was limited to the fall, and selling on the markets was banned, the woodcock stopped decreasing. Today they are holding their own, but changing land use patterns are more likely to hurt than help them in the future.

Philohela minor (Gmelin). Named in 1789 from Pennant's descriptions of the "Little (i.e., American) Woodcock" in *Arctic Zoology* (1785).

LOCAL NAMES: Timber doodle, whistler, bogsucker, etc.

FIELD CHARACTERS: The chunkiest of the shore birds, so thick-set that it seems neckless and tailless, but with very long bill. Warm, buffy cinnamon below, darker above, with strong "ruptive" patterns of blackish spots, including three or four broad *bars* on the crown (other species are streaked). Flushes explosively, towers, then zigzags on brown, *rounded* wings. Best located at dusk in spring, when its nasal *peent* notes are heard in brushy field borders. l. 10–12″, b. 3″, female heavier.

RANGE: From southeastern Manitoba and Minnesota on the west, thence almost straight south to Louisiana, with slight overlapping into the eastern edge of the prairie States; eastward to include all our northern States, and the southern half of Ontario, the St. Lawrence lowlands (not Gaspé Peninsula), New Brunswick and Nova Scotia, thence south to northern Florida. Winters as far north as frost conditions allow, but chiefly from eastern Texas across to South Carolina and central Florida.

19

COMMON SNIPE
(Wilson's Snipe)

Capella gallinago

WHEN bottom lands brighten beneath April showers, when red-wings whistle *Okalee!* along brooks in which the alewives throng up from the sea, then the snipe blow in on the south wind by night and pitch into their green meadow world.

Around Pilgrim Lake on Cape Cod I have frequent glimpses of them, flickering through the gloom or dropping among the cattails. Occasionally I spot one far up in the ruddy evening sky, zig-zagging across the darkening water. Even when bound for some definite objective this bird finds it impossible to travel in a straight line.

If you grow sunflowers in your garden goldfinches will come for the seeds as they ripen—appearing like magic from nobody knows where. How do they know that you have any sunflowers, and how do they guess that the seeds are ripe for picking?

Similarly, snipe will find a marshy pocket on a farm even if it is not half an acre in extent. Such a miniature marsh oozes from the bald top of a hill near Califon, New Jersey, in the center of a rocky pasture much frequented by killdeer plover. A single snipe will often alight there during migrations, almost as if it had scented the place while drifting past among the evening clouds.

When one pitches at Califon a hundred may revisit some larger fen at no great distance, for they often arrive in a cloud. As the woodcock is the genius of bosky crofts and upland alder runs, so the snipe is the familiar spirit of sweet-water swamps, grassy rivers, and brackish meadows.

Old time sportsmen accustomed to hearing the sharp, *Scape! Scape!* of snipe flushing before their dogs, never thought of this bird as a minstrel of the night.

Such, in a humble way, it certainly is. Its winnowing notes, strangely elusive and ephemeral, have a spirit-like remoteness when they float down from the gloaming above some verdant river-bottom. Sometimes one glimpses the singer, roding through the dusk in the spring. He circles at such heights that one frequently hears only the ventriloquial calls, now here, now there. The observer must take the bird itself for granted. The remarkable winnowing is a rhythmic *who-who-who-who-who,* repeated again and again.

These sounds are not vocal. The snipe rises at a steep angle and describes an immense ellipse. Then, slanting downward and side-slipping, the outer quills of its wings and tail produce the melody.

The mystery of snipe migration—here today but gone tomorrow— reminds us of woodcock ways. The two birds have many points in common: long, sensitive bills for probing in the fens, mottled plumage on the back and shoulders to match typical surroundings, a decided liking for the dusk, and a fast, nervous get-away when flushed before the dog. Both species revisit the same favored spots year after year, and both have been considered superb table birds, being all rich, dark meat.

The nest is a wisp of grass whirled into a circle in a marshy meadow, sometimes on a patch of floating-island, or knitted into a sedgy tuft at a slight elevation beside some creek or run.

Spring peepers hail its construction with shrill applause, but before the chicks pip the shell they will yield place to the *Trrrump! Trrrrump!* of aldermanic bullfrogs. While it is a-building the male snipe struts before his mate, head thrown back like a miniature turkey cock, wings trailing, and tail spread.

He is far from silent on the ground. Sometimes a marsh will suddenly become noisy wtih unseen Virginia Rails, all cackling at once. Similar cries from a sweet-water fen, *Kak! Kak! Kak!* may mean the presence of dozens of snipe hidden in the sedge.

The eggs of the snipe, large for the size of the bird, are pear-shaped, whitish or gray with heavy blotches of brown, umber or black on the larger ends. Lustreless when placed beside woodcock eggs, they bear patterns not readily spotted in the grass. While the parent broods, the solitary bittern drives his stakes in the mud not far away, the king-fisher winds a noisy reel, and a million tree frogs trill. When at length the chicks pip the shell and step forth into the fen, they will find insect food limitless.

The young are hatched when marsh flowers begin to glow, and be-fore they are fledged the air will be heavy with the perfume of water-lilies. They will see the Wood Duck lead her brood across vistas blue with iris, and green with cattail rushes. They will even learn to swim, dive, and wade with ease, and later, may even alight in brush or low trees.

Although snipe and woodcock wear somewhat similar protective patterns on their backs, their under parts are markedly different. The grayer speckled plumage of the smaller bird, and its whitish belly, con-trast sharply with the russet breast of the woodcock—as do the pointed wings with the rounded ones of the latter.

At the beginning of a day on the marsh in gunning days they lay well to the dogs, getting away with a dash, and baffling the novice by twisting and side-slipping for the first rod or so of flight. When several guns went into action the noise proved too much for their nerves. Al-most every snipe within hearing would take off and fly wildly round and round the meadow. Sometimes they would pitch again, but just as often they left the place for the season.

It is surprising how many snipe will congregate where cover seems inadequate. I recall a southern marsh notable, time out of mind, as a resting station for migrating birds. The grass was short the last time I went there, hardly high enough to be called cover, but it held a goodly number of snipe.

They clung close to the damp ground, and the first bird did not whirl up until my companion's Irish setter was almost upon it. This par-ticular bird had its wits about it, wheeling straight back overhead so that it was necessary to turn round to take it. The next rose wild, spun into a corkscrew and took two barrels to stop. We used number ten shot, a size not readily obtainable these days but heavy enough for snipe.

We walked on behind the weaving red setter, but before he came down on point several snipe flushed straight away, veering sharply when fired upon. They never rocketted so high as the usual woodcock amid birch whipe. Nor was it difficult to take them, once you got used to

their peculiar antics. Just as the woodcock gunner usually does not fire
until his bird starts to straighten out over the saplings, so the gunner
for snipe used to score best if he withheld his fire until the birds stopped
twisting and side-slipping. The assistance of a dog was always necessary
because a snipe falling at a distance was difficult to locate, its colors
blending closely with those in the swamp.

One never recalls his semi-occasional experiences with the elusive
snipe without inhaling again the aroma of autumn marshland, or ad-
miring its brown tapestry outlined by the carmine border of swamp
maples, or hearing the odd, staccato cries with which the game twisted
free of the grass. Such sport, although less spectacular than fowling, had
a peculiar seasonal charm, not easy to describe but never forgotten. The
sheer unexpectedness of snipe, their versatility and resourcefulness,
made their pursuit extremely fascinating.

Although is was difficult to guess just when a flight would arrive,
it was seldom difficult to tell where. Snipe keep to their ancient trails
and haunts almost as regularly as woodcock. Trudging home from a day
with the Black Ducks on Great South Bay many years ago, my guide,
Dan Chichester, pointed to a belt of sweet-water meadow land and re-
marked, "Dad always found snipe in that meadow after an easterly blow
—let's try it." We did so and discovered the place to be alive with snipe.
Nervous from the migratory urge, they seemed set on hair-triggers and
afforded lively shooting. Next day Dan told me that the entire flight
had vanished.

There are many records of individual marksmen killing 150 snipe
in a day's gunning a hundred years ago. None of us will ever see such
numbers again because the growth of human populations has, through
drainage and other manipulations of the landscape, eliminated over
50% of the breeding habitat in the southern half of this bird's range.
The decline in numbers was so drastic during the 1920's and 1930's that
the species was removed from the game-list for a few years. They have
shown a modest increase in numbers for a decade or more and have
recently been put back on the game-list. It seems doubtful whether this
is justified by conditions. For several consecutive years, while looking
for wild turkeys in northern Florida, I have flushed snipe here and there
in boggy stretches of wild palmetto—perhaps half a dozen in a forenoon.
If I were to put down a staunch setter and try in earnest to find snipe
after a northeaster during the autumnal migration, I might locate twice
that number. But having visited many snipe marshes from Maine to

Florida, I fail to find that the present numbers in any way suggest numbers sufficient to warrant a return to the hunt.

Then, too, if sportsmen and, particularly, boys are permitted to gun snipe, some of them will shoot yellowlegs, plover, and curlew, whether through ignorance of the species involved, or from disregard of the regulations. Not long ago I met a young fellow carrying home an Upland Plover. He admitted that he did not know the species at all. Any game warden along the coast will mention similar violations. Indeed, many game wardens, even in New England, know so little about shore birds that they are not equipped to differentiate among them, and to enforce the laws they have been hired to uphold.

Capella gallinago (Linneaus). Described in 1758, our race, *C. g. delicata* (Ord), in 1825.

LOCAL NAMES: Jack snipe, an unfortunate misapplication of the British term for a very different, smaller, shorter-billed snipe lacking the orange tail of this bird.

FIELD CHARACTERS: A tight-sitting, prominently streaked brown marsh bird with a long, straight bill, and a stubby orange tail. Best told by its explosive take-off and zigzag flight, and the raspy "scaipe" note. Head is striped (lengthwise), not barred (across) as in heavier-bodied Woodcock. Woodcock is stockier, has rounded wings; dowitcher has white lower back. A bird of wet meadows and grassy marshes, of sedge bogs in the north. l. 10¼–11¾″, b. 2½–2¾″, female larger.

RANGE: Circumboreal. Breeds in subarctic and north temperate bogs and fresh marshes throughout most of northern hemisphere. Our race breeds across North America south of the limit of trees, south to California, Nebraska and n. Illinois in the interior, and Pennsylvania and New Jersey in the east. Migration is done at night, in small flocks, and even along the coast in daytime on occasion, though their comings and goings are less regular than in other shore birds. Winters from s. British Columbia and s. New England south, except in mountains and arid regions, to n. South America.

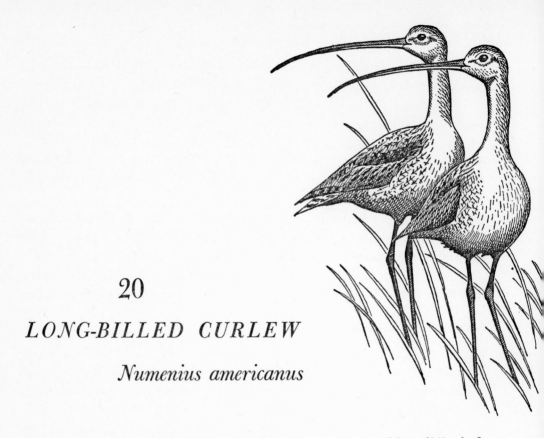

20

LONG-BILLED CURLEW

Numenius americanus

OLD Dan Chichester's boat-house on the "big crik" winding down to a famous eastcoast inlet was a fascinating salt meadow nook when I was a boy.

It straddled an inlet in such a manner as to accommodate a well-grassed Barnegat sneak-boat, with the usual paraphernalia—masts, sails patched until they were all patches, paddles, nets, oars, and hundreds of decoys. There were goose stool, canvasbacks, black-heads, mallard, pintail, teal, and a dozen others—old and new, hand-carved or factory-made, but all more or less battered and faded from use.

Those still in active service lay in heaps on either side of the miniature boat-slip, but there were dozens more overhead in a sort of attic beneath the sagging ridge-pole. Among these discards sat a magnificent swan decoy, one of the very few which I have noted anywhere along the Atlantic coast. It dated from the time of Dan's grandfather, who had been one of the great gunners of his day.

I climbed a rickety ladder to inspect this relic one morning when my eye fell on a pile of decoys, most of them headless, lying in a corner under the eaves. I pulled one out—an extraordinary stool, resembling a snipe, but standing three feet tall and with a prodigious, down-curved bill. Blowing off the dust I saw that it had once been painted cinnamon-red but that most of the pigment had weathered away.

Those dilapidated decoys, lying in the dust and trash of the bay-man's shack, remind me of the passing from our eastern seaboard of our noblest shore bird. The Long-billed Curlew, or "sickle-bill," is very striking. Its length runs from twenty to twenty-six inches, and its wing-spread from thirty-six to forty. The bill is somewhat variable, but some old females, which are larger than the males, have mandibles nine inches in length. One of these bigger individuals may weigh as much as two pounds.

Sickle-bills can be told from other curlews by their lighter tints, by the lack of brown stripes on the head, but more particularly by their splendid size. The general appearance of this bird is that of an ex-tremely large, cinnamon-tinted shore bird, and the slightly darker markings with which its upper parts are flecked serve merely to make its protective pattern almost perfect.

The Long-billed Curlew is not simply like the sand of the bars and beaches, but practically identical with them. Its voice sounds loud and vibrant, the cry being a startling, *Curlew! Curlew! Curlew!* Heard at a distance it blends pleasingly with the roar of surf or with the sigh of wind in the prairie grass.

In the old days flocks of these superb birds were more common on our Atlantic coast. I can recall a few stragglers on the barrier islands of North Carolina, where a few are again said to be spotted from time to time in summer today. They were too large to be inconspicuous on the meadows, and too excellent as food to escape in the age of market-gunning.

The Long-billed Curlew originally occupied desirable sites throughout the central grasslands of North America. The tearing up of the plains by agriculture, a process which culminated in the 1930's, extirpated these birds from vast regions. They continued to nest in iso-lated regions, however, in the Cache Valley of Utah and in the Bear River marshes fifty miles west and north of Great Salt Lake, in marshes frequented by the Avocet and Black-necked Stilts. With the trend to-ward larger holdings and a return to grazing and other less intensive uses of land since the thirties, the curlews began re-establishing them-selves in old haunts and have increased gradually since about 1947 in much of the northwestern grasslands.

In Oregon they commence to lay toward the end of May, but are slightly later in Idaho and in Utah. In the Bear River region, which abounds in shore birds, curlews deposit their large, gull-like eggs both in dry meadows and in more fenny expanses. An odd thing about their chicks is that their bills are perfectly straight and no longer than their heads. The superb length of mature curlews' mandibles is a matter of later growth.

Wherever these birds nest you are strongly reminded that they are all tattlers. They fly to meet you and scare you away from eggs or young. If you surprise a female with chicks she may roll away and scuffle like a partridge trying to delude an interloper. Meanwhile all the neighbor curlews circle around, crying, *Curleeoo! Cur-lee-ou!*

Although it has been my privilege to glimpse a few of these monarchs of shore birds, they were no longer gunned in my day. Old Dan once told me that when several curlews were shot down out of a flock, their companions would return and hover over the victims, uttering piercing cries.

Some, he assured me, were killed while doing this. Others which tried to lead pot-hunters away from their young, were shot on the breeding grounds—a piece of bad sportsmanship which appears incredible nowadays. When spring shooting was permitted, however, such occurrences were inevitable.

Audubon describes flocks of several thousand sickle-bills flying at twilight from their daytime feeding grounds on the salt meadows to offshore resting places where they passed the night. As darkness thickened the bands arrived more and more numerously but in absolute silence. They flew with heads and bills stretched out before and long legs trailing behind. They progressed by flapping for ten yards or more and then by sailing for a few seconds, somewhat after the manner of Brown Pelicans, but less deliberately:

"They flew directly towards their place of rest, called the Bird Banks, and were seen to alight without performing any of the evolutions which they exhibit when at their feeding places, for they had not been disturbed that season. But when we followed them to the Bird Banks, which were sandy islands of small extent, the moment they saw us the congregating flocks, probably amounting to several thousand individuals all standing close together, rose at once, performed a few evolutions in perfect silence, and realighted as if with one accord on the extreme margins of the sandbank close to tremendous breakers. It was now dark, and we left the place, although some flocks were still arriving."

Numenius americanus Bechstein. Described in 1812.

LOCAL NAMES: Sickle-bill, hen curlew.

FIELD CHARACTERS: A large, uniformly buff curlew with six or more inches of down-curved bill, a magnificent bird of coastal meadows or interior prairie. The head is not contrastingly marked as in the Whimbrel, and the under wing linings show bright cinnamon when the bird rises. Calls variable, from the delightful and long-drawn *curl-e-e-e-u-u,* or a willet-like *pil-will,* to guttural protestations and clearly whistled *quee-hee* notes. Length of bill varies greatly with age and sex, so depend most on *color* and general size. l. 20–26″, b. 2½–9″, female larger.

RANGE: Breeds from southern British Columbia to southern Manitoba south to Utah, New Mexico and Texas, mostly west of 100th parallel. The northern half of this range (from about 40° North latitude) is occupied by *N.a.americanus,* the southern race being *N.a.parvus.* The northern race tends to migrate and winter farther west, south to Guatemala; the eastern race to move up and down the western Great Plains, but there is a great deal of overlap in their winter ranges. Casual on the Atlantic and Caribbean coasts.

21

WHIMBREL

(Hudsonian Curlew)

Numenius phaeopus

THE Hudsonian Curlew, one of the most magnificent of shore birds, is smaller than the sickle-bill but resembles it rather closely. It may be readily distinguished by its shorter bill, by its grayer coloration, and by its head pattern. Whereas the head of the larger curlew is plain, the Hudsonian has a brownish crown with a buffy central mark and a dark lateral stripe running from the base of the mandibles through the eye.

Both species fly with neck extended and legs trailing behind, and both cry *Kur-leeeou! Kur-leeou!* Seen at a distance the difference in size is the only distinguishing mark, but as always this single criterion is deceptive in the absence of a standard of comparison. Both are birds of the tide, feeding on the bars and flats when the water is low but flying to grassy areas to rest while the tide swells high. Even their diet is largely identical, though perhaps the Hudsonian eats more insects.

Canadian ornithologist P. A. Taverner[55] once pointed out that this species has two rather widely separated breeding grounds, and that each population has distinct migration lanes. One group nests on the west side of Hudson Bay, the other in northwest Alaska and adjacent Mackenzie.

The first group migrates east to the Maritime region each fall, then hops from Nova Scotia to New Jersey in a fairly direct line, only a few making land on the New England shore. On the return flight from northern South America, however, these birds come up only as far as New Jersey, then head overland to the lower Great Lakes, pausing only briefly before going on to Hudson Bay. The western group simply moves across Alaska and down the west coast, including the Great Valley of California, and winters from central California to Chile. It retraces much the same route in spring.

Taverner suggested that, since these two groups are not racially distinct, it seems likely that the intervening territory was once occupied by another population, one which migrated down the Mississippi valley, and was wiped out during the orgy of waste that characterized the late 1800's, snuffed out, perhaps, like the Eskimo Curlew with which it may have associated in migration.

These big birds keep in fairly close formation when they migrate: clusters, strings or long bows, all speeding low over the bays and estuaries on powerful, curving pinions. The darker primary or flight feathers are stiffer and more durable than the plumage exposed to less friction, but like those of the far-voyaging gull, the curlew's are often frayed. Their loud and challenging calls may be heard at considerable distances as they come hurrying up on the south wind.

Prevailingly cinnamon-gray, with fine pencillings of a darker tint on breast and throat, the colors of Hudsonian Curlews match the hues of the reindeer moss and sedge tussocks among which the female lays her four large, spotted eggs. These are pear-shaped, like those of most shore birds, and bear protective coloration as perfect as that of the bird itself. This helps them escape the sharp eyes of the Parasitic Jaegers which prowl the tundra, forever on the lookout for raw omelette.

It is far from warm at Churchill in early June. The great bay is still one tremendous expanse of ice from horizon to horizon, but cold does not discourage these remarkable birds. The mother curlew sits low in the cover, pressing the double brood spots of bare skin on her breast against the eggs to keep them warm. When an intruder walks over the damp carpet near a nest, curlews jump up and fly to meet him, whistling loud alarms of *Kur-leeeou! Kur-leeeou!* Other brooding shore birds of several species join in the racket and soon the air is alive with them. And yet, when they settle again it is difficult to locate the nests even though the observer uses binoculars and knows where they should be.

When a flight is on late in August or in September, I have often spent the day in a pit on Cape Cod Bay watching all sorts of little migrants swing into a rig of old-time snipe decoys. Early in the morning as the tide rolls up, shore birds of a dozen different kinds come winging by. Once in so often I hear the glad cry of the curlew far up the beach and soon a big Hudsonian comes twisting by, a giant among throngs of migrating peep. Had it planned to land, it would have planed in on stiff wings for two hundred yards, surveying the area carefully the while.

When curlews decide to come in here they prefer remote tidal meadows, and if the area suits them they may linger a week. At Wellfleet, on Cape Cod, the muddy banks of the creeks at low tide are perforated with innumerable holes. Into these fiddler crabs by the thousands plunge for refuge, but Hudsonian Curlews thrust in their long mandi-

bles and yank them out. Elsewhere they feast on crayfish in the same
manner, for their bills are perfectly developed for just such work.
Selecting feeding grounds with an abundance of provender, these
curlews are always fat—one reason why they were sought after by epicures in the old days.

The come-back of these fine birds from the dark days of the turn of
the century coincided with the creation of numerous federal waterfowl
refuges in the mid-thirties, and the records kept by refuge managers[10]
sketch a pleasant picture. There was apparently a rapid build-up in
numbers from the early 1930's through the forties, and by the mid-
forties it had again become normal to see 5,000 of these curlews each
spring at Cape Romain in South Carolina or at Brigantine in New
Jersey. The fall flights were almost as good though of course less concentrated.

Numenius phaeopus (Linneaus). Described in 1758, our race in 1790.

LOCAL NAMES: Jack Curlew or Jack; in Europe, Half Curlew, a comparison with
the big Eurasian Curlew (*N. arquata*), which American tourists often take for
our Long-billed Curlew (*N. americanus*).

FIELD CHARACTERS: A large, brown shore bird with long downcurved bill. Resting, their bills are held horizontal (inclined in godwits). In flight, their flocks
may at first look like lines of ducks, even be wedge-shaped, but the sickle bill
and the trailing legs will soon spot them. Notes variable: a liquid *kur-leeeo*,
or a short, quick, whistled quintet of *kek* notes. l. 15–18″, b. 2¾–4″, female
larger.

RANGE: The Eurasian race (*N.p.phaeopus*) breeds from Iceland right across north-
ern Europe and Siberia. It is accidental on the northeast coast of North America (Cape Cod and Long Island) and easily told by its white rump. The
American race (*N.p.hudsonicus*) breeds from western and northern Alaska
eastward along the Arctic coast to northwestern Mackenzie, south to Mt. Mc-
Kinley National Park, southwestern Yukon, along western side of Hudson
Bay to northwestern James Bay. *Winters* locally on Pacific coast from central
California to the Galápagos Islands and southern Chile, casually on the coasts
of Texas, Louisiana and South Carolina.

22

BRISTLE-THIGHED CURLEW

Numenius tahitiensis

THIS remarkable wader is named for a few feathers, the shafts of which have no barbs, but project stiffly from its flanks. It is two inches longer than the Hudsonian Curlew which it resembles so closely. The pattern of its back is marked more strongly, the dark brown feathers of the scapulars having broader whitish margins which give the back a more checkered look. The broad white stripe over the eye, and the dark band above that, are the same in both species. The legs are lead-gray in both, but the barred tail of the Bristle-thigh is buffier.

Like the Wandering Tatler, the Bristle-thighed Curlew spends its winters on the islands of the south seas. It was discovered on what is now Tahiti, largest of the Society Islands, in 1769, by Sir Joseph Banks who was naturalist on Captain James Cook's round-the-world expedition during 1768–1771. When these collections reached Britain they came to the attention of ornithologist John Latham, who recognized that the large curlew brought back by Banks differed from the familiar European whimbrel. Latham named it the Otaheite Curlew after the original name for Tahiti, and Gmelin, some years later, christened it *Scolopax tahitiensis*. Later, when the genus name *Scolopax* was restricted to the European Woodcock and its relatives, the curlews were placed in the genus *Numenius,* and this bird became *Numenius tahiti-*

ensis (Gmelin). Gmelin's name, as the father of the first scientific name, was placed in parenthesis to show that his species had been shifted to a new genus. Such are the vagaries of nomenclature.

On Laysan Island, one of the outer Hawaiian group, it is notorious for its plundering of the eggs of Sooty Terns, Frigate-birds, Gray-backed Terns, Boobies, and others. Ornithologists have frequently observed it running around the shores of this island in the company of turnstones and occasional Golden Plovers, impaling eggs on their bills or lugging them away in their mandibles.

This is exceptional conduct for shore birds, but here are three rather distantly related species, banding together in banditry every day. Early morning and evening are the hours of their most intensive raids, but they probably snatch an egg whenever hunger moves them. This is no random plundering but a well-organized habit. After watching their stealthy operations in the Hawaiian Islands Bird Reservations, Dr. Alexander Wetmore[7] reported that "On close observation we found that curlews attacked the eggs of all birds indiscriminately, even pulling an egg from beneath a Frigate-bird when the incubating bird raised (itself) on the nest for a moment, the theft being committed so adroitly that the egg seemingly was not missed."

Thievery of this sort is not really surprising when one considers the innumerable eggs everywhere available on such heavily-populated sites as Laysan Island. The eggs offer unlimited food, easily obtained, and the habit of helping themselves probably developed from the frequent opportunity to sample abandoned eggs. It seems, in any event, characteristic of very high population levels. On some of the most successful nesting rookeries of White Ibis guarded by National Audubon Society wardens in Florida, it has been reported that Black-crowned Night Herons, normally "law abiding" birds, are regular predators on the eggs of the ibis. Similarly, on "Old Man Island" south of Cutler, Maine, I have seen swarming hosts of Herring Gulls devour many eggs laid by their neighbors, the eider ducks, and the Double-crested Cormorants which also nest in that rookery. In spite of such depredations the whole colony flourishes, all three species being on the increase, and already too crowded for comfort on their rocky isle. This egg-robbing, then, would seem to be a result of crowding.

Long listed among the most noteworthy over-water flights are the great migrations of this curlew. It is 5500 miles from Alaska to Tahiti, and even the shortest flight, from Midway Island in the Leeward chain, is nearly half that distance. They appear at a few places on the central Alaska coast after mid-May, pause here but briefly, and disappear. By early August they are back on the coastal tundra, here to gorge on berries while these are available. They have all departed southward before the end of the month.

For many years this status was noted by explorers, who failed, nevertheless, to locate the nesting grounds of the species, though several suspected that it had to be in the mountains near the coast. The mystery remained until the summer of 1948 when the indefatigable Dr. Arthur A. Allen,[1] together with his son David, led thither by Alaska schoolteacher and naturalist Henry Kyllingstad, found and photographed this bird at its nest on the dry, nearly birdless alpine tundra 20 miles north of Mountain Village and some 50 miles inland from the mouth of the Yukon River. The 179-year old mystery was ended.

Numenius tahitiensis (Gmelin). Named in 1789.

FIELD CHARACTERS: Slightly larger than Hudsonian Whimbrel, buffier, and more mottled above, with a clear, reddish-brown rump. The call seems distinctive also, being a Black-bellied Plover-like *wheeu-whu* rather than the simple *whe-whe-whe* whistle of the Whimbrel (Conover, in Bent). l. 17½", b. 3¼".

RANGE: Breeds on upland tundra back of Yukon delta in western Alaska. Winters mostly in central and eastern Polynesia, from Hawaii to the Marshall Islands and south to the Low Archipelago, migrating directly over water, a flight at least as spectacular as any the Golden Plover performs. This migration pattern is so firmly established that there are no records of occurrence in western Canada or the U.S. west coast.

23

ESKIMO CURLEW

Numenius borealis

A FALL flight of Eskimo Curlews was a thrilling sight in the days of their abundance. Hurrying out of the north on long, down-curved pinions, they came twinkling over the dunes of many a far-flung cape and settled like brown and wind-blown leaves. They thronged the salt meadows, brackish pools, and tidal basins by thousands, filling the air with melodious cries, *Tee! Tee! Tee!* flight notes all too easy for gunners to imitate from their rushy blinds.

Their colors matched so closely the sands where they fed that they were distinguishable from the surroundings only when they moved. When they flushed you would have thought that the grit itself was taking wing. At the same time, they were easy to recognize, being small for curlews. They had shorter, straighter bills than the larger Hudsonian. They could be told also by the paler under parts, by their dark greenish legs, and by the cinnamon-buff of the nether surfaces of the wings, which showed brightly as they sheared away from decoys.

Like the other curlews, the Eskimo, or "dough-bird," had remarkable powers of flight, sweeping down the length of the American continents and even occasionally spanning the Atlantic to Iceland and the British Isles. Most boreal of their kind, they made nothing of the long journey from the arctic tundra of northern Mackenzie to coastal Labra-

dor and Nova Scotia, the tidal marshes of Maine, or the coral sands of
Bermuda, en route to the pampas of Argentina. On these lengthy journeys they could swim if need arose. Although we sometimes think of it
as an eastern species because of reports that flocks actually darkened the
sky in Newfoundland in the old days, like Passenger Pigeons, this species was equally abundant in the west. Despite the attrition of the long
migrations and the perpetual bombardment they were subjected to in
South America, enormous flights passed up the Mississippi Valley in
spring.

In the Northeast they gorged themselves on curlew-berries (*Em-
petrum,* the crowberry), blueberries, and hog-cranberries, and were already extremely plump when they reached Cape Cod. Here, as the tide
ebbed, they explored every tidal creek, finding a great abundance and
variety of seafood. Whole colonies of little black and yellow fiddler
crabs, gallied by their approach, rustled into their holes on many a mud
bank, holding up monitory pincers to cover their retreat, but in vain.
The curlews deftly twitched them out again with long mandibles.
Bloodworms in half an inch of water slicked into the sand, but seldom
rapidly enough to escape those curved and probing bills.

Legions of shrimp-like prawns in shoal water under shelving banks
furnished a rich last course in this luncheon. Then the birds flitted into
fragrant meadows, purple with sea lavender, snatched a few crickets for
dessert, or plenty of those fat grasshoppers so abundant on the Cape,
and always gray as the dunes. Having stuffed themselves, they stood on
one leg, their beaks thrust into the scapulars, and dreamed long sea-
dreams while digesting their food. On waking an hour later, they
splashed themselves clean in the nearest creek and paddled a stroke or
two just for practice. They were never really wet, being protected by
body down similar to that of water wildfowl. Sometimes they loafed for
a week, but usually the migratory urge soon started them on another
leg of their long journey.

Living richly, Eskimo Curlews grew so heavy that they sometimes
split open on striking ground before the guns. When plucked, their
bodies showed white with fat, hence the vernacular name of "dough-
birds." As it was frequently spelled "doe," however, this derivation is
somewhat problematical.

This plumpness, and the fact that they were—like Woodcocks—all
dark meat, made them favorites among epicures at the time when
market gunners had thinned out the Passenger Pigeons and were look-

ing for available substitutes. Eskimo Curlews came only too readily to
decoys, and could be whistled down by any boy, whether he owned stool
or not. The boys usually then propped the first dough-birds bagged on
sticks thrust into the sand, as hunters did in the Bear River marshes of
Utah. They were also easier to shoot than the Hudsonian whose fall
flights were scattered and wary. The dough-birds showed a fatal tendency to concentrate in dense numbers on meadows, estuaries, and
beaches readily accessible to gunners and not too far from markets, to
which they were often shipped by the barrel.

Although they ran the gauntlet from Merrymeeting Bay in Maine
to Florida, they were gunned most heavily on Cape Cod, Long Island,
and the great sounds of Virginia and the Carolinas. Like Woodcock,
they followed their ancient flyways closely, visiting certain favored spots
all along the line. Baymen knew these places and always selected those
where they could kill the largest number of birds with the least effort.
The recollections of one Long Island bayman, who died about 1950 at
the age of 92, were recently reported as follows: [18] "I remember the
last fair-sized flock I ever saw. It was on a stormy September day (some-
time in the 1870's). For a couple of days a northeaster had flooded the
bay; the meadows (bay islands) were flooded. I was gunning south of
here not far from shore and a good-sized floating island of thick, dead
thatch was stirring around ahead of me. All of a sudden a close flock of
about forty Eskimo Curlews came by and alighted on the floating thatch
island. I shot and got quite a few, bunched as they were. Then instead of
flying off they returned and I got some more. They were easy to shoot,
always coming back; and do you know: I got every bird of that flock
down to the last one."

Many well-known sportsmen were enthusiastic shore bird gunners.
Daniel Webster, once as famous along shore as he was in the United
States Senate, used to put up every season at the old Sandwich Inn adjacent to the Barnstable marshes on Cape Cod. A room named for him
in that hostelry still keeps on display mementos of the great statesman.

When an easterly storm blew a big flight of curlews, yellowlegs,
and plovers to the shores of Cape Cod, Webster carried his decoys out
on the meadows. These immense green saltings were then and remain
today one of the great gathering and resting places for shore birds. They
are inferior in extent and beauty only to the boundless Marshes of
Glynn in coastal Georgia. From the Sandwich road they roll in green
waves to nine miles of glittering dunes on Sandy Point, which cuts them

off from the blue waters of Cape Cod Bay. Thousands of acres of reeds and grass, veined with tidal runs and bordered to the east by Barnstable Harbor, make a perfect haven for migrating shore birds.

Broad flats and bars bared at low tide make a marvelous place for every kind of beach waif to find sea food. Somewhere on these vast saltings Daniel Webster once shot a prime brace of Ruffs, wanderers from faraway Europe. These specimens are still in the collection of the Museum of Natural History in Boston. In Webster's day the flights of Eskimo Curlews seemed inexhaustible. Trudging across the green sea meadows at morning-glow, a gunner might flush clouds of them, criss-crossing in mid-air and making the foreshore ring with their cheery cries. Few foresaw their extinction.

But Webster was a true sportsman, limiting his bag of game to reasonable numbers. Meanwhile, in the west, these curlews were slaughtered by professionals who sent them to market in wagon-loads. There it was largely spring shooting because the northward migration swept up the interior of the continent. The curlew rapidly decreased between 1870 and 1890, and lingered on as a rarity for perhaps 25 more years. The last one shot on Cape Cod was a lone dough-bird bagged at East Orleans in 1913.

In my school days I occasionally saw a few Eskimo Curlews drifting into Race Run from Cape Cod Bay. This two-mile expanse of meadows not far from the northern tip of Cape Cod had long been a favorite resting place for Eskimo Curlews. By that time they had become extremely rare and were already regarded as a vanishing species. The last I saw was in 1922. I reported it to the features editor of the old *New York Evening Post* for whom I was then writing articles on birds and wildlife in general. He wrote me that I had probably mistaken a Hudsonian Curlew for a dough-bird.

Like other sportsmen who have spent much of their lives along the Atlantic coast, I still cherish the hope that at least a straggler or two may turn up in Race Run. A return of the dough-bird, although perhaps unlikely, is not yet beyond the bounds of possibility. Admittedly, our chief reminder of its former status as a game bird is an occasional dusty decoy for sale in some antique shop down east. Protective laws and a vast general change in public sentiment came very late, but not too late to help the great tribe of shore birds—perhaps even the Eskimo Curlew.

Numenius borealis (Forster). Described in 1772.

LOCAL NAMES: Dough-bird or doe-bird. SPANISH: Chorlo polar.

FIELD CHARACTERS: In 1947 Ludlow Griscom pointed out that this species has only half the body bulk of a Hudsonian Curlew, has a slightly-curved 2-inch bill, and is warm buff below and dark above. The under surface of the wings is conspicuously cinnamon-buff, and the legs dark green instead of bluish as in the larger species. There is the difficult possibility that leg color may vary with age, however, and the bird is today considered no more likely of occurrence than the Asiatic Least Curlew (*Numenius minutus*), from which it must therefore be distinguished. Except for minor anatomical characters, not useful in the field, the Least Curlew has buffy (rather than cinnamon-buff) underwing linings, and its legs vary from brownish to grey blue. Another characteristic of dubious value in the field is that the Eskimo has dark, unmarked primaries, while the inner webs of the outer primaries and both webs of the inner primaries of the Whimbrel are barred with buff. The voice also differs from the Whimbrel's, being "a soft, melodious whistle, *bee, bee,*" (Mackay) or a sharp squealing squeak like the single note of the Common Tern, but weaker (Griscom). l. 12–15″, b. 2–2½″.

RANGE: Formerly bred in northern Mackenzie and perhaps westward in northern Alaska. Wintered from the Mato Grosso of Brazil to southern Argentina and Chile. Last recorded specimens were taken in Argentina in 1914, Nebraska 1915, Maine 1929, Newfoundland Labrador 1932. The last carefully recorded sight observations are Nebraska 1926, Argentina 1939, and Texas 1945, 1959, 1960. As pointed out above, however, most sight records are open to question. Russian ornithologist N. A. Gladkov (*Birds of the Soviet Union,* 1951) treats the Least Curlew as a subspecies of our Eskimo Curlew. This caused British ornithologist James Fisher to quip, "Perhaps this species has been saved from extinction by systematics." At any rate, we hope no one will collect a presumed Eskimo Curlew just to be sure!

24

UPLAND PLOVER
(*Bartramian Sandpiper*)

Bartramia longicauda

I JOURNEYED recently to a flying field near Hempstead, Long Island, to observe Bartramian Sandpipers which had been reported as nesting in an expanse of grassy land west of the station. It proved just such terrain as they used to haunt in my childhood—flat or slightly rolling, and grown up to knee-high weeds and grass.

There I flushed a pair which whirled up and circled widely pouring forth their melodious flight notes, *Witte! Witte! Witte!* always thrice repeated and with a faintly ventriloquial quality.

Eventually I spotted their nest but found that it had been raided and the eggs devoured. The large, ovate shells, buff like the birds themselves, sparingly marbled with slightly darker hues, lay scattered about the site. The nest itself had consisted of a few handfuls of grass twisted into circular form, but some enemy had torn it to shreds. I suspected the identity of the plunderer when I picked up a black feather nearby, but whether it was that shed by an ordinary crow or by the more voracious Fish Crow, did not appear.

In those same open areas I flushed a few others of these "grass plovers," perhaps six in all. Although rather wild they kept circling back in such a manner as to suggest that some of them were nesting pairs. On that same day I put up another pair in a broad expanse given over to market-gardening. The birds were evidently nesting in a grassy croft beside which a number of women and boys were weeding garden-truck. I asked one of them whether he knew the species but found that he could not tell a hawk from a handsaw.

The flight-notes of those Long Island plovers carried me back to boyhood. I saw myself once more lying in bed at my Grandmother's house on the Island of Rhode Island. It was almost dawn. The caroling of robins, hardly loud enough to wake a light sleeper, drifted in through an open window. I remained listening until the notes of Upland Plover floated down from the red morning clouds. The call came again and again—more and more insistently as a flight of them passed high over-head—only two or three, perhaps, but infinitely thrilling. The big, handsome sandpipers had been growing scarcer for years, so that we boys used to hail their autumnal migration as an important event. We often flushed them in the fields of red clover, but never along the brooks nor on the shores of Narragansett Bay. Their haunts were the central grassy uplands of the Island of Rhode Island, all of it pastoral country in those days.

Hastily throwing on my clothes I sallied forth to have a look at the migrants. I had barely crossed the road in front of the rambling old mansion when the song sounded clearly from a field a little to the west. A plover might be there feasting on crickets and grasshoppers which they dearly love, so I climbed the stone wall to investigate. Before I could jump down on the farther side a magnificent, brown sandpiper whirled out of a far corner of the lot fully a hundred yards distant.

The startled cry of this bird put up another, and away fled the pair, sailing and veering in eccentric fashion. It struck me that these birds were extremely wild. They flew fully a furlong before pitching in the first pasture of the Redwood Farm on the old West Road. They settled beside a pool in the center of the fallow land, and there I tried to ap-proach close enough to see their color patterns.

I might as well have stalked a will-o-the-wisp. The long-winged migrants jumped wild and steered still farther downhill, uttering their musical but now somewhat tantalizing flight notes. There were then other plovers in the air and their calls reached me from verdant hillsides all around. I should have liked very much to watch them, but they proved intangible as moonbeams. Every bird seemed to enjoy marvelous eyesight, and spotted me even from the ground when screened by herbage twice their height.

Before I could get anywhere near they would take off on another lengthy flight, trilling cheerily as they skittered away. They commenced to seem winged personifications of the dawn itself—dawn not only visible but audible, tolling me on and ever on.

Nevertheless, I persisted. It was a joy merely to breast the bright morning air, fragrant with sweet grass and clover, growing heavier as the land warmed and the dew evaporated. But my shoes were soon soaking wet and I had eaten no breakfast; I was away from home without leave and in danger of punishment if I did not return pretty briskly.

I left those Upland Plovers to their broad, green fields, concluding that their skittishness might be due to a migratory urge so insistent that it would never allow them to stay still for more than a few moments. As day advanced I heard more of them in the uplands—the only shore birds which I had ever known on these rolling downs. Once in a while one passed overhead so high that its voice floated down remotely as if from another sphere—a spiritual, ethereal melody.

Forbush [20] wrote attractively of its voice and expressed a concern for this bird's future which it is pleasant not to have to echo: "Our children's children may never see an Upland Plover in the sky or hear its rich notes on the summer air. Its cries are among the most pleasing and remarkable sounds of rural life. They rank with the mating music of the Woodcock and the Wilson's Snipe. That long-drawn, rolling, mellow whistle as the bird mounts high in air has the sad quality of the November wind. Except the wail of the wind there is nothing else like it in nature. It is an ethereal sound which might well pass for the utterance of the fabled "wind spirit" and its *quitty quit,* as it rises startled from the grass, is a distinctive, unique and pleasing call unlike that heard from any other bird."

Hudson [27] loved them also, and stressed the spacing they seemed to maintain on their wintering grounds. "This species," he wrote, "differs from its fellow migrants of the same family from the north . . . in its wide and even distribution over all that portion of the pampas where the native coarse grasses which once covered the country have disappeared, an area comprising not less than 50,000 square miles. It begins to arrive as early as September, coming singly or in small parties of three or four; and, extraordinary as the fact may seem when we consider the long distance the bird travels, and the monotonous nature of the level country it uses as a 'feeding area,' it is probable that every bird returns to the same spot year after year; for in no other way could such a distribution be maintained, and the birds appear every summer evenly sprinkled over so immense a surface."

Bartramia longicauda (Bechstein). Described in 1812.

LOCAL NAMES: Grass plover, field-plover, hill-bird, all obviously drawn from the bird's habitat, and quaillie, and batitu (Spanish). Interesting is the name "Papabotte," supposedly a phonetic rendition of the bird's call used by Louisiana Creoles, among whom it was believed that the flesh of this bird is an aphrodisiac. Wells W. Cooke writes of one man in southern Louisiana who shot 117 birds in one day in 1899. Northern gunners did almost as much killing with no more incentive than gustatory anticipations. In England: Upland Sandpiper.

FIELD CHARACTERS: A tall, erect, plain buffy-brown shore bird of old fields and good pasture. The small-headed, short-billed, and thin-necked appearance, and, in flight, the long tail and yellow legs all combine to make it easy to identify. The Marbled Godwit is much larger and longer billed, the Buff-breasted Sandpiper much smaller. When disturbed on its breeding grounds, it hovers about like a kestrel or willet, its flight like the shallow stroking of the Spotted Sandpiper. Perches on posts, holding the wings high overhead on alighting. The voice is distinctive but difficult to describe. Alarm note an emphatic *quip-ip-ip-ip*. A number of rolling flight notes, a hawk-like courtship cry given from on high, and the much-described "song," a double series of long-drawn-out, wind-like whistles: *whooooleeee, wheee-looooooo*, the first part rattling and ascending, the second downward (Peterson). l. 12″, b. 1″.

RANGE: A prairie bird occurring, in suitably open areas, from Oklahoma east to Virginia and west to Washington, and north to southern Alaska and eastward, south of the muskeg, to Maine. Like the Prairie Horned Lark and the Cowbird, this species took advantage of man's openings in the eastern deciduous forest and actually increased for a short while. But it was then almost exterminated by the combined pressures of agriculture in the prairie States and the wanton slaughter of the turn of the century. Abundant until the 1890's, it all but disappeared between 1895 and 1920, and has increased slowly since, both in the west and the east. Migrates mostly through the interior of the two Americas and along the east coast. Large numbers pass through the Antilles and British Guiana in the fall on the way to wintering grounds which extend the whole length of Argentina. The migration lanes outside the United States are unfortunately still heavily gunned. Accidental in Europe.

25

SPOTTED SANDPIPER

Actitis macularia

THIS "tip-up" is familiar to every country boy from coast to coast and from Canada to the Gulf. Watch one bobbing and teetering along the margin of a brook and you may think it is hesitating, like a child trying stepping-stones for the first time. It moves like a feathered lady tucking up her skirts to keep them dry.

The Yellowlegs and other larger species do a good deal of bobbing. It may be merely a nervous reaction due to indecision, inasmuch as these birds often bob most when about to flush before an observer. But Common Snipe go through the same odd motions when they alight! Ouzels, waterthrushes, and wagtails show a similar tendency. All frequent the shores of streams and so give the impression that they are not sure what pebble to step on next. Several observers have even suggested that this tipping to and from causes the bird to blend into the lapping wavelets and the play of light and shadow they create on the shore, effectively camouflaging it. Be that as it may, the Spotted Sandpiper remains the champion teeterer and will nod and tilt its tail—more of a fore-and-aft movement than ordinary bobbing—whether on the beach or in some croft a mile from water.

Of all shore birds, its wings are held most stiffly in flight, vibrating through a narrow arc, and it flies closest to the surface of the water. When you follow it along the strand it invariably springs up with the staccato *"peet! weet!"* which has given it a familiar name. Alternately beating its wings for a few strokes and then gliding, it describes a wide arc out over the water before turning ashore again, perhaps five or six rods farther on. The more you pursue it, the longer the curve which it makes.

[As in many other shore birds, the female is credited with doing much of the courtship in this species, and letting the male do a good share, if not all, of the incubating. Here is a bird as versatile as any plant weed, occupying a vast range of varied habitats, from the rank lowlands of Okefinokee Swamp in Georgia to alpine meadows over 10,000 feet high, and northward almost to the edge of timber. I came to know it in a subarctic setting in the semi-barrens of northern Labrador in 1945. The break-up of river ice in mid-May had left the beaches littered with huge ice pans which were finally washed out by the ensuing flood. This too passed quickly, and during the night of June 7–8, the beaches once again became exposed. The very next morning Spotted Sandpipers arrived and soon occupied every gravel fan that marked the entry of sizeable brooks into the main water course. These birds had apparently been waiting somewhere upstream for this territory to become available. Migration ensued for a week, there often being five birds on our beach, but from June 16 onward, only the resident pair occupied our brook delta. On June 9 active courtship went on on this beach. Three birds were engaged in this contest, one of them calling loudly 'too-hee, too-hee' while stretched to its full height, wings held low and stiffly at the sides. Since the sexes are alike in marking, I did not surely identify the bird paying court in this way, but others have shown it to be the female.

[It was not until June 25 that I found the local nest, a cluster of four eggs—surprisingly like those of the Willow Ptarmigan, though of course smaller—in a depression under a dwarf birch where a little arm of the sand and rubble beach penetrated into the alder strand for several yards. The incubating bird decoyed me by flitting its wings overhead in a sprightly dance, but soon made off. (*R.C.C.*)]

My brothers and I used to chase Spotted Sandpipers from Oak

Glen all the way down our brook to Narragansett Bay. Near the mouth of the inlet there I once overtook a parent "spottie" with three chicks at its heels. The brood all fled, peeping frantically, spreading their wings and stumbling over blades of grass. I picked up the runt of the family, scarcely bulkier than a long-shanked bumblebee, but with a sure-enough snipe bill. The poor mite balanced on the palm of my hand, teetering nervously like a grown bird and uttering a peep so pathetic that the parent flew boldly to its rescue. It circled me with such anguished notes that I was glad to let the downy chick run and hide with its brothers among the flotsam of the beach.

Every country boy has such humble adventures and learns more about this small shore bird than about all the rest of its Order put together. He learns that the Spotted Sandpipers are extremely versatile. They alight on trees, walls, fenceposts, and upturned dories alongshore. And they can dive, either from the surface of the water or from the air. It seems as instinctive for them to take refuge under water when hard pressed as it does for the grebe. They can even go to the bottom in shallow water and run a short distance with head held low and tail raised like an Ouzel. Even the young take to water on occasion. While fishing in the Housatonic River in Connecticut I once came upon a Spotted Sandpiper with a brood of chicks about one third grown. I tried to catch one of the lively sprites but it dived from the margin of the stream and swam away under water, using its small wings vigorously.

Perhaps the most interesting of these diving observations is that of George M. Sutton [52]: "When the bird first flushed, its wings were fully spread, and it was headed for the open water of the lake. Upon seeing me towering above it, however, it turned its course abruptly downward, and without the slightest hesitation flew straight into the water. With wings fully outspread and legs kicking, it made its way rather slowly along the sandy bottom, until it was about eight feet out, in water three feet deep. I pursued the bird, thinking at the time, strangely enough, that it was wounded. When I reached it, it tried to go farther but apparently could not. Bubbles of air came from its mouth, and air bubbles were plainly seen clinging to the plumage of its back. At the time it was captured its mouth, eyes, and wings were all open, under water, and it remained at the bottom seemingly without difficulty. As it lay in my hands above water it seemed tired for a second or two, and then, without warning, shook itself a little, leaped into the air, and with loud, clear whistles, circled off a few inches above the water to a distant point of land."

Actitis macularia (Linnaeus). Described in 1766.

LOCAL NAMES: Tip-up, teeter-tail, twitchet, peet-weet, peep, etc. SPANISH: Chorlo o Gordillo manchado.

FIELD CHARACTERS: Our representative of Europe's Common Sandpiper. Summer adults, with round, Wood Thrush-like black spots below, are unique; other sandpipers are streaked, not spotted. The teetering and the stiff-winged flight are also characteristic. In fall, both adults and immatures are pale olive-brown, decidedly greenish in good light. A white line over the eye and a white patch forward of the folded wing may also help. A characteristic call, *ah-wheet, wheet, wheet,* is emphatic. In spring, a soft, rolling *toor-ee, toor-ree!* l. 7½", b. ⅞".

RANGE: Breeds across the continent from tree line, south to mountains of s. California and across the country at roughly the 35° parallel (southward in Appalachians, northward to Virginia on coast). Winters on U.S. west coast and south to Argentina and n. Chile; and from So. Carolina and Gulf coast (mostly) south to s. Brazil. Migrates right across the continent.

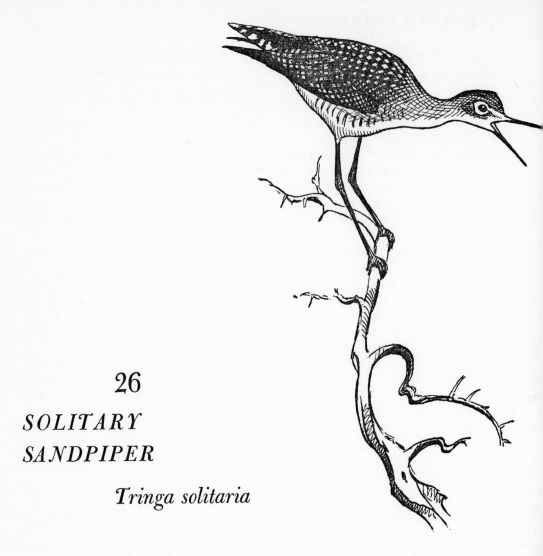

26
SOLITARY SANDPIPER

Tringa solitaria

THOUGH described as new to science by Alexander Wilson in 1813, this little forest dweller kept the secret of its nesting habits for ninety years, at which time an observant homesteader in the foothills of the Rocky Mountains of central Alberta, Mr. Evan Thomson,[7] discovered that the Solitary Sandpiper lays its eggs in the abandoned nests of robins and other song birds. This was on June 6, 1903, but the news was not released until 1904, after the observation had been repeated, and a parent bird taken at the nest as proof of the identity of eggs new to science.

Since then, the Solitary Sandpiper has been found using the old nests of grackles, Brewer's Blackbird, Rusty Blackbird, Cedar Waxwing, Kingbird, and Gray Jay, anywhere from four to forty feet up in some tree along the edge of a wet spruce-larch swamp, or muskeg. Considering the similarity of their ranges, this sandpiper certainly uses the nests of the Rusty Blackbird and the robin more often than any of the others mentioned. These nests are apparently all taken as they are, no additions of material being made by the sandpipers.

In Europe, the Green Sandpiper, and to a lesser extent the Wood Sandpiper, both share this habit of using old nests in which to lay their eggs. And though the Green Sandpiper was described by Linnaeus in 1758, not until 1863 did the English learn of this habit, though in that country the bird is a passage migrant only, although suspected of nesting on occasion.

That veteran Canadian naturalist, Dr. Harrison F. Lewis, once observed a ground display in this bird, writing to A. C. Bent[7] of it as follows: "The sandpiper, which was well aware that I was watching it, stepped slowly out unto the open surface of the mud of the bog, and, standing there with its left side toward me . . . spread its wings about halfway, holding them stiffly in the plane of its back, neither raised nor lowered, so that the dark markings on its axillars were slightly visible. At the same time it drew its head as far backward and its tail as far forward over its back as possible, and slowly lowered its breast until it almost seemed to touch the mud. After remaining rigid in this position for 10 to 15 seconds, it would suddenly relax and become its normal self, only to repeat the entire procedure almost immediately."

Joseph Grinnell,[23] in describing the birds of the Kotzebue Sound region of Alaska, called attention to a song flight indulged in by this bird, mostly in the early morning, "a slow circuitous flight on rapidly beating wings high over the tree tops, accompanied by the frequent repetition of a weak song somewhat resembling the call of a sparrow-hawk. At the close of this song-flight the bird alights, as if exhausted, and perches silently for some time at the top of the tallest spruce in the vicinity."

I have several times been assailed by territorial birds while passing along the edge of the small mossy bogs they occupy within the sub-arctic forest of central Ungava-Labrador. They call anxiously from the terminal spires of spruces and larches, raising their wings high on alighting, and engaging in a shallow flight like that of the Spotted Sandpiper when changing perch. We once counted 180 calls per minute in a bird that kept up its cries for 45 minutes as we sought its nest below.

No one seems to have witnessed the departure of young Solitary

Sandpipers from their elevated nests. Being precocial young, they must be ready to tumble out soon after hatching, and it may even be that the parent carries them down, though a drop to the cushiony moss carpeting of the muskeg would involve little risk of injury. So, like Wood Duck and American Goldeneye ducklings, they may simply jump down.

(R.C.C.)

Tringa solitaria Wilson. Described in 1813; a western race distinguished by William Brewster in 1890.

LOCAL NAMES: Black snipe, barnyard-plover. SPANISH: Chorlo o Gordillo solitario.

FIELD CHARACTERS: A medium-sized, dark-mantled sandpiper with a white eye-ring and a strikingly banded white tail. This is a bird of woodland pools, mud-bordered ponds, brooks and ditches, never seen on salt water margins. Its flight is buoyant, sometimes erratic as the snipe's, and it does a great deal of bobbing rather than teetering as the Spotted Sandpiper does. The usual calls are high pitched *peet-weet-weet* notes. Forbush described an ingenious foot-stirring trick in feeding, bringing organisms out of the bottom mud without roiling the water. Not truly solitary, but seldom more than six birds together on small woodland ponds. l. $8\frac{1}{2}''$, b. $1\frac{1}{4}''$.

RANGE: Breeds throughout the Canadian spruce forest, from central Alaska to central Labrador. Not proven to nest in U.S. though it may probably do so in mountains of New Hampshire and Maine, and elsewhere. Winters from Baja California, Gulf coast, s.e. Georgia, south to central Argentina. The northwestern population has been recognized as a slightly larger, darker-backed race.

27

WANDERING TATTLER

Heteroscelus incanus

THIS bird is a gray nomad of the South Seas, where summer reigns forever. It bobs and teeters along many a coral strand beneath the palm trees, and at the surf-bright bases of those vast green slopes above which the volcanic clouds of Hawaiian craters hang suspended in the blue air. It is familiar from there to the Galápagos, Tuamotu, the Society Islands, the Philippines, and even to Australia. It lives in a shore bird paradise spread over immeasurable areas of atoll-dotted seas, but also spends much time at inland ponds, behaving much as a Solitary Sandpiper would. Food is plentiful everywhere, the climate is heavenly, and there are no enemies.

If these tattlers were like human beings they might settle down as beachcombers and never leave this dreamland. But no—they will not do so. A few yearling tattlers remain in the Hawaiian Islands year-round, but most of these extraordinary birds annually forsake their South Sea haunts. Driven by the migratory urge, they take off as early as March and early April, reaching California, Washington, and Oregon soon afterward. From there they drift north to the cliffy shores of Alaska, and to the barren, rocky alpine tundra of the interior mountains to nest.

The ornithological history of this bird is indeed amazing. Described in 1789, from a specimen taken in the Society Islands, it became well known as a winter resident and transient on the American west coast, but no nest was found until 1912, and then on the Arctic coast of the Yukon. But this was a chance discovery, and not until 1923 was it found again, and a specimen of the nest and eggs taken to satisfy museum scientists beyond doubt. This was taken by the veteran naturalists, Olaus J. and Adolph Murie,[32] at 4,000 feet elevation in Mount McKinley National Park. Adolph, park biologist in this magnificent wilderness, has since come to consider the Wandering Tattler a common nesting bird in the park, and it was he who established the fact that both sexes incubate and brood the young.

In summer, then, this is a bird of seepage meadows above timberline and of the brook bottoms of tumbling glacial streams. The nest is usually built among the rubble of tumbled gravel bars after the freshets have passed. Here the young find pools in which to feed on the abundant emerging insect life. They are highly precocial, and Adolph Murie has seen them descend a fifteen-foot embankment grown to willow brush, moving downstream a hundred yards the day of their birth.

Although this bird, in true tattler fashion, flies to meet any intruder into its nesting territory, scolding noisily from rocks or bushes, its habits during most of the other nine months of the year are rather like those of the Purple Sandpiper or the Surfbird. It is then a lover of surf-chafed reefs and headlands. There its somber hues so blend with the surroundings that it is difficult to spot.

Heteroscelus incanus (Gmelin). Described in 1789.
LOCAL NAME IN ENGLAND: Grey-rumped Sandpiper.
FIELD CHARACTERS: Knot-like in size and shape, but slaty-gray above and heavily barred below in spring; throat and superciliary line white. Barring lost in winter; chest, sides and back then gray. No wing stripe. Legs yellow. Bobs and teeters a great deal. l. 11″, b. 1½″.
RANGE: Breeds at timberline in the Alaska Range and the Brooks Range. Migrates up and down west coast, wintering from California to Peru, and in eastern Polynesia. Accidental in Britain.

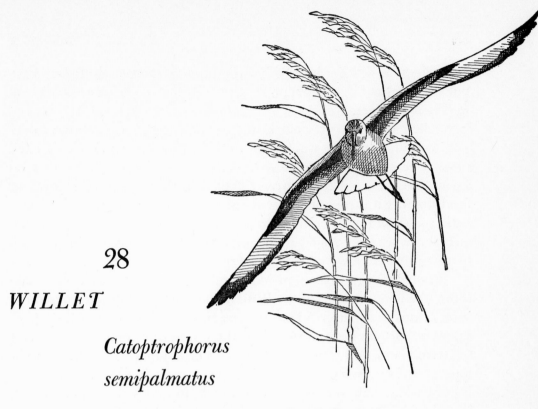

28

WILLET

*Catoptrophorus
semipalmatus*

*"Oh, what is abroad in the marsh and the termi-
nal sea?
Somehow my soul seems suddenly free
From the weighing of fate and the sad discussion
of sin,
By the length and the breadth and the sweep of
the marshes of Glynn."*
—SIDNEY LANIER, 1878

Will-will-willet! I remember well the first time I heard
that musical cry, which sounded as if the bird were spelling out the
letters of its own name. That was many years ago and I was sitting with
a crony behind a fragment of wreckage beside the estuary of Race Run,
Cape Cod.

"Willet!" he exclaimed, and presently a knot of them dropped
down out of the sunny air to our decoys. One alighted a rod distant, elevating its long, white-barred wings as it did so. The others settled on the
sand along the creek, six in all, perhaps a family newly arrived from
Nova Scotia where these big shore birds still nest.

They stood near enough for us to admire the long bluish bills and
legs. Their white under parts and lightly barred flanks reminded us of

Yellowlegs, as did the brownish pattern of their backs and shoulders, but they looked larger, being fifteen inches in length with a wingspread well over two feet.

Their brownish-gray cloaks were inconspicuous against the tawny background, but when we flushed them they seemed entirely different birds. There was so much white on wing coverts, primaries, and secondaries that these willets positively flashed in the sun. Steering away in level flight, with quivering wings rising barely beyond the horizontal, their snowy pinions dominated our impressions. Alighting a few rods nearer the sea they raised their wings high in the air, again showing black and white, lowered them, and disappeared from view.

William Vogt [66] has inquired closely into the significance of these zebra-like wing patterns of the Willet, asking "What is the value, to the bird, of this flash pattern? Has its chief function been that of intimidating enemies? Has it given the males the means of wooing reluctant and selective mates, and those mates a means of holding males through the long period necessary, every year, to perpetuation of the species? Does it exist as a signal, to other Willets, which, in part at least, makes flock life possible? Does it serve, like war-time camouflage, as a 'ruptive pattern' which, despite its brilliance, breaks the real outline and brings protection from stooping peregrines?"

Vogt noticed that the slightly larger, more demure female gives the same *will-will-willet* cries that can be heard half a mile away, but that the male also wails *ka-a-ty*, so he came to call the pair under his special scrutiny Will and Kate.

Both the male defending his territory, and other birds trying to invade it performed a "ceremonial flight" in which the flashing wings were prominently displayed: ". . . the whole performance might have been designed to display those wonderful wings! Widespread, with light piercing through to birds and man watching from the ground, vibrating through a few degrees of arc, they flickered like long tongues of black and white flame. As his mate, taking up the call and the flight, towered upward to fly just beneath the Willet, it was difficult for an excited ornithologist not to anthropomorphize the ceremony into ecstasy!"

In courting, also, the wings are displayed in "as exquisite a ritual as was the ceremonial flight. He would walk towards Kate, chipping slowly, and lift eloquent wings high above his back. At the same time the speed of the chips and the movement of the wings increased until he sounded like a cicada and wore, above his shoulders, a canopy of those same

flickering black and white tongues of flame. He was now directly behind her, and her eyes, set wide on the sides of her head, were manifestly watching every flash of the wings. If she were willing, she would incline slightly forward—sometimes calling softly—and the beating wings would carry him lightly to her. Thus, in a manner that has been fixed by centuries of success, the seed of the future Willet race is sown."

And even in distraction, after the nest exchange ceremony, the wings came into play. The climax came when he stood before her after a meticulously cautious approach through the grass. Now "Will bowed low before her, his bill pointed towards the ground near her breast, and gave utterance to his ringing pill-will-willet cry. Still no sign from her. Then, very deliberately, he walked unto the nest, stepping over Kate, and as his breast touched her, she darted out beneath him and flew away, accompanying the flashing of her wings with a clear pill-will-willet that, certainly, would have attracted attention away from the nest she had left. Thus male gave way to female, or female to male, without exposing the precious eggs, for an instant, to cold or enemy eyes."

From Fortescue in south Jersey, all the way to Tamaulipas in Mexico, the Willet breeds in considerable numbers wherever local conditions are suitable. It is a most picturesque snipe to watch. Visiting Cobb Island early one May, I noted that the Willets invariably stuck close to their nests, rocketing noisily a few feet ahead as I plodded through waist-high cover. This habit of flushing directly from the eggs is in marked contrast to the more subtle ways of many shore birds, especially of Killdeer, which are careful to steal away from their nests and rise at a considerable distance from them.

Not only did these Willets give away the location of their homes, but whenever one of them sprang, all the unattached birds, friends and neighbors, hovered towards me at a slight elevation, crying *Yip-yip-yip!* and *Pill-will-willet!* over and over again. They pursued me everywhere, settling in the grass only when I had withdrawn from the neighborhood of the nests. But they kept rediscovering me, leaping forth again and again, as clamorous as before.

These noisy Willet ways suggest why the birds were driven from the New England coast so early. In the days of shore bird abundance there were no closed seasons nor protection of any sort to inhibit gunners. Large plump snipe like these, hovering overhead and complaining loudly, must have presented pitifully easy targets to market-gunners. Old-time baymen did not limit their depredations to any one season. They bagged birds whenever and wherever they found them numerous enough to make it seem worth while. Moreover, Willet eggs, most of them over two inches long, were considered delicacies. They were easy to procure because the birds tended to nest in the same parts of a meadow, or bushy, seaside waste, and such spots were repeatedly betrayed by the birds themselves.

Catoptrophorus semipalmatus (Gmelin). Described in 1789, the western race in
     1887 by William Brewster.
LOCAL NAMES: Humility (another rendition of the cry), pied-wing curlew, white-
     wing, and the geographical prefixes eastern, or western willet.
FIELD CHARACTERS: The flashing, black and white wings make this big, gray sand-
     piper easy to recognize; only the Avocet and the Oystercatcher resemble it in
     this respect, but they are otherwise distinctive. But a standing Willet is an-

other matter. In spring, much like a Greater Yellowlegs in markings but with a somewhat stouter bill, bluish legs, and a much quieter demeanor. Flush if uncertain. Fall birds are paler, much like Hudsonian Godwits, but shorter billed. This is perhaps the only American shore bird in which distinguishing subspecies in the field is worth while. The eastern race is smaller, shorter-billed and darker, and is the only likely race on the Atlantic coast north of the Carolinas in spring. (l. 14–16″, b. 2–2¼″) In autumn, however, eastern birds apparently move southward offshore, and at least from Massachusetts southward, the western race is the common one. This bird is a head taller, has a longer bill, and is much paler throughout. (l. 15–17″, b. 2¼–2¾″) Females larger in both races.

RANGE: The eastern race breeds locally in So. Nova Scotia, southern New Jersey and Delaware, south to n.e. Mexico and a few of the West Indies. Winters from Virginia south to n. So. America. The western race breeds locally from central Utah to central Alberta, and from e. Oregon to e. So. Dakota. Winters from n. California to n. Chile; and from So. Carolina south to n. So. America.

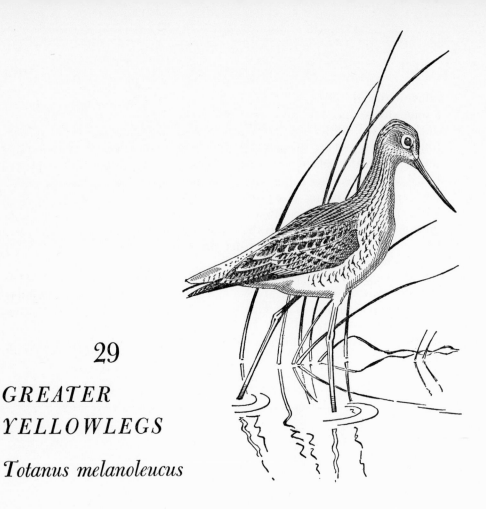

29

GREATER
YELLOWLEGS

Totanus melanoleucus

THE flight notes of shore birds, however humble as melody, have a magic of their own. Sufficiently individualistic to enable anybody to identify most species at considerable distances, they carry the listener up into the air with them, whether in the ruddy dawn, at midday, or in the thickening dusk. It is not necessary to see the bird itself. Just a ventriloquial whistle or two makes us visualize rippling wings. We listen a moment and share the mystery of migration with them.

Take the triple descending spiral notes of the Greater Yellowlegs. Those cheery, confident pipings sound as free and natural as voices of the air. It is impossible to hear them without seeing brown sea-meadows, green saltings, and tidal creeks twisting toward the broad blue buckler of the sea.

The salt fragrance of marshes grows strong in our nostrils; we hear the breeze sighing through the sedge, or feel it fanning our cheeks. Such sounds, as much part of the tidal world as the minnows which glisten in the shallows, not only arouse all our five senses but touch chords in our subconscious memory running back to childhood.

The whistle of the Greater Yellowlegs, loud and insistent, is easy to imitate. I have repeatedly drawn down wandering birds which passed somewhere overhead while I was fishing. The birds seemed to crave company and would circle over and over again, trying to locate their calling brother. Sometimes a bird would flounce back and forth for several minutes, whistling inquiringly, but always ready to come back and be fooled again.

Unfortunately for these handsome birds their music often cost them dear. In the old days tin snipe-calls were sold in sporting-goods emporiums, but they were really entirely superfluous. Any Down East boy could mimic the notes of these tattlers convincingly. Occasionally a bunch of prime birds, trailing their long legs, would plane in to his wooden or tin decoys on curving wings, suffer casualties and zig-zag to safety. They often returned for another look when skillfully called.

This gullibility proved a fatal weakness. Another handicap was their slowness as compared with swift-driving Black-bellied Plover. Not that they were invariably easy to stop. When fired upon they would occasionally flare or veer as unpredictably as jack-snipe, particularly in a high wind, when many escaped. They were plump, delicious prizes, although never quite the equals of woodcock or curlew as food.

The Greater Yellowlegs is one of the largest and most striking of shore birds. Its plumage pattern, gray and brown above but mainly white below, with very conspicuous white tail coverts, long bright yellow legs and a bill over two inches in length, identify it almost at once. Its forceful treble whistle will put any doubt to rest.

Migrating coastwise in spring and fall Greater Yellowlegs are more partial to drowned flats and tidal basins than to the outside beaches. I recall a circular pool not far from Great South Bay, Long Island, to which a shore bird enthusiast used to take me once in so often. Although brackish this basin was unaffected by ordinary tides and always harbored a goodly school of minnows.

There was no cover near the water excepting marsh grass and so we always gathered big mounds of sea lavender (tumbleweed) to screen us. The last time we visited the place proved balmy for the season, with a soft, perfumed breeze breathing on us from the boundless meadows.

My companion had expected a big flight of birds, but they failed to materialize, presumably because it was slack tide and they were busy feeding elsewhere. Both of us presently fell asleep. We were roused by loud, clear whistling very near at hand. About a dozen Greater Yellowlegs were drifting in and alighted so close that we could watch their every movement. One or two were bobbing and teetering like tip-ups, but the rest promptly started to feed in the shallows where they stood almost belly-deep.

From a similar hide-out on a creek near Provincetown I once watched half a dozen of these snipe catching minnows. I lay so close to them that it was easy to study their methods. They would form a line and chase a school into some triangular nook where it was easy to dash in and seize a full meal. During migrations the stomachs of these birds are sometimes crammed with fish about an inch in length. They also eat mussels, crabs, clams, small hoppers and seaside insects, but almost never probe for food as so many shore birds do.

On the ocean beaches the few Greater Yellowlegs which we see fly up wind as a rule. Were it not for this it might be easy to mistake one for something torn loose by the breeze as it comes twisting past the decoys with cheery whistle. Its long bill in front and legs trailing behind add to its apparent size. The bird pitches about a hundred paces away, runs up the slope to the weed belt, and glances suspiciously about for a moment. Then seeing me wave a hand, it leaps into the air, startling by its outcry all the birds in the vicinity. This snipe has certainly earned its familiar name of "tattler."

Greater Yellowlegs are even noisier in defense of their nests and eggs. They fly round and round an intruder, whistling and scolding with incredible boldness, and stirring up their friends and neighbors to join in the outcry.

They do not breed so far north as most of their order, but nest well within the timbered zone from British Columbia east to Labrador and Newfoundland. They prefer sheltered nooks at the forest's edge whereas most snipe and sandpipers of that region have homes out on the wet tundra and muskeg.

It seems likely that the protection afforded shore birds may lead eventually to the full recovery of the cheerful Greater Yellowlegs. Already, larger flocks gather for migration, particularly in the North, and as they are no longer shot for game, more and more survive the perils of the long pilgrimage.

Only a few years ago while tramping across salt meadows northwest of Moose Factory on James Bay, some 300 miles below Churchill, I witnessed a flight which must have been comparable with those common in earlier days. A cloud of birds kept lifting on the green horizon, too distant for identification, but suggesting a vast concentration of waterfowl.

When the birds drifted nearer I saw that they were Greater Yellowlegs. They were not flying quite so thick as I had surmised while they were far away, but in more or less detached companies. All formed parts of one splendid snipe division, and all were southward bound, for it was already August.

Totanus melanoleucus (Gmelin). 1789, though first described as the Stone Snipe in Pennant's *Arctic Zoology* (1785).

LOCAL NAMES: Winter yellowlegs, horse yellowleg, winter turkey-back, cucu, greater tattler, tell-tale, etc. SPANISH: Chorlo or Gordillo mayor patas amarillas.

FIELD CHARACTERS: A tall, large sandpiper with long bill and long, bright yellow legs. Speckled on breast in spring, almost white in winter; the back is dark grayish-brown with white speckles, somewhat streaked. The plain dark wing and white rump are helpful when the bird flies. An active, noisy bird usually seen chasing about madly in minnow pools on tidal marshes or inland. Its ringing, 3-syllabled *whew-whew-whew* call is generally diagnostic and the safest criterion for distinguishing small individuals from large examples of the Lesser Yellowlegs.

Carefully compared, the Greater Yellowlegs' bill is proportionately longer, stouter, and is slightly upcurved. More important than the bird's larger bulk are its relatively longer legs and more ample wings. It is less gregarious, wilder, and does more bobbing than the Lesser.

In spring its yodeling, a rolling *toowhee, toowhee,* mellow and musical, is a pleasant sound of wetlands. Variable. l. 12–15″, b. 2¾–3½″, female larger.

RANGE: Breeds in the muskeg country of the transcontinental spruce forest, from south-central Alaska to Newfoundland. Migrates across the continent and off the Atlantic coast (earlier in spring, later in fall than Lesser Yellowlegs). Winters regularly from central California and Chesapeake Bay south to southern tip of South America.

(*l-r*) Solitary Sandpiper, Greater and Lesser Yellowlegs

30

LESSER YELLOWLEGS

Totanus flavipes

I FREQUENTLY hear the glad whistling of these delicate waders before the birds themselves appear. I recall, particularly, a flock whose mellow pipings reached me across a meadow one glorious August morning. I could not catch the flicker of a single wing for a moment, but presently saw a flash of silver low on the green horizon—unmistakably sunlight reflected from the white breast of a wheeling shore bird. It vanished when they steadied on their keels, because the birds were still too remote to be visible when only their darker mantles were touched with light.

Presently they seemed to hatch from the air itself, and came winging steadily along a creek like silvery ripples in flight. Such airy motion

is in the nature of a song without words. Every movement of both species of yellowlegs is incredibly graceful and pleasing to the eye.

Like the Greater Yellowlegs, this bird includes in its range most of
North and South America, but the migratory routes of the two birds
differ markedly. Coming north from Patagonia in spring, the Lesser
Yellowlegs spills over up both coasts of North America somewhat; but
by far the greater number migrate up the western side of the Mississippi
valley. Even birds which start up the outside coasts gradually leave them
to pass inland. As a consequence the bird is scarce in spring north of the
Carolina capes, rare north of Delaware.

The few that appear in spring on the southern New England shore
are conspicuous among the smaller peep because of their greater size
and the nervous haste with which they devour the sea-spoil. They soon
disappear northward, or northwestward if we could but follow them,
and do not return until early July, when the southward trek commences. The fall migration reaches a peak in late August or early September in the New York City region, and goes straight down the coast.
This coastwise flight is the major fall movement, and its present day
magnitude is suggested by the fact that Ludlow Griscom reported and
estimated 4000 birds on the flats of Monomoy, Cape Cod, on Aug. 6,
1947.

The meadows of Race Point Run near the northern tip of Cape
Cod were a famous resting place for these "summer yellowlegs." Crossing the upper stretches of that basin with a friend late one August, I
came suddenly upon a goodly flight of these birds in the grass which was
here about three feet tall and half drowned in salt water. That was before the dyke was built nearer Cape Cod Bay to dry the region and rid
it of mosquitoes. Better to have flooded it permanently.

As we plodded seaward, yellowlegs flushed before us at almost
every step. The farther we walked, the thicker they became. There must
have been several hundred, as the grassy stretches of all Race Run
seemed crowded. All were summer yellowlegs, without a single larger
wader accompanying them. These birds are considerably more gregarious than their larger cousins. But, often, somewhat mixed flocks alight
on our broad sea meadows. When a sizeable lot whirls up it often draws
along a throng of smaller peep, with perhaps a big willet, and a Hudsonian Curlew or two.

Wherever Yellowlegs appear in considerable numbers nowadays,
we may be sure that they were gunned in our grandfathers' time. A fair

shot could kill almost any number of these waders. They rose in the open, with neither bush nor tree to shield them, and most of them flew straight away over the grass, legs dangling, or circled overhead whistling at you. To gun them under those circumstances was senseless slaughter. Gathering in much bigger flocks than Greater Yellowlegs, and being markedly less wary, they sadly needed the protection that came just in time to save them from serious decimation.

This bird nests in the more open muskegs of the Canadian spruce forests, those almost impassable stretches of small bogs and ragged Black Spruce woods struggling through a foot or more of peat moss. In the Churchill region, where muskeg meets open tundra, the Lesser Yellowlegs is common "to the point of being a common nuisance, as its loud protestations and wild dashes on the appearance of an intruder put all the birds of the vicinity on the *qui vive* and spoil many a quiet approach." [56]

Both yellowlegs are difficult birds to come to know on their breeding grounds, and as a consequence we know little of their courtship or the details of their breeding biology. That skillful egg collector, Richard C. Harlow,[7] has reported that this bird may scratch out a number of nest hollows within a radius of 50 yards or more, and even line some of these depressions with dry leaves before selecting one and laying the eggs. This may probably represent the type of formalized courtship ceremony described by Niko Tinbergen for the Northern Phalarope.

Totanus flavipes (Gmelin). Described in 1789 from a New York specimen described in Pennant's *Arctic Zoology*.

LOCAL NAMES: Summer yellowlegs (east coast). Yellowshank (England). SPANISH: Chorlo o Gordillo menor patas amarillas.

FIELD CHARACTERS: This slim bird is a third smaller than the Greater Yellowlegs, more delicate, and slimmer, but size is only occasionally helpful. Their plumages are almost identical though this species is often paler above. Both have long, bright yellow legs. The Lesser's bill is more slender, perfectly straight instead of slightly upturned as in the Greater. Most helpful is the rather flat, one- or two-syllabled *cu-cu* note given on flushing or in overhead flight. Like the Greater Yellowlegs (which see) it has an attractive springtime yodel. l. 9¼–11″, b. 1¼–1½″, female larger.

RANGE: Breeds in open muskeg, or in fire clearings, in spruce forest, from north-central Alaska on the west to the eastern shore of James Bay on the east. Winters on the coasts of eastern U.S. (south of New Jersey mostly) and most of Mexico (commonest on eastern lowlands) south to southern South America. Chief autumn migration down eastern seaboard; principal spring flight passes up the Mississippi Valley. Much scarcer on Pacific coast.

31

KNOT

Calidris canutus

"THE Knot, good reader, is a handsome and interesting species, whether in its spring or in its winter plumage, and, provided it be young and fat, is always welcome to the palate of the connoisseur in dainties. As to its habits, however, during the breeding season, I am sorry to inform you that I know nothing at all, for in Labrador, whither I went to examine them, I did not find a single individual. I have been informed that several students of nature have visited its breeding places; but why they have given us no information on the subject, seeing that not only you and I, but many persons besides, would be glad to hear about it, is what we cannot account for."

Thus did Audubon,[5] in a sense, chide all of us, though admitting, later, that he too had been guilty of remissness in failing to study and report closely. Actually, the nest of the Knot went undiscovered until Admiral R. E. Peary paused to photograph one on June 27, 1909, after his dash to the North Pole, and not far from Cape Sheridan, Grinnell Land. And details of its nesting went undescribed until A. L. Manniche reported on his fine northeast Greenland studies, and Dr. W. E. Ekblaw sent detailed notes to A. C. Bent,[7] who used them at length in his Bulletin 142.

When New England's apple orchards are oceans of pink and white blooms all musical with bees, and the bluebird carols cheerily, the adventurous "robin sandpiper" is crossing the Magic Circle, northward bound. About the time our robin commences to line her nest here, the Knot pitches somewhere up in northern Greenland.

It chooses for a summer home some flinty tableland or a patch of dry tundra near the Arctic Ocean. Having selected a site, the sandpiper hollows out a shallow cup, and lays three or four pear-shaped eggs, remarkable only because of the remote and inaccessible places where they are hatched. Indeed, the Knot is thought to brood its eggs (the male apparently does most of this) farther north than any other shore bird.

Whether or not the Knot's northern flights date back to some warmer interlude in the geological calendar, it is obvious that even the brief Arctic summer of today is warm enough for this hardy bird. The chicks are extremely precocial and sprout flight feathers with surprising rapidity. The adults start south rather early, and appear on the New England coast from mid-July onward. The young, then, are abandoned almost as soon as they can fly and have achieved parental independence. Within two weeks or so they follow the departed parents southward, bound they know not where, but driven by an almost unerring instinct.

In August, on Cape Cod, Sanderlings are the most abundant birds at times, and by far the most curious concerning decoys. They often associate with other shore birds and sometimes bring with them flights of Knots, many of them still red as Woodcock and nearly as plump. These ruddy birds appear gigantic beside the various peep. They turn and twist in flight and are as likely to whirl back over the beach as to skim along its margin. A group of Knots frequently comes several times to the decoys before giving up the unresponsive images as ingrates. When they alight on the shore at a distance it is useless to follow. The migratory urge goads them so sharply that they seldom delay more than momentarily except at high tide.

A few generations ago Knots were incredibly numerous despite the varied perils of lengthy semi-annual migrations, inhospitable nesting sites, and the small size of their clutches. During the southbound migration they alighted in ruddy-silver clouds on the flats of Cape Cod, and were there subjected not only to heavy shooting but to a vicious commercial practice called "fire-lighting." The procedure, according to George H. Mackay, "was for two men to start out after dark at half tide, one of them to carry a lighted lantern, the other to reach and seize the birds, bite their necks, and put them in a bag slung over the shoulder. When near a flock they would approach them on their hands and knees, the birds being almost invariably taken on the flats. This practice continued several years before it was finally prohibited by law." The southbound flocks were hunted everywhere, especially on Long Island and New Jersey in addition to Cape Cod, since these shore areas were within easy reach of markets in Boston and New York. They seemed fated to follow the Passenger Pigeon and the Eskimo Curlew into extinction.

Since legal protection was extended to them, Knots have increased gradually. A flight of them paints pictures on the sunny air against a background of white dunes and blue sea not readily forgotten. They are swift of wing and a delight to the eye, especially those occasional individuals that retain their red bridal plumage for weeks after their fellows have taken on the gray tints of winter. Such were the first I ever saw—a squad of five which came twisting past my decoys while I was trying to photograph Black-bellied Plovers.

Calidris canutus (Linnaeus). Described in 1758; our race separated, by Alexander Wilson, in 1813.

LOCAL NAMES: Robin snipe, red-breasted sandpiper, rosy plover; whiting, grayback, silver-back, blue plover, wahquoit, the latter a Cape Cod name. The name Knot itself is given a flavorful history by Dawson[14]: "When King Canute, or Knut, had dined on a dish of strange coast-faring birds, he was gracious enough to express to his blushing chef the royal appreciation of the flavor. Whereupon the eager courtiers dubbed the waders Knuts, or Knots, and so they have come down to us—at least so Pennant says; and Linnaeus, not over-serious (he was a busy man with all Adam's task to finish) accepted the tradition in *Tringa canutus*" [now Calidris canutus]. SPANISH: Chorlo rojizo.

FIELD CHARACTERS: The only short-billed shore bird with a red breast in spring. In fall, it flies and feeds in dense flocks, is grayish. Then almost as large as a Black-bellied Plover, but dingier, shorter-legged. Whitish rump and wing bars inconspicuous. At close range, the back is beautifully scaly because of white feather-edgings. The flight note is a double whistle, soft and rolling, *wha-quoit;* the other, a single soft honk or croak, *skeuk.* l. $10\frac{1}{2}''$, b. $1\frac{3}{8}''$.

RANGE: Circumpolar. From Southampton Island, north through the central portion of the Arctic archipelago to Taimyr Peninsula in Siberia. The limits of the two recognized races of this species are not yet worked out. The nominate race (*C.c.canutus*) migrates chiefly down the European and Asian coasts. Ours (*C.c.rufa*), in fall, chiefly along Atlantic coast to winter from New Jersey all the way to Tierra del Fuego; in spring turning inland to pass northward along west coast of Hudson Bay. Some birds thus span the length of the continents from extremity to extremity.

32

PURPLE SANDPIPER

Erolia maritima

SOMETIMES the winter fisherman, Gloucester-bound with cod, his decks and rigging coated with tons of ice, passes some ledge round which the breakers boil. Perhaps he is watching a flock of snowy eider drakes picking mussels from the reef, or diving for sea clams.

All at once he descries a group of sandpipers, short-legged little fellows, slightly larger than Sanderlings but much darker in color. They look blackish-brown above, save for their heads which show buffy streaks and their shoulders on which may glow a faint, purplish iridescence. Their flanks are gray, but the under parts are white, as with so many others of their Order.

When the ocean covers the rockweed from which these sandpipers gather prawn, periwinkles, mussels, sea-worms, and even iron-clad barnacles, the birds crowd together on the dry portions of the islet—if that may be termed dry over which spindrift is blown whenever a roller thunders against the seaward rampart. There they rest or play as unconcernedly as if they were on summer sands. When the tide falls they feed where every surge lifts the floating sea-wrack in a welter of foam. Occasionally they scamper up the icy reef to escape a particularly menacing breaker, or swim a few strokes to some neighboring rock, or fly in a wide arc over the waves, then complete the curve back to the reef.

Pack ice or bergs seem to please them better than sun-kissed sands. Fog, cold, and the whine of wind have no terrors for them.

Purple Sandpipers normally reach the southern New England coast after mid-October and drift northward again in early April. We knew rather little of their northward passage until Soper[48] found this to be one of the abundant summer birds of the Nettiling Lake region, on the flat, sea-level plains of western Baffin Island. Tens of thousands swarm through this region, their legions covering the small patches of bare tundra while snow still occupies much of the ground in mid-June at this high latitude. The picture of the height of migration conjured up by Soper's notes is one to rouse the envy of every field naturalist. There, while the lingering snow restricts the available feeding grounds, large numbers of Purple Sandpipers, together with Snow Buntings, Lapland Longspurs, White-rumped and Baird's Sandpipers; Golden and Black-bellied Plovers; Snow, Blue and Canada Geese, and Brant crowd together on narrow strips of muddy tundra along the ice-choked streams and feed sociably.

Whether in the uplands or near the coast along the northern seas it calls home, the Purple Sandpiper prefers to nest in patches of heath tundra among the rocky outcroppings. Its chief display seems to be a variable "wing-ceremony," in which one or both wings are raised high as the bird stands facing or running toward a potential mate or competitor. This display may be alternated with a display flight on stiffly held wings, during which it gives voice to a musical *to-wit-to-wit-to-wit-towit*. (*H.M.H.*)

All of us, when face to face with an unexpected antagonist, are prone to make two "instinctive" choices of reaction—we may fight or flee. If the fear that grips us is strong enough, purposeful reaction is completely inhibited and we say that we were "frozen" by fear. Birds face the same choices, but instead of trying to reason a way out of their dilemma, they have evolved more or less stereotyped patterns of behavior, patterns which have proved sufficiently successful over the ages to permit the survival of the species. But *successful* only in the face of the *usual* challenges to their adaptive powers, because when confronted with circumstances that are out of the ordinary, birds are usually quite incapable of responding appropriately. This is not to say that birds are unintelligent, but simply that they do not rely on intelligence to solve the everyday problems of life.

It is this fascinating chain of behavioristic patterns that the modern student of comparative animal psychology, the ethologist, tries to unravel. His professional jargon is currently overloaded with big and little words, confusingly used, but he has struck upon a new and powerful tool of enquiry, and it behooves us to be patient because many of his findings will prove helpful to an understanding of ourselves.

One of these behavioristic patterns is the distraction display of the Purple Sandpiper which includes an unusual form called the "rodent run," and is one shared by several other species of the open tundra. This has been interestingly interpreted by Kenneth Williamson.[69]

In those high latitudes, where the fox, the jaeger and the snowy owl are the chief predators, the lemming and various mice are the chief prey animals. But birds, too, must bear part of the brunt of the incessant demands of the larger predators. That some shore birds should adapt to this threat by simulating the most sought-after prey animal of the arctic, the lemming, is one of the extraordinary facts of the struggle for existence.

Invade the nesting territory of this sandpiper and it will fly at you while you are still a hundred feet from the nest, attract your attention to itself by a call or two, then alight and walk away from the nest with apparent unconcern. If you succumb to this lure and approach the bird more closely, it will fluff out its feathers till they stand on end like fur, droop and quiver its wing tips which may then look like hind legs, and zig-zag away through the rocks and low plants with head and body low, the while perhaps uttering a thin call, and looking for all the world like a lemming, even to the dark dorsal stripe!

Several trained observers have seen dogs and native guides completely fooled by this trick, and therein of course lies its survival value and its unbird-like name, the "rodent run." If this seems fanciful to you, the ethologist will remind you that owls, for example, are so addicted to the texture of fur as a component of fair prey that they have been known to lift the coonskin cap off a man's head and engage in other such unwise but owlish acts. If you pursue the Purple Sandpiper which is luring you, it will lead you away a hundred feet or so before flying off in quite bird-like fashion and circling back to its eggs or young. (*R.C.C.*)

Erolia maritima (Brunnich). Described in 1764.
LOCAL NAMES: Rock-bird, rock snipe, rock sandpiper, winter snipe.

FIELD CHARACTERS: Dark, tame, and portly sandpipers frequenting rocky points and islets of the north Atlantic coasts in winter. Sooty brown above and on chest, with paler throat and white belly; base of bill and rather short legs yellowish. Voice, seldom heard above the noise of the waves, a low *weet-wit*. l. 9″, b. 1¼″.

RANGE: Breeds on shores of upper North Atlantic and adjacent arctic waters, from Ellesmere Island, Southampton and Belcher Islands in Hudson Bay; Greenland and east to New Siberia Islands archipelago; south in Europe to the Faeroes, central Sweden in mountains, and the Murmansk coast. This bird learned to use stone jetties, groins, etc., along sandy stretches of the Atlantic coast after the 1930's and consequently enjoyed a remarkable extension of winter range. It now winters south regularly to North Carolina [in 1954 a large flock of 75 or more were identified on the rocks of Fort Sumter, S.C. by J. H. Dick] (casually to Georgia and Florida) on our side, and to Baltic and North Sea coasts in Europe. Casual inland. It has recently wintered on the Great Lakes.

33

ROCK SANDPIPER

Erolia ptilocnemis

(*l*) Rock Sandpiper in breeding plumage.
(*r*) Purple Sandpiper.

THE wife of the head trapper for Revillon Frères used to spend the winter at Moose Factory on lower James Bay, Canada. She felt too far away from her summer home up in Baffin Island, and told me that Hudson and James Bays are too far south for comfort. She was truly homesick for the white North.

The Rock Sandpiper reminds me of her. This species breeds on the desolate, fog-bound islands of the Bering Sea. That is well up toward the top of the world.

This little bird is the north Pacific coast analogue of the Purple Sandpiper of other northern seas, and was not distinguished from it until 1873. Indeed, the Russians consider them conspecific. Today four races of the Rock Sandpiper are distinguished by taxonomists, each of which formerly bore a species name to confuse us utterly; today, at last, we use double adjectives to designate subspecies, if we try to distinguish them at all outside the museum. Of these the Aleutian race is very sedentary, being a permanent resident in that chain of chilly islands. Even more circumscribed in distribution is the Commander Rock Sandpiper, resident of the Komandorskie Islands of eastern Siberia. The Pribilof race breeds on St. Matthew, Hall, and the Pribilofs, famous haunts of the fur seal, and winters somewhat farther south, from Nunivak Island to Juneau on the southern Alaska coast. The fourth race, though it perhaps deserves the appelation less than its confreres, is the Northern Rock Sandpiper which nests on the alpine tundra of Siberia's Chukotski Peninsula on the west side of Bering Strait, and in similar habitats on the Seward Peninsula of Alaska, including way stations on the peaks of St. Lawrence and Nunivak Islands.

The Rock Sandpiper, whatever race we may be observing, is one of the conspicuous summer birds of the tundras of the Bering Sea region. Their love-making and noisy defense of the eggs and young obtrude upon the summer visitor to these outposts and help animate, in their small way, even the seal islands.

Dr. Ira N. Gabrielson's [21] report of hundreds of these sandpipers sunning themselves on the wharves and roofs of the cannery buildings at Petersburg in southern Alaska during winter months, reminds us how closely related to the gulls the whole tribe of waders is. Seen in silhouette, without benefit of size comparisons, and at a distance sufficient to blur the details of bill and foot, many of them would seem to have interchangeable forms.

The recently discovered southern outpost of this bird's winter range is a lesson in ecology, indeed. For many years now, the accepted limits of the wintering grounds for the Northern Rock Sandpiper have been "from the Alaska Peninsula south along the Pacific coast to Washington and Oregon, rarely to Humboldt Bay in northwestern California." But off the otherwise hot and arid coast of Baja California, 100 miles below San Diego, oceanographers have shown that upwelling currents of cold ocean water create a peculiarly "northern" habitat in a zone otherwise subtropical. And here, in the company of other familiar cold water forms, the Rock Sandpiper has been added to the list of winterers by Carl L. Hubbs.[29] How, one may wonder, do these birds learn to bypass some 800 miles of unsuitably warm coast to find this small area of cold water outside Punta Piedras Blancas at 31°19′N. latitude?

Erolia ptilocnemis (Coues). Described in 1873, the other races in 1880, 1920, 1937.
FIELD CHARACTERS: Plain, thick-set, and dark bluish-gray birds with black rump
and gray tail. Breast and flanks heavily mottled with dark gray; sides show

whitish when wings are lifted. Lower belly white. The bill is olive, with a
more yellowish base and a black tip; the legs are dull yellow. Spring birds
rufous above, with black patch on breast. A bird of the coastal rocks, where it
associates with Black Turnstones and Surfbirds, being more numerous than
those two, and even plainer in color. Shows a white wing-stripe in flight.
Winter birds indistinguishable in the field from Purple Sandpipers (except
by range) but summer birds show more reddish in the plumage. l. 9″, b. 1⅛″.
RANGE: Nests on coastal tundra and islands on both sides of Bering Strait, south
to the Kurile Islands on the Asiatic side, to the Aleutians, the Alaska peninsula, and the Shumagin Islands on the American side. Some races are sedentary, others shift southward to middle Kurile Islands and coasts of Canada
and U.S., south to northern California except for local outposts off cold water
coast of Baja California.

34

PECTORAL SANDPIPER

Erolia melanotos

THIS chunky, rather short-legged sandpiper, nearly as large as a small Knot, looks somewhat like a large edition of the Least Sandpiper. It is, however, more strikingly marked, its brown head, neck, and breast being streaked with dusky hues. This distinctive brown pattern is cut off abruptly by the white of the under parts, making a contrast recognizable at moderate distances.

Migrating north from South America in May, the great majority pass directly to their tundra summering grounds throught the interior of the continent, and are rare on both coasts in spring.

I have often admired the gentle, confiding notes these birds utter when resting or feeding with companions along New England pond margins. These sounds, like those of most "peep," convey a sense of ease and contentment. But to fully appreciate this surprising bird's vocalizations one must go to the arctic tundra north and west of Hudson Bay. Quite different here are the resonant, musical booms which the larger males give vent to on territory. These are made by inflating the throat to an amazing size, like an enormous bubble, and then letting the air escape. What a peculiar wind instrument for an ordinarily quiet, inconspicuous little shore bird. When not inflated, this sac hangs like a dewlap, a pendulous skin flap about an inch and a half wide, causing the bird's brown bib to stand out sharply. This extroverted, Prairie Chicken-like performance makes the Pectoral Sandpiper one of the most conspicuous shore birds of the tundras it occupies.

Let Dr. E. W. Nelson[34] tell you of his discovery of this amazing territorial song:

"The last of May, 1879, I pitched my tent on a lonely island in the Yukon Delta and passed the several following weeks in almost continual physical discomfort, owing to the rain and snowstorms which prevailed; however, I look back with pleasure upon the time passed here among the various waterfowl, when every day contributed new and strange scenes to my previous experience.

"The night of May 24 I lay wrapped in my blanket, and from under the raised flap of the tent looked out over as dreary a cloud-covered landscape as can be imagined. The silence was unbroken save by the tinkle and clinking of the disintegrating ice in the rivers, and at intervals by the wild notes of some restless Loon, which arose in a hoarse, reverberating cry and died away in a strange gurgling sound. As my eyelids began to droop and the scene to become indistinct, suddenly a low, hollow, booming note fell upon my ear and sent my thoughts back to a spring morning in Northern Illinois, and to the loud vibrating tones of the Prairie Chicken. Again the sound arose nearer and more distinct, and with an effort I brought myself back to the reality of my surroundings and, rising upon elbow, listened. A few seconds passed and again arose the note. A moment later . . . I stood outside the tent. The open flat extended away on all sides with apparently not a living creature near. Once again the note was repeated close by and a glance revealed its author. Standing in the thin grass, ten or fifteen yards from me, with its throat inflated until it was as large as the rest of the bird, was a male Pectoral Sandpiper."

Pectoral Sandpipers appear, indeed, to be unique among North American shore birds in several other respects. The size disparity in the sexes is unusual and perhaps related to the fact that the pairing bond between mates is very brief. The males occupy from six to fifteen acres, depending on the density of the population, and pay very little attention to the females after mating. The latter tend to all domestic duties alone, and the males often leave the tundra before the eggs are hatched, during the first week of July. This behavior has led Dr. Frank A. Pitelka [39] to suggest that the Pectoral Sandpiper's reproductive pattern represents an evolutionary step toward the lek behavior of the Ruff (see page 196).

Recent studies [24] of the behavior of transient flocks of adult birds on the Delta Marshes of south-central Manitoba, where the birds linger for two or three weeks during July and August, have revealed interesting vestiges of the summer mores. Apparently as an aftermath of the breeding-ground territoriality these birds have practiced, nearly one third of the flock insists on establishing and defending individual territories, and these may vary in size from only ten to as much as two hundred square meters in area. There is a concentric arrangement of birds throughout the day during this post-nuptial vying for position, the less territorial birds at the center of the group being satisfied with maintaining no more than an individualistic sort of lebensraum. The "over-conditioned," still rival-minded, individuals must perforce hold territories along the periphery of the flock. Here, with head high, they posture, bluff, threaten and even fight occasionally, as though there were still females to joust for. At night, however, they give up these atavistic performances and gather in a peaceful social group to roost together on another part of the marsh. This sort of autumnal display has also been noticed in lapwings.

Every season a few drop in along the creek back of Wood End on Cape Cod and several of the tidal ponds which are flooded only by high course tides. These latter, of which Milk Pond near Provincetown is typical, are stagnant and brackish. Near such water Pectoral Sandpipers, alone or in little groups, trip about contentedly in the dusk, picking up insects and minute crustaceans. When surprised in the grass and flushed, they make off with a loud *Creaker! Creak!* zig-zagging away almost like snipe.

Somewhat larger flights of Pectoral Sandpipers alight on grassy stretches in the drier, upper portions of runs and hollows being gradually reclaimed from the sea. Such, for example, is the two-mile bottom of Race Run near Provincetown. Once an arm of Cape Cod Bay, this place has been silting up for years. Mosquito-control engineers have dammed the lower part, so that only a narrow creek makes inland there. In old times, Race Run was a famous place for the Eskimo Curlew and is still visited by flocks of Hudsonian Curlews and summer yellowlegs every fall after easterly storms.

Crouching in the rank grass of such retreats Pectoral Sandpipers are rendered inconspicuous by their remarkable protective coloration. They like grasslands even better than creek margins and mudflats. Feeding largely on insects, they become prime birds and were once considered among the most desirable game birds in Massachusetts. Their plumage looks lighter after midsummer molts, but the distinctive brown neck, collar and breast band, or bib, together with yellowish legs, still make field marks easy to recognize.

The common names of this species suggest its former status as a game bird, its typical coloration, and some of its distinctive habits.

Erolia melanotos (Vieillot). Described in 1819 from a specimen taken in Paraguay. SPANISH: Chorlito manchado.

LOCAL NAMES: Creaker, grass-bird, marsh-plover, brownie, brown-back, squatter, grass snipe, etc.

FIELD CHARACTERS: Females often distinctly smaller than males, and size thus variable, since the sexes are otherwise very similar. Summer and winter plumages also almost alike. The dark brown crown, pale eye stripe and throat, in combination with the close-striped brown breast sharply demarked against the white lower breast (bib-like), and the yellowish legs, are distinctive. The back has snipe-like buff *stripes*. The head is often held up alertly, giving it a more ploverine appearance. Dark wings and erratic flight, along with the grating *"crrriek"* notes given on jumping, are all characteristic. Grassy stubble is a preferred habitat. l. 8–9½", b. 1–1¼", male larger.

RANGE: Low-arctic breeder, from Taimyr in coastal Siberia east to Southampton Island, south to central coastal Alaska and southern Hudson Bay. Winters mostly in southern half of So. America. Migrates chiefly through interior of No. America in spring; rather rare on both coasts. In fall, small numbers overflow onto U.S. Pacific coast and to Japan, the bulk of the flight being eastward along Atlantic coast, from Newfoundland southward.

35

WHITE-RUMPED SANDPIPER

Erolia fuscicollis

ALEXANDER WETMORE'S [68] observations on the bird life of the Argentine are a classic source of information on our waders in their wintering grounds. They complement and enlarge on the better known essays of W. H. Hudson.

The following sketch attests to this view:

"Occasionally when the fall sunlight came warmly I sat in the mud and let little bands of white-rumps work up around me until they were feeding and call-ing within a meter or so, eyeing me sharply for any cause of alarm. At such times, their twittering choruses came sweetly and pleasantly, clearly audible above the lap of waves and the rush of the inevitable winds of the pampas. Between songs the search for food continued without cessation. At short intervals, activated by the warmth of the sun, they suddenly indulged in dozens of combats with their fellows, bloodless affrays, of bluff and retreat, where they lowered their heads and with open mouths ran at one another pugnaciously. The one attacked sidled quickly away or fluttered off for a short distance, save where two of equal tempera-ment chanced to clash when first one and then the other threatened with raised wings in alternate advance and retreat until the fray was concluded to their mutual satisfaction. At such times the movements of these otherwise plain little birds were sprightly and vivacious to a degree. Their loquacity at this season was marked as it contrasted strikingly with their silence and quiet during the resting period of southern summer. Flocks frequently rose to perform intricate evolutions and then returned with a rush to sweep along the shore and join less ambitious comrades. As they passed the white rump flashed plainly, certain advertisement of the species. At times the chattering of these active flocks reminded me of the twittering of swallows."

Nearly 8000 miles to the north, on the arctic barrens of Southampton Island in the mouth of Hudson Bay, another famous student of shore birds found these same White-rumps well worth watching. "Most of their time," George Miksch Sutton [53] wrote,

"they spent running along the beaches, probing nervously for food, stopping for an instant to preen their plumage, lifting a foot up behind a dropped wing to scratch an ear, then racing off anew to continue their feeding. They were noisy and excitable. Often they paused for a moment in their feeding; then, without any sort of warning, so far as I could see, suddenly leaped into the air to dash away at terrific speed, as if pursued by demons. These flocks milled about near me, turning now this way, now that, the gray of their backs melting into the monotone of mud and distant moss, the gleaming white of their breasts flashing as they twisted in their flight. They seemed to be curious, whirling near me again and again, and sometimes coming so close as to confuse me with the rush of their wings and the sharpness of their squeaking cries.

"The tactics of the flock had, no doubt, to be mastered, for these little shore birds were constantly pursued by Parasitic Jaegers, and irregularly by Duck Hawks. When a jaeger came by, the flocks rose as they did when I disturbed them; then, instead of racing away as rapidly as possible from their persecutor, they made straight for him in the most amazing way, whirled about him, mounting higher and higher, twisting, turning, flying at him, separating into two or three bands, then joining again. The little birds seemed to realize that, as long as they kept closely together, they were safe. It was the jaeger's problem to cut *one* bird off from the flock, for individual pursuit. So long as the flock kept the jaeger from deciding upon a victim, all were safe. The problem became more complex, of course, when two or three jaegers gave chase."

Southampton Island helps close Foxe Basin on the south. To the north, east and west lie over 8000 square miles of low-lying, horizontal sedimentary rocks which hold a grass tundra with an extraordinary wealth of bird life. Here in addition to dominant geese, ducks and gulls of a dozen species, there is a rich mixture of Red Phalaropes, Purple, Baird's and Semipalmated Sandpipers, Black-bellied and Semipalmated Plovers, and lesser numbers of American Golden Plovers, Ruddy Turnstones, and Red-backed Sandpipers. Especially on the east shore of this basin, about Nettiling Lake in western Baffin Island, the White-rumped Sandpiper is the most plentiful breeding shore bird.

In the spring in Baffin Island a migratory surge of these peeps begins in early June, attains peak proportions for a week or so in mid-June,
and leaves a large resident population in its wake. The males precede
the females by a week or so. Sutton wrote that the courtship cries of the
males are so different from the disyllabic mouse-like squeaks we know
on migration that he more than once found himself pause, "as if a
rattlesnake or some other reptile had given warning nearby." These
buzzing notes are not loud but have a ventriloquial quality to them.

A final quotation will help us picture these broad lowlands and
gain an insight into the survival value they have for shore birds. "One
has to cross this flat, monotonous grass tundra afoot," Sutton [54] wrote,
"mile after mile of it, to appreciate its character. Off in every direction,
as far as the eye can see, there are ponds. A distant lake, seen through the
binocular, looks good for birds, for there is a scattering of little islands
along the shore. Reaching this lake requires a circuitous route around
and between a score of lesser ponds, for nowhere is the water shallow
enough, or the bottom firm enough, for easy wading. By the time one
has reached the lake, visited the nearest of the little islands, and followed
a stretch of the shoreline, one realizes how birds nesting at the very tips
of the long peninsulas, or off in the middle of the big marshes, escape
predators by the sheer circumstance of being where they are."

(R.C.C.)

Erolia fuscicollis (Vieillot). Described in 1819 from a winter specimen taken in
Paraguay. SPANISH: Chorlito rabadilla blanca.

LOCAL NAMES: Bonaparte's Sandpiper (in Europe, especially), bull-peep, white-
tailed stib.

FIELD CHARACTERS: In fall a small grayish peep, larger than the Semipalmated,
smaller than the Dunlin, with a white rump and straight black bill. When
standing among Semipals, its folded wings give it a long-tailed appearance
which is helpful. Brownish in spring. The usual call note is a thin *jee-jeet*
note reminiscent of the Pipit's; or a mouse-like *chit-chit,* or a sucking in-
drawn *tsch, tsch,* not very loud, and nearly always disyllabic (Sutton). Rowan
called it a loud bat "tzeet." Allan Brooks wrote that unlike all other peeps,
this one never visited dry pasture, sticking to the shore lines. l. 7½", b. 1".

RANGE: A North American species, breeding on the arctic coast from Point Barrow, Alaska, to Baffin Island, south to Southampton Island. Migration chiefly
through the interior in spring; in fall, both through the interior and along
the Atlantic coast. Winters the length of Argentina east of the Andes. A
vagrant in Europe.

36

BAIRD'S SANDPIPER

Erolia bairdii

SHORE birds are such an engaging tribe that there are as many characterizations of them as there are kinds. Among the small, unobtrusive kinds we lump as 'peep,' however, the Baird Sandpiper is the most difficult to identify with certainty without long practice. And though it is a common nesting bird over almost all of the wide expanse of the North American tundra, we have—perhaps because of its high plains migration route and the difficulty of recognizing it quickly—rather little written information about it.

Joseph S. Dixon[17] who, in 1917, wrote what is still the most personalized account of this bird's home life, called it an extremist in its choice of proper places to spend the different seasons of the year. It summers entirely within the Arctic Circle and winters in far southern South America, being apparently fond of high places while in passage, because it has several times been taken at elevations exceeding 10,000 feet in the cordilleras of both Americas.

The shortness of the arctic summer enforces such a compression of the usual pattern of courtship that even so good a field student as Dixon failed to hear any "song" in this species. Actually, in the right season—and this may be very short indeed—this species has characteristic vocalizations of its own. Alfred M. Bailey,[6] a more recent student of the

Alaskan tundra's bird life, wrote of it thus on one June 15th: "Cutting down the opposite side of the ridge, I heard many calls which reminded me of home in the early spring, for the combined totals sounded like the singing of many little grass frogs in a meadow pond. It was . . . the spring song of the Baird's Sandpiper." One can almost visualize the spring-like qualities of that June day, as rare in the arctic as in the sonnets. No wind blew that day, we know, because normally it is a feat of concentration to hear any but the closest and loudest of small bird voices—the incessant winds whisk them away so quickly.

Reynold Bray,[9] who died in 1938 in the eastern arctic he helped explore ornithologically, found them noisy birds, and common, on the bleak limestone hills above Fury and Hecla narrows, Melville Peninsula, where their trill was the most characteristic sound of the tundra.

The sequence of distraction and territorial displays in this bird remains to be worked out by some future student of these cruel but fascinating polar lands. Only fragments have so far been recorded. Dixon wrote of the male's fluttering flight above the female—with Nighthawk-like wing strokes, and of a raised-wing display. More recently, V. C. Wynne-Edwards,[71] who came to know it on the inhospitable shores of Clyde Inlet in northeastern Baffin Island, gave it credit for a vigorous distraction display when approached, a "screeching and trembling with the wings arched, and all the feathers raised."

Dixon was impressed with the way this bird and its clutch melted into the surrounding tundra, and although his conclusions about the role of predation in the population economy of this and related shore birds are not shared by those who have studied it more objectively since, it is an interesting commentary on the precarious existence of these small waders:

"This method of nesting seems to be the most effective way of escaping one great danger at least, namely, the notice of the countless Jaegers, both Parasitic and Pomarine. These robbers subsist almost entirely during the breeding period on the young and eggs of other birds, and cruise continually back and forth over the sandpipers' nesting ground, looking for the least telltale feather, bit of windblown down, or other object which might afford a clue to the whereabouts of a nest.

"On June 26 I found a nest of the Baird Sandpiper by nearly stepping on the bird. It contained three fresh eggs, and was in the usual exposed position on the tundra, there being only the slightest of depressions lined with dead willow leaves which were also well strewn

over the tundra in general at this particular point. I marked the nest
by placing a fresh chunk of turf on a little mound about ten feet to one
side. Upon taking my departure I noticed a Pomarine Jaeger following
in my wake, and as I looked back the bird spied the upturned clod and
promptly lit and began to walk around on the ground to see the cause
of the disturbance. It is perhaps needless to add that the three eggs were
gone when I returned. I found that the only way to mark down a nest
was by placing two guides in a line, keeping them at least fifty yards
away from the nest site."

This is another species in which the male apparently does half or
more of the incubating. He sits tightly, confident of his protective markings, but once flushed he is nervous and wary. While circling back to the
nest after being so disturbed, he is likely to give vent to a low, whining
bark, a habit which has led the Alaska eskimo to call it "the bird that
sounds like a man with a bad cold."

Even at the very northeastern extremity of its range, on the ice-free
apron of Bylot Island, Louis Lemieux [61] found 900 Baird Sandpipers
feeding on a two-acre patch of mud flat on August 24. This is at 73°
north latitude!

Closer to home, Forbush's [20] sketch of its haunts and habits describes the bird well: "On the south shore of Martha's Vineyard where
in West Tisbury and Chilmark shallow pools are formed from the overflow of ponds and marshes just inside the beach ridge—there Baird's
Sandpiper loves to feed. In late August or early September when the
grass has been cut, this bird comes in small parties of four to eight and
hunts about the margins of partly dried out pools, threading its way
among the stubble or poking about upon the bare mud. It is very intent
on its own business, assumes a crouching attitude as if near-sighted, and
works slowly along, weaving in and out among the Least or Semipalmated Sandpipers with which it associates."   (R.C.C.)

Erolia bairdii (Coues). Described in 1861.
LOCAL NAMES: Bull-peep, grass-peep. SPANISH: Chorlito unicolor.
FIELD CHARACTERS: In spring (in the interior), very much like a White-rump in
    size and general appearance, but buffier and back scaly rather than striped.
    Fall White-rumps are gray but Baird remains brownish buff. Early-returning
    Sanderlings are rusty about head and breast, but lighter otherwise, and with
    conspicuous wing stripe; Baird is a late migrant, when Sanderling is much
    paler. Baird is somewhat like Least in color, but larger than the grayer Semi-
    palmated; smaller than a Pectoral. All three of these "peep" have streaky

backs, not scaly. Young Bairds are almost unmistakable because of the broad, buff feather margins that give the back a conspicuously scaly look. Legs black. This bird goes its own way rather than racing around with the smaller peeps, walks about deliberately with a hunched-up look, prefers drier, sandier reaches of the beach or the flats. Flushing note, a rolling *kreeep*. l. 7½", b. ⅞".

RANGE: Common breeder throughout the arctic of North America, from Bylot Island west to arctic Alaska and adjacent Siberia. Winters locally in the mountainous western half of South America, mostly from Ecuador south. Migrates north through the interior of North America on the plains, spreading out across Canada to reach extremities of tundra. In July and August retraces this route but overflows onto both coasts. more so on Atlantic coast than westward.

37

LEAST SANDPIPER

Erolia minutilla

To HAVE close-up views of shore birds it is necessary to reach the shore of some shallow bay while the tide is making, but very early. Scoop a hiding place some four feet deep among the flotsam at the beach crest. Then set out a dozen snipe or plover decoys, matching them in groups facing the breeze and so far down the incline that the skirts of the breakers trail about them every little while. That is the best place for them, although you may have to shift some every so often, as the tide creeps in.

Meanwhile only the tide disturbs the birds at their breakfast, driving them up the beaches or forcing them to flit elsewhere for better fare. The stool (decoys) are scarcely in place when there comes a ripple of light as a flock of Least Sandpipers, tiniest of the Order, flash in from nowhere.

Steady and close as a school of minnows slipping over a shoal, they settle among the lures, but if you raise a hand they vanish in a flurry, just as fish do. Once in a while you will see them coming from a distance, seeds of light that grow visibly, flower in the air, and are gone. They remind you of flying fish that flitter away when some old hooker noses them out of the weed in the Gulf Stream, but plump into the first big wave they meet.

These smallest of shore birds are extremely tame and unsuspicious. They will trip past your blind so close that you can see them wink their little brown eyes or scratch their heads. If a man could move his legs as fast as the little yellowish legs of this sandpiper, he might run a hundred yards in five seconds.

Bands of these peep sometimes trip along the strand, pausing every second to seize some minute crustacean from the weed uprooted by the rollers. Sometimes several stand around a stranded goose-fish and swallow the flies buzzing above its squat carcass.

Every time a wave slides back hoppers by myriads kick themselves from the foam only to be gobbled by the sandpipers, which dash down and snatch them before another breaker can chase them to dry places once more. Not that they run any danger, for like all shore birds they can swim when sudden need arises.

Running on the sand they are difficult to distinguish. Their necks and breast show a brownish wash, their backs are mottled gray-brown, with darker flight feathers, and below they are white. You might think that they had taken these hues from the sand on which they scamper. They have silver bosoms but their brightness blends with that of the breaker which puts them to flight. When they drift ashore a few rods farther on, they seem to vanish. They appear and disappear like ripples which spill their lustrous lining on the beach and then subside.

Least Sandpipers are even more abundant on the harbor flats and on the muddy margins of brackish ponds or creeks, and are thus characterized as "mud peep." Almost everywhere their small size and thin cries distinguish them from larger shore birds with which they throng the flats. The late Ludlow Griscom, who counted the waders of Monomoy Point assiduously, several times estimated swarms of over 20,000 of these small peep there.

Like so many others of their kind they nest far to the north, but are not truly arctic. They lay their buffy eggs, three or four to a set, in a grass-lined cup, perhaps on some rocky island off the Aleutian or the Labrador coasts, or more often, in some sphagnum and sedge bog of the subarctic regions in between. The female is a trifle larger than the male, but the latter, like a phalarope or several other relatives, is thought to do most of the brooding. When distracted they perform much the same "rodent run" display described in our discussion of the Purple Sandpiper.

They are cheerful, social little creatures, consorting, in migration, with Semipalmated or Western Sandpipers, Sanderlings, and other larger birds. And what brave mites they are! The smallest of all shore birds, they sometimes span the broad Atlantic and have been observed in the British Isles, Finland, and France, blown about the world like spindrift. They seem at home everywhere.

Erolia minutilla (Vieillot). Described in 1819.

LOCAL NAMES: Peep, mud-peep, oxe-eye, American stint.

FIELD CHARACTERS: The smallest of the small, streaked brown "peep." A minia-ture edition of the Pectoral Sandpiper, with brownish breast and yellow-green legs. The Semipalmated, its look-alike, is gray rather than brown, and has black legs. Bill also thinner, slightly drooped. A mud peep as a rule. Voice a thin, drawn out *kreee-eet* note (Peterson). l. 5–6¾″, b. ⅝–1″, female larger.

RANGE: Chiefly subarctic, from central Alaska in a broad band extending from the low arctic tundra into the sedge bogs of the muskeg, across to Newfoundland and Sable Island. Winters from Oregon, the Gulf Coast (and inland about 150 miles), and North Carolina coast south through the Caribbean to central Peru and Brazil's Mato Grosso. Migrates across the breadth and width of North America.

38

RUFOUS-NECKED
SANDPIPER

Erolia ruficollis

ALTHOUGH at least five records of nesting have been made since 1933 when Alfred M. Bailey's Cape Prince of Wales colleagues found the first nest, Bailey's account is still the most detailed available.

He wrote,[6] "Small sandpipers look so much alike from a distance that it is difficult to distinguish between them. We have little information on this species but I believe it nests regularly at Wales in small numbers. The first I observed was secured (July 11, 1922) on the high tundra at the base of Wales Mountain, an adult female which proved to be the first definite record for North America. A pair was observed building a nest on June 14 along a little stream bed, and their antics were of enough interest to cause me to make field notes at some length as follows: 'The male would give up his searching among the dried grass stalks to demonstrate his love for his little partner, after which she would take to wing and circle about. Finally she entered a little tussock of grass, standing on her "nose" and fluttering her tail and wings. Soon the male pushed his way inside, too, and after a few more rustlings about, they took to wing. I looked in the grass and found a little cavity which they were just lining with leaves. Upon examining their nesting clump, I found a small pit, exactly similar to the nest of the Western Sandpiper, in which they had deposited about twenty small willow leaves. I marked the spot carefully, but upon my return found the nest abandoned.'

"During the years that have followed, I have examined each shipment of specimens from Wales with interest, expecting to find birds or eggs of this species, and my expectations were realized in 1933 when Tevuk sent me a beautiful set of four with the adult. With the skin and eggs was the nest material of dry willow leaves, tundra moss, and a characteristically marked scapular feather."

Erolia ruficollis (Pallas). Described in 1776, from a specimen taken in eastern Siberia.

OTHER NAMES: Red-necked Stint (New Zealand).

FIELD CHARACTERS: The same size as a Least Sandpiper but more rufous about the head and throat in spring, and with black legs. The Spoon-bill Sandpiper is almost identical in spring except for its peculiarly broadened bill. Some authorities consider it merely a race of the Little Stint of Eurasia. Flushing call a *pit-pit-pit* (Pough).

RANGE: Breeds in northeast Siberia and adjacent Alaskan coast (Cape Prince of Wales). Winters on southwest Pacific coasts, east to New Zealand where it is the common small sandpiper, occurring in flocks up to 2,000 birds from September to March.

39

CURLEW SANDPIPER

Erolia ferruginea

THE Curlew Sandpiper, or pigmy curlew as it is called in England, is one of the most wide-ranging of all shore birds. As a bird of passage it is found throughout the Eastern Hemisphere, and is casual in both Americas. It occurs frequently enough along our eastern coast to be considered in any book on American shore birds.

The bird is well named, its rather long down-curved bill, long legs, and upright stance making it resemble a miniature curlew. It is taller than other species of about the same size. Its diagnostic field mark is the white rump, and in spring the rusty head, neck and under plumage distinguish it easily. In autumn, however, it is white below and gray-brown above, and is then uncommonly difficult to distinguish from the Dunlins it often associates with, unless, that is, flight reveals its white rump.

The translation of Theodore Pleske's [40] great work on the *Birds of the Eurasian Tundra* by Glover M. Allen in 1928 introduced to the English-speaking world the remarkable field studies of A. Bialynicki-Birula, a mammalogist turned ornithologist, made while a member of the Russian Polar Expedition of 1900–1903. Birula published these studies in 1907 as a Memoir of the Academy of Sciences of St. Petersburg entitled *"Sketches of bird life on the arctic coast of Siberia."*

In the spring of 1901, after wintering in Western Taimyr, at 76° North latitude, where the snow-free season is no longer than one hundred days, Birula made the following notes on the habits of the Curlew Sandpiper during the breeding season: "On 18 June 1901, the wind went down in the afternoon and the weather turned fine; the parts of the tundra bare of snow on the south slope of Bonnevie Isle have become very animated, particularly through the presence of Snow Buntings and pairs of Lapland Longspurs—on almost every spot from which the snow has melted are seen Knots and Curlew Sandpipers; the Knots are already paired, while the Curlew Sandpipers, the commonest sandpiper of late in the tundra, are still flying about and running over the tundra in little flocks, without the least appearance of pairing off.

"Four days later, 22 June, I found the first nest with a complete set of four eggs and on 24 June my second nest, likewise with four eggs. Evidently some of the pairs of Curlew Sandpipers had commenced nesting the day after their arrival. Since at this time it was only the southerly slopes of the hills in the tundra that were bare of snow and somewhat warmed, these sandpipers were obliged to occupy them in preference as nesting places, and almost formed nesting colonies on the driest of these slopes. . . . It even seemed to me that many pairs contented themselves with the nests of the year before."

The Curlew Sandpiper, again according to Birula, apparently "never attempts the ruse of trying to attract the enemy away from its nest but evidently depends chiefly for protection upon the concealing tints of the surrounding tundra, a view that explains why it leaves its nest so soon; if it stayed for a longer time on the nest, as the Knot does, it would run the risk of betraying the spot where the nest is. If the nest contains well-incubated eggs, the bird returns to it very soon, approaches directly toward it without any precaution, stands on the ground at a little distance, looks about it and at once settles upon the eggs.

"When crossing the tundra at about the end of June or in early July, one frequently drives them from their nests or young. Even as late as 27 July I saw them still in pairs, but at the same time noted rather large flocks of adult birds which showed me that most of them were through breeding and that the old birds, having reared their young, were preparing to depart." He noted roving flocks of immature birds from August 7 to 13, but they disappeared from Taimyr thereafter.

(R.C.C.)

Erolia ferruginea (Pontoppidan). Described in 1763.

FIELD CHARACTERS: A Dunlin-like bird and consort of this abundant species, but longer-legged, more upright in posture, and more slender. White eye-line and white belly snowier than Dunlin. The bill is also usually more slender and slightly curved throughout its length rather than merely drooped at the tip as in the Dunlin. One for the experts unless the white rump is seen, or in spring when it is rusty below instead of black-bellied as is the Dunlin. Prefers mud flats, is an active, erratic feeder, often wading deep. Flight said to involve a series of switch-backs, finch-like. From the White-rumped Sandpiper, by larger size and curved bill. l. 8″, b. 1½″.

RANGE: Breeds in the high arctic tundra of central Siberia. As stated in the text, it has been recorded almost throughout the world. Though perhaps regular on Cape Cod, Long Island and in New Jersey, it remains unrecorded except almost by accident elsewhere. One, two or three individuals have been recorded spring and fall in the Jamaica Bay region of New York City almost every year during the last decade and more, though, as elsewhere, disturbance of favored feeding and resting spots in recent years has upset the chain of observations.

40

DUNLIN
(Red-backed Sandpiper)

Erolia alpina

The Dunlin are in the air and all, as by an invisible broom, are swept into a perfect unison of movement . . . thousands of leaderless birds with the cohesion of one body, supported from one pair of wings.

H. J. MASSINGHAM

THE sands, shores, and reedy wilderness find vocal expression in the flight-notes of many shore birds. Every region and every hour of the day seems to have its minstrel. Night cries out in the notes of birds that fly by night. In the humble lay of the woodcock, water lilies under stars and moonlit swamps may be heard. The ethereal winnowings of Wilson's Snipe render audible the mystic silences of sweet-water meadow land and northern bogs. And in the same way the play of sunlight on the sand, the moan of distant surf, and even the wild beauty of barren lands find echoes in the lays of dozens of other shore birds. We hear only a few of them in our middle latitudes. They are far louder and more ecstatic towards the top of the world, where the sandpipers nest amid a profusion of flowers known only to northern explorers.

Though the Dunlin's voice is not among the noteworthy ones, its legions and the marvelous unison of its aerial evolutions mark it as one of those who contribute importantly to the character of the open shore. So adaptable a bird is it, and so widespread as a breeder, that it is the most abundant sandpiper in Europe, where it is said that all peeps are dunlins until proved otherwise. When flocks of thousands pour into an English estuary they make a picture long to be remembered because they fly, wheel, or scatter on the saltings as if the whole immense throng were moved by a common impulse. The American population ranks about fifth in abundance with us, being outnumbered here by stints (peep), whereas these are rare in Europe. But since it comes late in its southward passage, massing its ranks only after the autumnal equinox, it often has the beaches and flats almost to itself. Thus, wildfowlers know them well, whereas summer observers miss them entirely. Hence, also, the names "fall snipe" or "winter snipe."

To witness the spring migration one must seek the barrier beaches of the Carolinas and more particularly of Virginia. Red-backed Sandpipers in bridal array throng the small, muddy islets between the mainland and Cobb Island on the Virginia coast early in April. On my visits to the nesting colonies of Willets, Clapper Rails, and Black Skimmers on nearby sandy Wreck Island, the racket of our motor-boat always flushes sizeable flocks from beach to beach at this season. They are then as restless as Sanderlings, dashing frantically along the flats, probing for the worms and other sea-spoil that maintain their numerous clans. When flushed, they whirl up, bunch, and make off at great speed.

T. T. McCabe [31] wrote that whereas in his own flying about the San Francisco Bay region of California, he had always been disappointed that the flocks of shore birds he flushed from feeding grounds seldom exceeded speeds around fifty miles an hour in moving from one area to another at low altitude, he was struck by the distinctly different mode of flight of these birds at high altitudes. Heading west over Oakland airport at 1500 feet altitude and at an air speed of ninety miles per hour at dusk one early April day, he was overtaken by two small, tight flocks of a hundred or so birds each, mixtures of Red-backed and smaller sandpipers. "The two flocks were in close echelon, the individual positions fixed, the wing-beats rhythmic and powerful, in extreme contrast to the desultory, easily deflected flight of the lower flocks" he had encountered earlier. Although these flocks crossed his path at an angle, familiarity with aircraft movements of known speed convinced him that these birds were moving at an air speed of at least one hundred and ten miles per hour. So struck by this incident was he, that he felt he had stumbled on a near view of true migratory flight, and that this high speed movement was characteristic of true migration, something perhaps strictly seasonal, and at most latent or even impossible for these birds during non-migratory intervals.

Herbert Brandt [8] points out that these birds are among the first to return to the Alaskan tundra in spring, arriving in flocks whose members are not yet all paired. Mr. Brandt's comment on the song, like the "tinkling of ice in a glass," will be interesting to compare with E. W. Nelson's [34] spring notes:

"Soon after they arrive in spring they are engaged in pairing, and the males may be seen upon quivering wings flying after the female and uttering a musical, trilling note, which falls upon the ear like the mellow tinkle of large water drops falling rapidly into a partly filled vessel. Imagine the sounds thus produced by the water run together into a steady and rapid trill some five to ten seconds in length, and the note of this sandpiper is represented. It is not loud, but has a rich, full tone, difficult to describe, but pleasant to hear among the discordant notes of the various waterfowl whose hoarse cries arise on all sides. In his moments of excitement he rises 15 or 20 yards, and, hovering on tremulous wings, pours forth a perfect gush of music, until he glides back to earth exhausted, but ready to repeat the effort a few minutes later. They generally choose some dry knoll, or other dry elevation, overlooking the neighboring lakes and pools. Here, upon a bed of last year's grasses, but without the trouble of arranging a formal nest, the female deposits three or four large eggs of pale greenish varying to pale brownish clay color with dull chocolate and umber brown spots and blotches."

Artist Peter Scott has called attention to a remarkable tendency this bird has to associate with the Golden Plover in Iceland. Icelanders have therefore come to call it "Plover's Slave" or "Plover's Page."

Erolia alpina (Linnaeus). Described in 1758, our race, *E.a.pacifica* (by Coues) in 1861.

LOCAL NAMES: Winter snipe, lead-back, red-back, simpleton, little black-breast, among others.

FIELD CHARACTERS: In spring, the only "peep" with a black belly patch, rusty-red above. In fall, the plainest of its tribe: a soft mouse-gray above and dull off-white below. The rather long, stout black bill is down-curved *at the tip only*. These birds "hunch up" as they run on the flats, are almost always in groups, small or large. Call "a nasal, rasping *cheezp*" (Peterson). l. 7½–9¼″, b. 1⅜–1¾″, female larger.

RANGE: As a breeder, circumpolar, south to southeastern Alaska and Hudson Bay (but not inland), and southern Wales and the Baltic states. Winters from southeastern Alaska, Massachusetts, and Great Britain south, only, to the tropic of Cancer. Our race (*pacifica*) migrates up and down the Pacific coast, but the eastern population, in spring, cuts inland up the Chesapeake to the Great Lakes and west of Hudson Bay. In fall down the same route but spreading eastward to New England and westward down the interior of the continent.

41

SHORT-BILLED DOWITCHER

Limnodromus griseus

ALTHOUGH perhaps too parochial, the popular names of shore birds are often more meaningful than the scientific ones. For this, I suppose, we may blame the influence of the rules of priority, which pin the first monicker, no matter how ill-conceived, given by the first describer. The quavering whistle of the dowitcher, for example, is supposed to sound out the book appellation, but to my mind, does so rather badly. Henry David Thoreau could sometimes render such shrill syllables in words, and the American Indian, living closer to nature, did even better, but in general most word renditions fail to satisfy the outdoorsman. On the other hand, the more familiar terms of red-breast, red-breasted snipe, and robin snipe suggest the beauty of the dowitcher in bridal plumage.

Standing on the eastern shore of Monomoy Point toward sunset one day in May, I was enjoying the play of sunlight on the surf. The migration of shore birds was at its height and the vast, rolling beaches, scoured white by the waves, were alive with birds. Suddenly, a flock of Short-billed Dowitchers came rippling in from the sea. Nearing the strand, all espied me, mounted sharply and veered overhead at a terrific pace, the slanting sun illuminating their ruddy under parts. I could not help reflecting that the popular name for this species—red-breasted snipe —was the true one.

"Fool plover" is less descriptive, though it was often used by old time pot-hunters. They found these beautiful sandpipers absurdly tame, inclined to doze in flocks on exposed bars or mud flats. They stood so close togehter that a dozen might be killed by a single charge of shot. Being fat as butter and large as snipe, they were often shot for the market. Photographers and bird watchers can today take innocent advantage of this innate tameness, and many of them call the dowitcher "Honest John."

In spring, these birds are cinnamon-breasted, variously spotted and flecked with darker markings depending upon the race involved. The pattern of the upper plumage does not differ much from that of the Wilson's Snipe, but is darker, hence the popular name of brown-back. The rump and upper tail coverts are white, however, and the tail whitish but finely barred with black. Diagnostic as is the white rump, structural characteristics and the bird's habits are equally helpful in identification. Its long bill and the short, yellowish-green legs remind us of Wilson's Snipe, but snipe feed on the marginal mud, or in very shoal water. And they seldom venture far from the shelter of some tuft of weeds or sedge, and are always set for precipitate flight.

A band of dowitchers presents a marked contrast. They frequent wide sand flats on sheltered inner beaches, and along the estuaries of tidal creeks. There they stand belly-deep, sometimes resting on bent tarsi, probing with their bills almost straight down. At times they even paddle a stroke or two with their half-webbed feet, nodding and shaking their short tails like newly-emerged diving ducks. The mandibles are thus often submerged to the nostrils while feeding, the birds moving here and there leisurely, never with the greedy haste of Sanderlings or Yellowlegs.

When satisfied with food they sometimes stand for half an hour almost without motion. Towards noon they may lift into the air together—for dowitchers often act and react like a single bird, as if the flock had but one guiding mind. They flit over the nearest bank and line up on a pan of marl sheltered by beach grass, or in the full glare of the sun. Then they thrust their bills backward under their coverts and doze through the heat of the day. At such times an observer can approach them closely, but if he makes a sound the sleepy birds whirl up and make off in a body.

Not long ago I watched a flock of over a hundred dowitchers feeding in the water of a lagoon west of the causeway leading south through the federal wildlife refuge at St. Marks in northwest Florida. They kept very close together, with only a scattering flanker or two at no great distance. Wishing to make them display their flight patterns, I decided to flush them. They allowed me to approach within forty yards or so but then took off at great speed, their white wing linings and white rumps showing alternately. After speeding off for a furlong they stooped to the water, alighting gently and elevating their long pinions like willets. I did not expect them to return, but in ten minutes back they flew, alighted again on their favorite bar, and went back to feeding complacently. (*H.M.H.*)

Bays of this type, sheltered from the sweep of the wind, where the birds may find plenty of food in shallow, brackish water, are the favorite resorts of Short-billed Dowitchers during winter and the migration season. On the great bays of the New Jersey coast, this species ranks second in abundance both spring and fall in most years, being outnumbered only by the Semipalmated Sandpiper. The principal migration here is from April 29 to May 25, and from July 6 to August 25. At Alameda, in San Francisco Bay, the western race of the Short-billed Dowitcher passes southward from August 16 to September 15.

The racial stocks of the Short-billed Dowitcher remained a source of great confusion for over fifty years. Prominent ornithologists, possessed of only partial knowledge of the geographic extent and variability of this species, became inextricably involved in error when they tried to distinguish various groupings. The commonest error was to label all western birds Long-billed Dowitchers. Finally, in 1950, came Dr. Frank A. Pitelka[38] to show that the Short-billed Dowitcher was actually composed of three geographical races, grading in an unbroken series from a smallish eastern bird with an unknown breeding range, to a slightly larger race in southern Alaska.

Most intriguing was the confident prediction, by him and others before him, that central Ungava would prove to be the breeding area of the eastern race, even though no one had yet discovered these birds nesting there. In the summer of 1958 two independent teams of investigators finally uncovered this breeding ground in the sedge bogs of the folded-rock province which is the iron ore belt of the vast Ungava-Labrador peninsula in the subarctic of eastern Canada. Though nests and eggs remain to be discovered, territorial birds and flying young still showing down about the neck were found that summer.   (*R.C.C.*)

Limnodromus griseus (Gmelin). Described in 1789 from a Long Island, N.Y., specimen.

LOCAL NAMES: Red-breasted snipe, robin snipe, brown-back, driver, German snipe, Deutscher. The common name, dowitcher, may very probably be derived from the German Deutscher.

FIELD CHARACTERS: Chunky, medium-sized shore birds with long bills, yellowish-green legs, and a conspicuous white patch on the lower back. They probe methodically in salt and brackish waters while with us, often belly-deep and immersing the bill completely. Cinnamon-red breasted in spring, grayish all over in winter. The common flushing note is a double *tu-tu*, sometimes trebled, softer, more rolling than a yellowlegs' call. (See long-billed Dowitcher.) l. 10–12½″, b. 2–2⅝″, female larger.

RANGE: Breeds in muskeg of northern Canada, from interior Ungava-Labrador to southern Alaska. The eastern race, *L.g.griseus* (Gmelin), nests east of Hudson Bay, migrates down Atlantic coast. *L.g.hendersoni* Rowan occupies the interior of North America, west of Hudson Bay and east of the Rockies, and migrates down the Mississippi and from Chesapeake Bay south on the Atlantic. These races winter in the eastern Caribbean and northwestern South America, south to Brazil, *L.g.caurinus* Pitelka, the Alaskan race, migrates down the west coast and winters from Baja California, perhaps to Peru. These races are not positively distinguishable in the field.

42

LONG-BILLED DOWITCHER

Limnodromus scolopaceus

HERBERT BRANDT [8] called "the wild inspiring sky song of the dowitcher, as it cruises aloft on swift, saber pinions, one of the most unforgettable of Arctic voices. All this, too, in a land where the very air is vibrant with bird cries and melodies as the various plumed minstrels join the strange aerial chorus of the high north." For this is a tundra bird, restricted to the upper portion of the arctic coasts of Alaska and adjacent Siberia and Mackenzie.

. Frank A. Pitelka [38] who has studied the problem of species distinction closely, suggests that the relatively longer bill and legs of this bird are adaptations to feeding in the deeper, steeper-sided fresh water pools this bird uses. They are, in effect, a compensation for the tidal fluctuations that continually expose feeding areas for the Short-billed Dowitcher. A bird which habitually feeds deep in water will profit from a shorter wing for more effective take-off, and this the Long-bill has evolved. The great size disparity between sexes in this species would seem to be another adaptive trend allowing the population to exploit its limited habitat more completely. These characteristics, it seems safe to presume, evolved during one of the periods of maximum ice advance of the last glaciation, when Long-bills were isolated in the unglaciated portions of central and western Alaska, and the short-billed forms remained in contact with one another south of the ice in the United States.

The provisional nature of so much of our knowledge is well illustrated by the history of our attitudes toward this bird. The argument as to whether it was a valid species, or whether it should even be given subspecific ranking, has raged for over a century.

It was first described by Thomas Say in 1823 in James' *Account of an expedition from Pittsburgh to the Rocky Mountains under the command of Major S. H. Long,* the first, or type, specimen having been collected near Council Bluffs, Iowa. Thomas Say was a brilliant investigator who had the good fortune to be turned loose in virgin territory. He became the scientific hero of Major Long's otherwise futile expedition, and brought back, and described as new to science, literally hundreds of new insects and shells, plus the coyote and eight species of birds. After being argued over for a full century, however, his Long-billed Dowitcher was rejected as a species, and relegated to the rank of a subspecies of the eastern (short-billed) dowitcher by the American Ornithologists' Union in 1931. Dr. Pitelka's inclusive studies of the problem, published in 1950, caused the Check-list Committee to reverse this judgment and restore the Long-billed Dowitcher to full species rank in the 1957 edition of *The A.O.U. Check-list of North American Birds,* where it will probably remain.

Reproductive isolation is the best test of a good species in higher animals at the present time, but since the Long-bill is not known to overlap the breeding range of the Short-billed Dowitcher, ornithologists don't have the comfort of this conclusive test to point to.

The Long-bill's breeding range lies northwest of the main Short-billed Dowitcher nesting grounds. But ninety per cent of the Long-billed Dowitchers seem addicted to fresh-water habitats during migration, whereas Short-bills, given the opportunity, will usually feed on marine flats. The wintering range, though marked by the same northern limits, is considerably more restricted in the Long-bill. In California, where we know most about the seasonal status of these birds, the migration periods of these two species are discrete, the Short-bill passing through in a month's movement ending September 15, the Long-bill in the following four weeks. A few Short-bills winter in California, but seventy-five per cent of the winterers are Long-billed Dowitchers.

Though there is no way of knowing what proportion of these birds were actually Long-billed Dowitchers, as he thought. Elliott Coues' sketch of these birds is an attractive scene worthy of quotation:

". . . nowhere have I seen them so abundant as in Dakota during the fall passage—everywhere on the ponds, and especially in the saline pools of the alkali region along the Upper Missouri. There the birds were loitering in great flocks, wading in water so loaded with alkali that it looked sea-green and blew off a white cloud with the slightest breeze, while the edges for several yards all around were snow-white with solid efflorescence. Around such pools, the water of which was utterly undrinkable for man or beast, were numerous ducks and waders, especially Teal, Plover, and these Snipe, swimming, wading, or dozing in troops on the banks in the yellow light of autumn, all in excellent order for the table. They were loaded with fat, though it seemed incredible that they could thrive in such bitterly nauseating and purgative water.

"As we approach a pool we see numbers of the gentle birds wandering along the margin, or wading up to the belly in the shallow parts, probing here and there as they advance, sticking the bill perpendicularly into the mud to its full length with a quick, dexterous movement, and sometimes even submerging the whole head for a second or two. All the while they chat with each other in a low, pleasing tone, entirely oblivious of our dangerous proximity." [12] (R.C.C.)

Limnodromus scolopaceus (Say). Described in 1823.
LOCAL NAMES: Same as for Short-billed Dowitcher. SPANISH: Becasina migratoria.
FIELD CHARACTERS: Separable from Short-billed Dowitcher by a *combination* of
   characteristics (color, markings, measurements) not always obvious in the
   field. Although extreme examples may possibly be differentiated in the field,
   the "rule of percentage" will apply and leave individual identifications open
   to question.
       Pitelka's studies show that Long-bills are more completely salmon below
   in breeding plumage, with dense spotting on throat and upper breast *only*.
   The sides of the breast and belly are heavily barred. The back and upper side
   of tail are dark (reddish-buff with broad black bars).
       Short-billed Dowitchers are lighter above (light buff with narrow bars)
   but variable below, depending on the race. The eastern race (griseus) is ex-
   tensively white below but heavily spotted; the interior race (*hendersoni*) is
   very buffy below but sparsely spotted; the Pacific race (*caurinus*) tends to produce combinations of these extremes, being salmon-breasted throughout or
   with considerable white on the belly, but with well *scattered* spotting (light
   when colorful, heavily spotted when pale) and *no flank barring*. Although
   young birds tend to be darker above in the Long-bill, few winter specimens
   are safe to "call." And since the bills of the longest Long-billed Dowitchers

exceed the maximum length of Short-bills by only 12 mm. or so, this is hardly a safe field mark. These differences, observable enough in a long series lying side by side in a museum tray, have been discussed chiefly to impress the binocular wielder that even good species (let alone subspecies) may be outside the scope of field identification. The thin *keek* note heard away from the breeding grounds may turn out to be truly diagnostic. l. about 12″, b. 2⅛ to 3″, female larger.

RANGE: Breeds in upland tundra of northeastern Siberia and northwestern Alaska and adjacent Mackenzie. Migrates chiefly through western half of U.S. and Canada, spreading east in fall to Atlantic coast from New England (rare), increasingly from Chesapeake Bay southward to Florida. Winters from latitude of central California and central Florida south to Guatemala, being more numerous in the west.

Dowitchers (*l*) Short-billed, (*r*) Long-billed

43

STILT SANDPIPER

Micropalama himantopus

IT MAY prove comforting to beginners who have come to feel that the identification of the shore bird tribe is as difficult to master as the "all-alike" sparrows, that Arthur Cleveland Bent, the monographer of our North American bird fauna, never came to know this bird in the field. This may be a clue to the comeback this bird has staged in the last twenty-five years—for it is considered a regular fall migrant on the southern New England coast Mr. Bent worked—or a measure of our advances in the technique of field identification. We shall probably never know.

Nor could Mr. Bent quote a single worthwhile account of the nesting behavior of this bird from the literature. Neither can we, thirty-five years later, even though this is one of the commonest breeding shore birds on the wet tundra at Churchill, Manitoba, where a score of good students have known it. One of these, Dr. Ralph S. Palmer, tells me that its aerial display is a hovering flight accompanied by a donkey-like "hee-haw."

Like the Buff-breasted Sandpiper, the two dowitchers, and the Surfbird, this sandpiper is uniquely American; together they typify genera unrepresented in the avifauna of Eurasia. And like the Buff-breasted Sandpiper it uses the most direct route in moving up and down our continent, staying close to the 100th parallel. Unlike that colorful bird, however, it has never wandered to the Old World continents.

Especially interesting is Elliott Coues'[12] experience in mistaking his first flock of these birds for dowitchers until he had one in the hand. He writes, "They gathered in the same compact groups, waded about in the same sedate, preoccupied manner, fed with the same motion of the head, probing obliquely in shallow water with the head submerged, were equally oblivious of my approach, and . . . swam with equal facility. The close structural resemblances of the two species are evidently reflected in their general economy."

Most of us, less observant of structural and behavioral traits, would first mistake the Stilt Sandpiper in fall plumage for a Lesser Yellowlegs. In that plumage, however, it is grayer (less brown) above, and less speckled. Its bill droops a bit at the end, but best of all, it has a rather conspicuous white line over the eye, and greenish-yellow legs. Spring birds are handsomely barred below, and have broad buffy-brown stripes through the eye and on the crown. (*R.C.C.*)

Micropalama himantopus (Bonaparte). Described in 1826 from a New Jersey specimen.

LOCAL NAMES: Frost snipe, mongrel, bastard yellowlegs. SPANISH: Chorlito patas largas.

FIELD CHARACTERS: Resembles a smallish Lesser Yellowlegs in fall (see text for other details). Common flight note resembles the single whistled *whu* of the Lesser Yellowlegs, but is lower pitched and hoarse, sometimes reedy. John T. Nichols, on whose notes the above comment is based, suggested that there has been imitative convergence in the habits and voice of this species, the Lesser Yellowlegs, and the Dowitcher. l. 7½–9¼", b. 1¼–1¾", female larger.

RANGE: Breeds on arctic tundra from northwest Mackenzie around to west side of Hudson Bay south to Cape Henrietta Maria. Migrates mostly through the interior, overflowing to Atlantic coast, from Massachusetts southward in fall, rarely to California. Winters in middle South America.

Peeps, showing bill size and length.

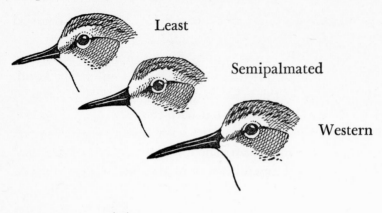

Least

Semipalmated

Western

44

SEMIPALMATED SANDPIPER

Ereunetes pusillus

I OFTEN watch the Semipalmated Sandpiper on the outer shores of the ocean while migration is at its height. Sometimes I am following a hundred or more of these peeps scampering over the swelling beach ahead, and looking not much bigger than a swarm of ants. A vast wave stumbles on the bar, bending up a rainbow in spray as it thunders into ruin. The drops, or so it seems, float directly toward me. Just when I am wondering why they do not fall, I see that they are a goodly cluster of these birds, the commonest of our beach waifs.

Twinkling out of the east, they appear to ride on the rays of the sun. The entire flock, bunched so tightly that wing must almost touch wing, veers, settles, or darts off to sea like a single bird—an instance of group control which reminds us of fish.

Alighting on the strand, they chase the retreating waves precisely as do the Sanderlings, feasting on the hoppers washed out by the rollers. And, like Least Sandpipers, they can swim at need, but I have not seen them try this in the surf, which is violent and terrible. Sometimes I see them afloat for an instant on quiet creeks, quivering their wings as if to wash out parasites. Swimming seems purely accidental—merely a paddle of a yard or so from one shoal to another.

You need binoculars to tell this little fellow from its frequent companion, the Least Sandpiper. Its feet are partially webbed, but more important, its legs are black. The Least Sandpiper's legs show greenish-yellow. The "Semi" averages a half inch longer than the other, but even field glasses will seldom tell you that. The Semi is a grayish bird, the Least a brownish one. Looking closely at specimens in a museum tray, you see that the bill of the Semipalmated Sandpiper is thicker at the base, stouter and straighter throughout its length, but in the field such differences are of dubious help. The leg color remains the chief reliance.

Semipalmated Sandpipers seem always hungry, not to say greedy. They feast on minute mussels, clams, starfish, sand fleas, and the like, swallowing as if they were famished. They also consume flies, sea worms, grasshoppers, locusts, beetles, bugs, and the seeds of various seaside weeds.

These sand-peep throng north along our Atlantic shores in May and early June, after which they steer for the tundra of the arctic coasts to breed. Like the Woodcock and Wilson's Snipe, the Semipalmated Sandpiper comes to New England with a song, a real flight song, early in the season. It does not wait until reaching its nesting grounds but sings among our dunes and saltings. Here we sometimes see it circling on twinkling, down-curved wings, pouring forth a musical twittering and trilling before pitching to the ground again. On its breeding grounds, its flight song is a conspicuous feature of the early summer.

The rapidity with which they hatch their chicks is suggested by the fact that by the second week in July they once more crowd our beaches in companies and whole armies. In the mid-forties Ludlow Griscom several times estimated aggregations of over 50,000 of these peep on the great flats of Newburyport, Mass., during the early August migration peak.

Many of these delicate sand-peep linger through the summer on southern beaches, failing somehow to join in the ritual of reproduction but adding life, beauty, and a touch of gentle melody to a thousand miles of wave-washed sand, otherwise so desolate. By the middle of October their swarming numbers commence to disappear over the endless sandy trails to Central and South America.

Ereunetes pusillus (Linnaeus). Described in 1766 from a West Indies specimen figured as "la petite Alouette-de-mer" by Brisson.
LOCAL NAMES: Peep, beach peep, sand-peep, bumble-bee peep, oxeye, hawk's eye.
SPANISH: Chorlito enano.

FIELD CHARACTERS: One has to "soak" in the small peep a while to separate them accurately. It is when we fail, for lack of time, patience or skill, that we lump them as "peep." This one is the least distinctive of the lot, a grayish-brown bird with blackish legs. The Least is browner, streakier, especially on breast; the Western rustier above and longer-billed. Its note is a louder, fuller *cherk* or *cher*, less drawn-out, and with less of an "eee" quality than the Least's. Flocks in motion often sound soft, short, snappy *chips* (Nichols). l. 5½–6⅞", b. ½–⅞", female larger.

RANGE: Breeds on low-arctic tundra from northwestern Alaska across to Baffin Island and Ungava Bay, south along shores of Hudson Bay in suitable places. Migrates *eastward* from Alaska in fall, moving south down Mississippi valley and Atlantic coast, and reversing in spring. Winters from South Carolina and Gulf coast through Caribbean to northern Chile and southern Brazil.

45

WESTERN SANDPIPER

Ereunetes mauri

It is one of the intriguing facets of the evolution of species that this bird should have so restricted a breeding range, whereas its eastern counterpart, the Semipalmated Sandpiper, has the run of the arctic tundra from Cape Prince of Wales in Alaska around to Ungava Bay in Labrador. And yet, the Western is the number one bird in abundance on the beaches of California, just as the Semipalmated outnumbers all others on the flats of New Jersey. They are so similar in appearance that even the most experienced field students do not pretend to separate them all.

All these small peep are tame. "Nothing, to my mind," wrote Leon Dawson,[15] "could exceed the flattery implied by the near approach of these trustful creatures. If the compliment were really deserved, the cunning little souls would undoubtedly respond to the most familiar advances short of actual handling." Nowhere is this trustfulness more evident than on the nesting grounds, but here it is characteristic of almost all the shore birds once they have become strongly attached to eggs, or have newly hatched young. Though the modern student knows that this behavior is born of instinctive drives so strong they are hardly to be denied, the trait is nonetheless endearing. Like the visitor to the Galápagos, the arctic explorer easily falls under the spell of the romantic notion that all God's creatures would be as responsive if man would but let them.

Leon Dawson confessed that the blank pages in his notebook section on this species were due to the fact that its very abundance, in the west, and the difficulty of distinguishing it among other small peep, had combined to make it less well known than many a rarer form. Most of us do not bother with "common" species. And though it would be exaggeration to say that modern students have not written interestingly of it (Herbert Brandt[8] did, for one), we go back, as so often in discussing northern birds, to the writings of E. W. Nelson[35]:

"The warm days towards the end of May cause the brown slopes and flats to assume a shade of green, and among the many pretty bird-romances going on under our eyes none is more charming than the courtship of this delicate sandpiper. They have forsaken the borders of icy pools and, in twos and threes, are found scattered over the tundra, showing a preference for small dry knolls and the drier tussock-covered parts of the country in the vicinity of damp spots and small ponds.

"The female modestly avoids the male as he pays his homage, running back and forth before her as though anxious to exhibit his tiny form to the best advantage. He trails his wings, elevates and partly spreads his tail, and struts in front of his lady in all the pompous vanity of a pigmy turkey-cock; or, filled with ecstatic joy, (he) springs from the earth, and rising upon vibrating wings, some ten or fifteen yards, he poises, hovering in the same position, sometimes nearly a minute, while he pours forth a rapid, uniform series of rather musical trills, which vary in strength as they gradually rise and fall, producing pleasant cadences. The wings of the songster meanwhile vibrate with such rapid motion that they appear to keep time with the rapidly trilling notes, which can only be likened to the running down of a small spring . . . in a fine high-pitched tone. This part of the song ended, the bird raises its wings above its back, thus forming a V, and glides slowly to the ground, uttering at the same time, in a trill, but with a deeper and richer tone, a series of notes which may be likened to the syllables *tzur-r-r-r, tzur-r-r-r*. The word "throaty" may be applied to these latter notes as distinguished from the high-pitched key of the first part of the song. By the first of June, and earlier in some seasons, they have eggs. Their nests are usually upon the drier parts of the tundra, generally on a mossy hummock or slight swell. A sheltering bunch of dwarf willow or a few grass stems in a tuft form a favorite cover."   (R.C.C.)

Ereunetes mauri Cabanis. Not distinguished until 1856.

LOCAL NAMES: Most of the names applied to the Semipalmated Sandpiper.

FIELD CHARACTERS: The problem is to distinguish it from the Semipalmated. Like it, a brownish-gray peep, but rustier above in spring, and usually with conspicuously rusty scapulars in fall. Slightly larger and somewhat more coarsely marked than Semipalmated. Bill longer (but only those with 1″ or more of bill are safely assigned on this character alone), slightly thicker at the base, and drooped at the tip. Tends to feed in deeper water than the Semipalmated, and to carry the bill down-pointed, even in flight. Peterson calls the note a "Thin *jee-rp,* more like the squeak of a White-rump" than the note of a Semipalmated. l. 6–7″, b. ⅞–1¼″, female larger.

RANGE: Breeds only on the northwest coast of Alaska, on both coastal and upland tundra. Migrates up and down the west coast, spreading eastward to winter on both coasts of Mexico, the Caribbean, and northern South America. A few move eastward to New England in the fall, where, however, it is rare in spring.

Greater Yellowlegs with Western Sandpipers

46

BUFF-BREASTED SANDPIPER

Tryngites subruficollis

THIS little gold and silver bird is at once one of the most beautiful, rarest, and least known of our shore birds. Dr. Milton B. Trautman, who had, like many of us, already come to consider the autumn migrants he knew the most beautiful of their tribe, wrote me that he was quite unprepared for the full beauty of these birds in spring flocks. Most striking, perhaps, are the golden, butter-yellow legs which can be seen farther away than the light, buff-breasted bird itself. The back is a deeper, golden brown which so blends into the brown earth backgrounds of the open fields these birds frequent as to cause them to disappear from view at no great distance. But the silvery wing linings flash so startlingly that they make flocks on the wing visible at great distances. W. H. Hudson wrote of them, you may recall, as "buff-colored clouds" materializing on the southern horizon and passing northward rapidly in the long-ago days of their abundance.

Hudson's [28] nostalgic accounts are perhaps our only real clue to the original numbers of these birds, too often referred to as having occurred in "millions." Here is his oft-quoted account of their spring passage:

"Now, one autumn, when most of the emigrants to the Arctic breeding grounds had already gone, I witnessed a great migration of this very species—this beautiful sandpiper with the habits of a plover. The birds appeared in flocks of about one to two or three hundred, flying low and very swiftly due north, flock succeeding flock at intervals of about 10 or 12 minutes; and this migration continued for (at least) three days. I sat each day for hours on my horse watching them pass, each flock first appearing as a faint buff-colored blur or cloud just above the southern horizon, rapidly approaching then passing me, about on a level with my horse's head, to fade out of sight in a couple of minutes in the north; soon to be succeeded by another and yet other flocks in endless succession, each appearing at the same point as the one before, following the same line, as if a line invisible to all eyes except their own had been traced across the green world for their guidance. It gave one the idea that all the birds of this species, thinly distributed over tens of thousands of square miles of country, had formed the habit of assembling previous to migration at one starting point, from which they set out in successive flocks of a medium size in a disciplined order on that marvelous journey to their arctic breeding grounds."

Recent studies of the role of tradition in molding specialized migration lanes confirm Hudson's intuition. A century later, the much diminished flocks frequent only two major stopping places in spanning the length of the North American continent. Night migrants, they strike the United States near Rockport, Texas, after crossing over water from South America. They rest and feed here a month or so, and jump northward some favorable evening in mid-May, to reappear again in numbers only near Edmonton, Alberta, where the late Professor William Rowan [44] studied them in the 1920's. From here they apparently fly directly to the tundra of Alaska's arctic slope, where they nest.

The converging of flocks, too, was observed by Trautman, his wife, and the discoverer of this stopping place, Mrs. Connie Hagar, on the dry prairie west of Rockport, Texas. Here, on April 26, 1952, they estimated that at least 1000 Buff-breasts were scattered over two large fields bisected by a road. Dr. Trautman's field notes comment on their behavior as follows:

"When feeding, the birds scatter rather evenly over the field and each is usually more than 25 feet from its nearest neighbor. If two get

closer together than 10 feet, the invader is usually chased. The bird
stands upright with its neck outstretched as if peering over tall grass
(though the grasses are here only 2″ high). Suddenly it runs forward
and picks up something, presumably an insect, stops abruptly and looks
about again. The whole flock normally feeds against the wind. Those
reaching the edge of the field may rise and fly to the windward side of
the field. The birds frequently stand upright and flap their wings,
flashing their silver wing-linings; obviously to attract other birds and
passing flocks, just as is done among Black Ducks.

"When I slowly walked among these birds they would part in front
of me and close in behind me. When several acres of birds became
alarmed, they jumped upwards at a sharp angle to a distance of four or
five feet. Then all the birds in an area of an acre or so in extent, depending on their density, flew together to a central point. First you see the
birds on a plane about five feet above ground; then you see a rapid converging of about 25–60 birds toward a common center, which quickly
becomes a flock, the number of flocks depending on the number of birds
that rose. Individuals in these very rapidly flying flocks flew closer together than do Pectoral Sandpipers, and with the greatest precision,
first showing their golden backs and immediately thereafter, the silver
wings. When a flock alighted they chose an unoccupied portion of the
field. As the flock swooped earthward, the birds rapidly radiated out-
ward from the common center so that they were four or five feet from
each other when alighting; whereupon each bird ran as quickly as possible from its neighbor until it was ten feet distant. Then it would stop
and begin to feed."

Rowan[44] described similar habits in the flocks he saw near Edmonton: "One can easily walk into a flock without knowing it till the birds
get up almost under foot. They stand immobile on being approached,
not necessarily crouching, generally the very reverse, but without movement they readily enough escape observation. If they start moving as
one gets nearer, it is always on the run. They then carry their necks
'craned,' scatter widely, and zig-zag hither and thither."

Or, again, "A flock will seldom rise in unison, but the nearer birds
will merely fly over and settle on the remote side of the farther ones.
Even when the buff-breasts are amongst sandpipers, such as Baird's,
Semipalmateds, etc., five times out of ten they will remain on the spot
if the others are scared up. A really large flock is rare. We estimated the
number of buff-breasts on a few acres of grass one morning at about

2000, and we spent several hours in trying to photograph them. They were scattered in clumps in all directions. Although we walked through them from one end to the other more than once, thus tending to herd them, the largest number we were able to put up together was about 150."

Trautman saw no hint of courtship in northbound flocks in Texas, but by the time they reach the latitude of Edmonton they are in active display. Rowan gave extended accounts of these actions—a variety of wing tiltings—in the most characteristic of which the birds raise both wings high and rotate them forward so that the white linings show prominently. Stretched to its full height, a displaying bird gives voice to rapidly repeated *"ticks,"* each note accompanied by a sympathetic jerk of the whole body. On the breeding grounds, these displays reach the peak of intensity when displaying birds thus face each other and "tower" together to a height of 30 feet or so before drifting off down wind.

The tameness of these birds, and their fondness for company, militated against them when the shore birds were slaughtered for the market and for sport. Rowan and others have pointed out that every bird of a flock could be killed provided only that the first shot brought down a bird. The others would then return again and again to the wounded and the dead until all had been killed. In this fatal habit, in its choice of habitat and in its attachment to particular migration lanes, even to particular fields along this route, the Buff-breasted Sandpiper thus closely resembled the Eskimo Curlew. It too was so fat that it oozed grease when shot, a characteristic which helped focus the cupidity of the gunner until the law belatedly forebade their killing. They escaped the curlew's fate by a narrow margin, and even now, a half a century after the low point in their numbers, have hardly recovered from these attacks.   (R.C.C.)

Tryngites subruficollis (Vieillot). Described in 1819, from a specimen taken in Paraguay.

Local Names: Hill grass-bird, grass-bird. SPANISH: Chorlito ocraceo.

Field Characters: Slightly smaller than Pectoral and, like it, carries head high, often "craning" upward for a look; but evenly buffy below, with bright yellow legs. Small-headed, with pale eye-ring and short-billed, so dove-like. Tameness and flock habits described in text. Uniformly buff except for contrasting white underwing, marbled near the tip. A grass bird, usually in association with plovers, etc., when in small numbers. Head lagging (as in European

Stone Curlew) has recently been reported. Winter notes include a robin-like *schwup* and a low trilled *pr-r-r-reet* (Wetmore); in spring a pebbly *tik* (Rowan). l. 7½–9″, b. ¾″, male larger.

RANGE: Breeds on dry tundra of arctic Alaska and adjacent Canada, from Point Barrow perhaps east to 100° West Longitude. Few recent breeding ground observations. Spring migration up the interior of both continents (Great Plains of U.S. and Canada); in fall down the same route, but spreading eastward to New England, thence apparently southwestward across Appalachians because rare on southern coastal plain. Winters in central Argentina.

47

MARBLED GODWIT

Limosa fedoa

ALMOST all shore birds are known by their cries. This one pronounces its own name, *Godwit! Godwit! Godwit!* with a sharp emphasis on the final syllable. Once we know this great bird, it is easy to wish that one had known it in the days of its abundance. Elliott Coues [12] did a century ago, and wrote of it admiringly as the Great Marbled Godwit. "I found it," he wrote, "on the plains bordering the Red River in company with Long-billed Curlews and great numbers of Bartramian Sandpipers, nesting, like these species, on the prairie near the river and about the adjoining pools, but not necessarily by the water's edge. In its habits at this season it most nearly resembles the curlew, and the two species, of much the same size and general appearance, might be readily mistaken at a distance where the difference in the bill might not be perceived. On intrusion near the nest, the birds mount in the air with loud, piercing cries, hovering slowly around with labored flight in evident distress, and approaching sometimes within a few feet of the observer."

Farther north, on the plains of southwestern Saskatchewan in 1905, the late Arthur Cleveland Bent[7] made a superb photograph of one of these great birds flat in the grass, with the long mandibles and the protective pattern of its back showing perfectly. It was not concealed in any way, and Mr. Bent photographed it repeatedly, finally taking the picture which is Plate 48 of his classic Bulletin No. 142 at only two feet. He then actually lifted the bird off her nest to photograph the eggs!

A century ago Marbled Godwits migrated along the Atlantic and Pacific coasts in large numbers, lending beauty and life to many a barren promontory and sandy islet. Their great size and magnificent wing-spread were familiar everywhere alongshore. Unfortunately, they were far too large and plump to be safe during the reign of the market-gunner, and so were quickly killed off on the Atlantic side. In that era, every household of any standing in our South employed specialists termed "game cooks" in addition to the regular culinary staff. There were no game laws, nor closed seasons, and these splendid shore birds were regarded merely as so much desirable raw material for the cook.

On March 14, 1952, while watching a flight of dowitchers near St. Marks lighthouse, south of Plainfield in northwest Florida, I saw a pair of Marbled Godwits among the smaller shore birds, the first I had enjoyed in many years on the eastern seaboard. They fed on the sandy shores of an impounded, brackish lake some fifty paces from the Gulf of Mexico. These birds seemed rather tame, allowing me to walk up within forty paces. They then bobbed a bit nervously and sailed away, crying *Wick! Wick! Ker-wick!* I rejoice that this bird is once again seen every autumn on the flats of the Atlantic coast, from Cape Cod to Florida. Like the Long-billed Curlew, this species' future is largely dependent upon the type of agriculture we pursue in the plains States.

Limosa fedoa (Linnaeus). Described in 1758 from a specimen taken in the Hudson Bay region.

LOCAL NAMES: Marlin, brown marlin, big marlin, badger-bird, brant-bird, straight-billed curlew.

FIELD CHARACTERS: A large, tall, richly mottled buff-brown shore bird with a straight or slightly upturned bill. The long legs are bluish and the wing-linings a rich cinnamon. P. A. Taverner called the breeding ground cry a "loud exasperating *eradica-radica-radica-radica*"; the usual cries may be represented as *ker-wick* or *godwit*. l. 16–20″, b. 3–5½″, female larger.

RANGE: Now limited to northern Great Plains, from Edmonton, Alberta, to west-central Minnesota. Winters from central California and coastal South Carolina, south to British Honduras on the east, and Chile on the west. Chief migration through western interior to and from California, scattering eastward in fall.

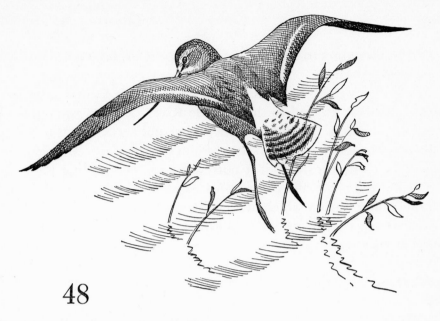

48

BAR-TAILED GODWIT

Limosa lapponica

DR. E. W. NELSON [35] in his classic report on the Alaskan tundra of some eighty years ago, wrote, "I found them arriving at St. Michaels in flocks of from 25 to 200 from the 13th to 20th of May. These flocks were shy and kept in continual motion, wheeling and circling in rapid flight over the low land, now alighting for a moment then skimming away again in a close body.

"By the last of May the flocks are broken up, and the birds are distributed in small parties over their breeding ground. Their courtship begins by the 18th or 20th of May, and is carried on in such a loud-voiced manner that every creature in the neighborhood knows all about it. The males continually utter a loud ringing *ku-wew, ku-wew, ku-wew,* which is repeated with great emphasis upon the last syllable, and the note may be heard for several hundred yards.

"They frequent open grassy parts of the country and are quick to protest against an invasion of their territory. At the mating season the males have a rolling whistle also like that of the ordinary field plover, but shorter. When the birds fly at this time they hold the wings decurved and stiffened and make a few rapid strokes, then glide for a short distance. On the ground it walks gracefully, its head well raised, and frequently pauses to raise its wings high over the back and then deliberately folds them."

Today we know that it nests from the Koskokwim River delta on the west coast around to the Colville River delta on the north, being most common in the Yukon delta region and occurring as much as one hundred miles inland southeast of Point Barrow.

Everyone considers it a noisy bird on its breeding grounds, the equal of the notoriously vociferous Avocet, Black-necked Stilt, and the Long-billed Curlew which nest farther south. On the other hand, the female sits as closely on her eggs as any species, refusing to leave them until almost trod upon.

These Alaskan birds are an overflow from the Eurasian mainland, and apparently return to Siberia across Bering Strait before beginning their long migration across the western Pacific. Winter flocks of up to ten thousand birds occur in New Zealand which, with Australia, is the principal wintering ground, but stragglers may be found from China to Hawaii at that season. The main migratory movement appears to take place not far west of the International Date Line, i.e., west of 180° west longitude. In his *New Zealand Birds* (1955), Dr. W. R. B. Oliver tells how important these godwits were as an item of food to the Maori who ate them whole after cooking. Flax snares or nets were spread horizontally above the night resting places of these birds with the aid of stakes. After nightfall, natives equipped with flares rushed into their midst and flushed the frightened birds so suddenly that they jumped up and were tangled in the snares they had calmly walked under earlier that evening.   (R.C.C.)

Limosa lapponica (Linnaeus). Described in 1758; our race, *L.l.baueri,* by Naumann in 1836 from an Australian specimen.

LOCAL NAMES: Pacific Godwit.

FIELD CHARACTERS: A brown godwit without the wing stripe of the Hudsonian and Black-tailed Godwits. White rump and barred tail makes it look like a small European Curlew or Whimbrel, though the bill is of course straight or curved upward rather than down. Lacks the head stripes of whimbrel. 18".

RANGE: Eurasian tundra (low arctic and subarctic), overflowing Bering Straits to occupy Alaska tundra from Kuskokwim to Colville River deltas. Migrates up and down Aleutians, passing southward over western Pacific to winter in southwest Pacific islands, mostly from Philippines to New Zealand. Accidental in British Columbia.

49

HUDSONIAN GODWIT

Limosa haemastica

SOMEHOW, a white lower back or rump on a retreating shore bird is its most conspicuous feature, like the flag on a White-tailed Deer, or the bobbing signal on Molly Cottontail. The Hudsonian Godwit is so equipped, and is thus easily distinguished from the Marbled Godwit in any plumage. The Black-tailed Godwit of Eurasia resembles it, however.

Like the American race of the whimbrel, this species has, apparently, two discrete breeding populations, one along the western side of Hudson Bay, the other in the lower MacKenzie region. But these vast low arctic and subarctic reaches are still but partially explored, and connecting populations may yet be found.

Though reportedly never a common species, it has increased measurably since the early 1920's when protection helped it and others. The most interesting clue to its numbers is that provided by Canadian naturalists Hope and Shortt [26] who, on July 23, 1942, saw flocks totalling at least a thousand birds pass their camp on the west side of James Bay, all in less than two hours at midday. These flocks, of 60 to 70 birds as a

rule (the largest was of 125 birds), flew swiftly and directly, in broad flat
V's and crescents, with little changing of formation. "The wing beats
were rather shallow but powerful, and the sound of the rush of wings
was plainly audible as a flock passed over at their usual altitude of about
200 feet. The flight call was a modulated trill which we found virtually
impossible to distinguish from the flight notes of the Hudsonian Curlew," though these birds were less noisy than curlews.

We know so little of the habits and migrations of this bird that the
thousand birds reported above may have represented the better part of
the total population, as seems the case with the Buff-breasted Sandpiper
when seen concentrated near Rockport, Texas, or near Edmonton. We
do know that they move eastward to the Maritimes of Canada from
James Bay in the fall, and then apparently fly directly to South America,
passing well off the New England shore, and landing on the eastern seaboard only when the overwater flight is interfered with by storm or fog.

Eastern gunners thus never made much impression on their numbers, mostly for want of opportunity. They were much more numerous
on the Argentine pampas a hundred years ago, but it is not clear, yet,
whether their decline is to be laid to shooting on the wintering grounds
or on the American prairie. For, this species is another bird whose migrations trace a vast ellipse, passing off our coast in autumn, but through
the interior in spring.

One March 7, some years ago, I watched a pair on the beach
north of Daytona, Florida, wanderers from the main inland flight lane.
Two godwits might not seem to you particularly notable, but they made
a picture long to be remembered—the endless crescent of glistening
beach, rimmed with white surf and alive with the wings and *yap-yaps* of
Black Skimmers. In the center, the two ruddy-breasted godwits stood
meditatively on one leg, or, awakening abruptly from midday dreams,
chased each other for a few paces, and returned to their somnolent posture.

One may again regularly see Hudsonian Godwits on the great flats
of the New England coast, and on Long Island and New Jersey. They
come in late August and September, and when the winds have favored
us, it may be possible to see from two or three birds up to a dozen or so,
though the larger counts are few and far between.

John J. Elliott [17a] has reported an interesting incident involving
this big wader and one of its lesser kin on the sandy flats of Moriches
Bay, Long Island, one September 15 some years ago. "Suddenly," he

writes, "a Sanderling approached to avail itself of the efforts of the big
sandpiper. It advanced gingerly, pivoting back and forth to avoid the
digging godwit. The godwit dug with upthrust strokes, pushing the
mud up and out and using its decurved bill as a tiny spade. The poach-
ing Sanderling appeared at the front of the digging bill and remained
there dabbing occasionally, and apparently once getting food. The
godwit flew soon afterward, but the Sanderling remained a few moments
to further search the disturbed area. The smaller bird, however, kept
its "meal ticket" in mind and soon tracked off after the godwit." The
godwit's moving about suggests that the Sanderling was not entirely
welcome, though the larger bird at no time showed antagonism.

The success of duck restoration projects across the continent,
whether by individuals, or private or governmental agencies, points in
the right direction. Direct help to ducks and geese redounds to the benefit of shore birds. This is easily seen at Malheur Lake in Oregon, along
the Bear River marshes in Utah, and elsewhere. When regions too
hastily drained for agriculture are once more flooded for ducks, the
shore birds take advantage of the new habitat, and since nobody shoots
them nowadays, they not only find protection here but are aided in their
migrations, and their increase is encouraged.

Limosa haemastica (Linnaeus). Described in 1758 from a Hudson Bay specimen.
LOCAL NAMES: Ring-tailed marlin, straight-billed curlew, spot-rump, brant-bird.
    SPANISH: Becasa de mar.
FIELD CHARACTERS: Slightly smaller than Marbled Godwit and, in spring, more
    chestnut below, with more and darker barring, and with a nearly black back
    (with chestnut markings). The slightly larger females are separable by the
    great amount of white flecking throughout, due to brown feathers with white
    tips. The white rump contrasts strikingly with the squarish, black white-
    tipped tail. Fall birds are a very nondescript plain gray, willet-like, but
    longer-billed and with distinctive white rump and black tail. The axillars are
    black and the under-wing linings sooty. l. m. 14", f. 16"; bill c. 3".
    We should be prepared to distinguish two other species as visitors:
The Black-tailed Godwit (*Limosa limosa*), a very similar Eurasian species, breeds
    as close to us as Iceland, is accidental in Greenland and Newfoundland. Its
    wing linings are white, and the white wing stripe is more prominent than the
    Hudsonian's. The legs protrude well beyond the tail, and there is no white tip
    to the black tail. The bill is always straight. Probably silent as a visitor. 15–
    17", bill c. 4".
The Bar-tailed Godwit *(Limosa lapponica)* of Eurasia (see text).
RANGE: Breeds locally in northwestern Mackenzie and on west side of Hudson Bay
    (Churchill). Winters in southern half of South America. Migrates north

through interior North America, west of Hudson Bay. In fall, moves eastward, down west side of Hudson Bay, then east to Maritime Provinces, then
over Atlantic to South America except as driven ashore by storms, or as
scattered individuals and small groups.

Some measure of the scanty nature of our knowledge is evident in the
unexplained occurrence of winter visitors to New Zealand. Did they skirt
Antarctic seas from South America, or come the length of the Pacific from
Mackenzie and Alaska?

50

RUFF

Philomachus pugnax

(*foreground*) Fall plumage
(*background*) Male in Spring

PERHAPS the most remarkable of our European visitors is the Ruff which is noted almost annually on our Atlantic shores, though we seldom see it in the full glory of its remarkable plumage. The male is rather large but the female is much smaller and so different in color that in Europe she is known as a Reeve.

The male in winter plumage and the female at all seasons somewhat resemble our Upland Plover. In breeding plumage the male wears an extraordinary erectile ruff on neck and shoulders, capped by a pair of owl-like tufts at the back of the head. No two of these showy ruffs are alike: they may be brown, white, black, or a speckled mixture with purplish iridescence. Few other birds, and certainly no wader, show so much variation in courtship dress. So conspicuous are the enormous ruff and ear tufts of the Ruff that they give the bird a peculiar, thick-necked appearance in flight.

During the mating season Ruffs congregate at special meeting places called "ruff hills." Each male bird squats on its own mound, expands its great ruff and ear tufts, and defies all the other males. Sometimes two will sit beak to beak for minutes, each trying to bluff the other by sheer display, but never actually mixing it up. Instead they growl and gobble maledictions until one bird backs down and leaves the dominant bird in possession of a small territory on the hill. This whole performance illustrates both a very specialized type of territorial behavior and a highly ritualized form of fighting for, or defending this territory. The nearest they come to violence as a rule is chasing each other off their respective hills while the reeves look on nonchalantly. The Black Grouse of Europe defends similar meeting grounds called leks, and this formalized jousting is thus called lek behavior. Far from being a mere show of aggressiveness, however, this "fighting" is probably essential to successful reproduction because of its role as a social stimulant.

The very specialized adornments of the Ruff are worthy of further comment. Are these extraordinary feather tracts a product of sexual selection in evolution, an advantage in attracting females and thus assuring the perpetuation of the showiest Ruffs, generation after generation? Charles Darwin suggested that this was their function. But modern biologists, whose regard for Darwin seems to grow with every passing generation, disagree with him on this point.

Bird behaviorists tell us that the prime function of showy plumage is not attraction but intimidation, i.e., an aid in territorial defense. An unregulated society would wreak havoc with reproduction because the chaos of continuous fighting over females would leave the males neither time, opportunity, nor energy for actual mating. By establishing dominance over a territory which he can defend with a minimum of effort, by a sort of symbolic jousting instead of by open warfare with his neighbors, the male can then concentrate on courting the females which come to the ruff hill. Actually, however, the females seem to select a male rather deliberately, solicit him by assuming the attitude of readiness to mate, head down, and the mating which follows, either on the hill or nearby, is not interfered with by other Ruffs. There are no jealous swains!

The sexes appear more alike after the nesting season, and in winter. Both then have sandy-colored backs, buff breasts, and whitish underparts. The female wears a few thrush-like breast spots. The bills and legs vary greatly in color. Winter Ruffs and Reeves then resemble our Greater Yellowlegs, with which they often associate while here, and are probably often overlooked by American observers. But the legs of the Ruff are never bright corn-yellow, and a trained observer can learn to identify it by other markings.

Although Ruffs have been observed on our eastern shores from the

Maritime Provinces of Canada to North Carolina and Barbados, and inland to Ohio, Indiana, and Iowa, they are always casual visitors with us. Their real home is the eastern hemisphere. They are everywhere great wanderers, breeding from the arctic coasts of Eurasia south to France and almost throughout the Soviet Republics. They are also casual east to the Pribilof Islands, Japan, and the Philippines.

(R.C.C.)

Philomachus pugnax (Linnaeus). Described in 1758.

FIELD CHARACTERS: In size, between our two yellowlegs, but shorter-legged. Summer males unmistakable. Winter birds rather nondescript. Bill shorter and heavier than Lesser Yellowlegs, yellowish at base; legs variable, from dull yellow to olive-green or grayish. In flight, spread tail shows a black central stripe with oval white patches on either side, a diagnostic pattern. Always browner than yellowlegs. Rather silent birds, deliberate in action. l. 9½–12½″, b. 1¼–1½″, males much larger than females.

51

SANDERLING

Crocethia alba

THE flight of shore birds on a rising tide shows a wild ecstasy capable of carrying them considerable distances before the impulse fades and hunger makes them pause. Our coastal measurements mean little to their long pinions—a hundred miles from the mouth of the Kennebec River in Maine to Highland Light in Massachusetts—what do such insignificant intervals mean to migrants which flit from Baffin Bay to the Argentine?

Taking off from some northern strand, many of them have barely struck their stride when they sight the tip of Cape Cod, flung like a golden sickle in the sea. Whether they will stop or not depends largely on the tides.

They seem to follow the air trails so long as the water is rising, particularly when driven by storms. The very instant the ebbing water bares flats and bars, the migrants arrive like magic, as if they had timed their voyage accordingly. Before the sea has receded a foot, I frequently hear their voices high overhead, and presently a few yellowlegs or plovers drop down out of nowhere. They whirl alongshore for a few minutes, as if looking for a place to land, and when the tide is half way out, they throng the flats as fast as these appear.

It is the same story all the way from the St. Lawrence to Plymouth, and thence round the Cape to Chatham and Monomoy. Everywhere the

emerging land crooks a beckoning finger to the shore birds, the green
peace of the meadows tolls them in and soon a sandy universe affords a
playground for their twinkling feet.

Just as the outside beaches give the best glimpses of migrating
shore birds, so the inshore flats and lagoons are the most convenient
places to observe their feeding habits. The sands of Barnstable, Wellfleet, Monomoy, Martha's Vineyard, Montauk, Barnegat, and dozens of
other harbors or promontories on the Atlantic coast, are visited by innumerable sandpipers, snipe, and plovers from the arrival of the first
Ringneck early in July to the disappearance of the last flight of Sanderlings in mid-October or later.

Almost any day between these dates, I can watch many different
species without stirring from my Provincetown wharf. When the tide
ebbs, flurries arrive everywhere and alight, elevating their wings and
peeping complacently. They start feeding immediately and keep it up
almost without interruption until the next high tide chases them into
the air. They seem the winged embodiment of the tide—their flight a
ripple, or series of ripples, and their bodies, aerial minnows, dark above
but glistening underneath.

Myriads of little beach waifs run around devouring minute crabs,
hoppers, sand-worms, and various insects and molluscs. All feed eagerly
but none can compete for an instant with those greediest of sandpipers,
the beautiful Sanderlings. The latter dash about as if actually famished,
often holding their mandibles submerged to the nostrils but working
like scissors. This incessant predation of shore birds plays a significant
role in the ecology of the beaches and flats. Sand crabs and mud worms
are importantly reduced by sand or mud-frequenting species, respec-
tively. Mollusk populations, on the other hand, are little disturbed in
proportion to their numbers. Sanderlings and the other species that
feed over the glasswort flats (*Salicornia*) take appreciable numbers of
the larvae of the alkali fly (*Ephydridae*).

In May and early June Sanderlings pass along the New England
coast bound for their nesting grounds on the shores of the Arctic Ocean.
They are almost circumpolar in summer, and their southern migration,
during which we see them in greatest numbers, takes them to southern
Argentina, South Africa, Ceylon, Borneo, Hawaii, Australia and New
Zealand. It is among the most cosmopolitan of birds.

Despite this wide dispersal, considerable numbers of Sanderlings
winter all along our Atlantic coast in the middle latitudes, where they
add a touch of life and beauty to the sinister and deserted sands.

Although common on the inshore flats at low tide, these birds are pre-eminently the sandpipers of the sounding ocean beaches, and are appropriately termed "surf snipe" there. They prefer those vast, tide-scoured, rolling strands where breakers crash and roar. When the tremendous backwash seethes down the slope, baring minute crustaceans and hoppers, these bold little birds dash after the water, snapping up the insects that kick themselves clear of the spume.

Often, too, Sanderlings probe the hard, wet sand for sand fleas, leaving rows of holes two or three feet in length and deep enough to survive the scouring of several waves. Following a flock of these birds along the barren, outside strand it is pleasant to hear their contented peeping and whistling, and to watch them at a distance swarming over some rise in the sands.

At other times the observer may be surprised to see a flock spring from the margin of the sea, where a light, protective coloration renders them indistinguishable until they move.

Their heads and upper plumage are rusty in the breeding season, with blackish speckling above. The under parts are then white, the bill short and black, and the legs blackish. In winter plumage, after summer moults, Sanderlings lose most of their rusty tints and look as gray and white as the sand on which they scamper.

Crocethia alba (Pallas). Described in 1764.

LOCAL NAMES: Beach-bird, whitey, whiting, surf-snipe, skinner, etc. SPANISH: Chorlito blanco.

FIELD CHARACTERS: The commonest and whitest of the beach sandpipers (in fall); plump, black-billed and black-legged. The white wing stripe is more contrasting than in other small peep. In spring, the reddish breast, head and back make it more difficult; early autumn birds often show confusing vestiges of this rustiness. Depend on habitat and prominent wing stripe until you have "soaked in" these variations. Flushing birds call *"twick,"* a shrill note that becomes distinctive with practiced listening; feeding flocks twitter softly to themselves. l. 7–8¾", b. ⅞–1⅛", female larger.

RANGE: Breeds circumpolarly at very high latitudes, mostly on arctic islands. Females brood but are probably helped by the males. Winters on almost all coasts south of British Columbia, Massachusetts, and Ireland and China, reaching Hawaii and Polynesia in small numbers. In South America as far as southern Argentina and Chile. American populations migrate north along both coasts, but head inland over British Columbia and New England to Hudson Bay coasts. Same routes in fall, but increased numbers spread out to hit coasts north of spring departure points. Almost cosmopolitan.

CHAPTER 7

THE AVOCETS AND STILTS

TALL, long-legged, and striking waders with long bills —straight in stilts, recurved in avocets. Widely distributed in temperate and tropical regions around the world, either along coastal marshes or inland sloughs and saline lakes.

More or less gregarious throughout the year, and colonial during nesting season. Sexes nearly alike. Eggs usually 4, laid in a scrape in the sand or on a platform of reeds.

Four species of avocets are recognized: the Old World Avocet of Eurasia and Africa, the Australian Avocet, the American Avocet and the Chilean Avocet. All are very much alike.

There are two stilts: the Black-necked with three races (Australia and New Zealand, the New World, and Eurasia and Africa) and the Banded Stilt which occurs in the interior of Australia.

A seventh member of the family, the Ibis-bill, an avocet-like bird, occurs at high altitudes in central Asia.

52
AMERICAN
AVOCET

Recurvirostra americana

WHILE driving across the desert from Salt Lake City to Wendover, Nevada, some years ago, I noted a magnificent pair of these great shore birds fidgeting disconsolately as they gazed round on ninety miles of glittering salt flats. Once or twice those big pink birds bobbed like tip-up snipe. No doubt my desert pair were stragglers from Bear River, where avocets still nest in numbers, along with sickle-bill curlews and their closest relatives, the Black-necked Stilts.

Avocets are admirably equipped by nature for life on these big lakes and sloughs. The down of their under parts is as dense and thick as that of a grebe, completely insulating them from the chill of cold water. They wade like herons, swim like ducks, dive smoothly, and can flush from the water like rocketting teal.

Much farther east, near Vincennes, Indiana, the great Audubon[5] enjoyed watching a group of these birds in 1814, and gave us, later, one of the most picturesque accounts of their behavior our literature contains, even a century later:

"On alighting, whether on the water or on the ground, the American Avocet keeps its wings raised until it has fairly settled. If in the water, it stands a few minutes balancing its head and neck, somewhat in the manner of the Tell-tale Godwit (Greater Yellowlegs). After this it stalks about searching for food, or runs after it, sometimes swimming for a yard or so while passing from one shallow to another, or wading up to its body, with the wings partially raised. Sometimes they would enter among the rushes and disappear for several minutes. They kept apart, but crossed each other's path in hundreds of ways, all perfectly silent, and without showing the least symptom of enmity towards each other, although whenever a Sandpiper came near, they would instantly give chase to it. On several occasions, when I purposely sent forth a loud shrill whistle without stirring, they would suddenly cease from their rambling, raise up their body and neck, emit each two or three notes, and remain several minutes on the alert, after which they would fly to their nests, and then return. They search for food precisely in the manner of the Roseate Spoonbill, moving their heads to and fro sideways, while their bill is passing through the soft mud; and, in many instances, when the water was deeper, they would immerse their whole head and a portion of the neck, as the Spoonbill and Red-breasted Snipe are wont to do. When, on the contrary, they pursued aquatic insects, such as swim on the surface, they ran after them, and on getting up to them, suddenly seized them by thrusting the lower mandible beneath them, while the other was raised a good way above the surface, much in the manner of the Black Shearwater (Black Skimmer), which, however, performs this act on the wing. They were also expert at catching flying insects, after which they ran with partially expanded wings."

Somewhat as cranes indulge in fantastic and ludicrous dances, so avocets occasionly stage mass demonstrations indicative of some strange collective agitation. One observer reports a hundred and fifty of these showy birds crowded together on a muddy islet only about twelve feet in diameter in the estuary of the Bear River, Utah. The avocets milled about in such a manner that the entire mass revolved slowly like the hands of a clock. They seemed to be marching at half step, or marking time, and occasionally crowded some of their number into the water. Those thus ousted flew to neighboring islands while others swooped down to take their places. Turkeys perform similar "ring dances." These dances, however, are not considered courtship performances.

Recurvirostra americana (Gmelin). Described in 1789, mostly from Pennant's description in *Arctic Zoology*, 1785.

FIELD CHARACTERS: A large, long-legged wader with long, slightly decurved, awl-like bill. Strikingly black and white, especially in flight. Feeds with a sidewise sweeping of the bill, often in deep water, and swims easily. Adults have pale blue legs, warm pinkish-buff heads and necks. Young, and winter adults, have gray tints instead of buff. The voice is a strident *wheep*. l. 16–20″, b. 3¼–4″, male larger.

RANGE: Formerly bred throughout most of temperate America except New England; now restricted to suitably wet areas west of 100th meridian and common only about shallow marshes of high plains and alkali lakes of Great Basin region. A concentration of ten thousand Avocets along the Salton Sea of California in 1949 is a high point we may not see again because agricultural changes in that area have drastically altered available habitats. Winters from north-central California and southern Texas south to Guatemala. Migrants have increasingly revisited the Atlantic coast, from New Jersey to Florida, in recent years.

Avocet in aggressive pose

53

BLACK-NECKED STILT

Himantopus mexicanus

AVOCETS and stilts belong to the Recurvirostridae, a family name suggesting strongly recurved mandibles, yet even the Avocet's long bill is only slightly recurved. The Black-necked Stilt's delicate mandibles are nearly straight, long and pointed like needles, but they never give the impression of being out of proportion to the bird itself. Its legs are most striking, being so slender and lengthy that the stilt is often called the "daddy-long-legs" locally. Only the flamingo has longer legs in proportion to its size. And these legs are bright pink or carmine, with half-webbed feet, though the stilt swims much less than the avocet.

Elliott Coues [12] wrote interestingly of a small group near Los Pinos, New Mexico, in June of 1864:

"They offered a very striking and pleasing effect, wheeling in easy flight, the flock appearing one moment black, the next white, as they showed alternately the upper and under parts, with the long bright-tinted legs heightening the contrast of color. Although not heedless or unduly familiar, they were not very shy. . . . Besides being almost unacquainted with the danger that may lie in man's approach, they appeared of a gentle, unsuspicious nature, the more noticeable in contrast with the restlessness and watchfulness of most waders. Thus I remember to have approached, on one occasion, within a dozen paces of a large flock, with no other artifice than stooping a little and walking quietly and slowly. The birds had observed me, of course, as the grass was only a few inches high and the ground perfectly flat, but they stood motionless, looking with more of curiosity than fear. It was a picturesque group, still as statues the birds stood in the water, raised only a little above it, on their firm, though so slender, supports, their trim bodies drawn up to full height, and their large, soft eyes dilated in wonder. In an instant, however, as if they had but one mind in common, a thought occurred, and quick as the thought they were off. . . ."

Recently I had the privilege of holding a pair of Black-necked Stilts in my hands. They had been caught by a helper at a "rare bird farm" in eastern Florida. Very likely they had been attracted to the place by the array of aquatic birds swimming in the pools. At any rate, there they were—a male in superb plumage, black head, wings and scapulars, with a slight greenish reflection in the black, and a flush of pink at the throat, and pure white under parts. The female was similar as to pattern, but with brownish-black scapulars, and a slightly paler head and nape. They were beautiful and graceful birds. Even the attendant, who had never heard their name until I told him, greatly admired their extremely long pinions.

The birds were alike in size, about that of a winter yellowlegs but more slender. They peeped gently while their captor thrust them into a paste-board box perforated to admit air. He apparently contemplated feeding these stilts on grain, like the rest of his charges, and seemed surprised when I said this would not do. I suggested that he liberate the birds, but fear that they are still part of a permanent exhibition advertised along the pike. They were taken on February 20th, the earliest date on which I have observed the species in breeding plumage.

Whenever one approaches the nest of a pair of these tall waders, or even passes it at a distance of three hundred yards, they fly to meet him and lead him away from their eggs or young. The clamor they raise is truly startling and generally stirs up all the other birds nesting in the vicinity. The stilts do not limit their efforts to this outcry, however. They alight in the water, bob up and down by bending their knees, and strike the surface with their breasts so as to make a series of splashes.

Then they run ashore, trail a wing as if broken, and scuffle like a mother grouse leading an interloper away from her chicks in northern woods.

At present they are casual east of the Mississippi, except in Florida, but still nest in small colonies in the west, as well as in Central America and northern South America, and even out on the Galápagos Islands. They are still fairly numerous in Utah and California, often associating with avocets around the salt lakes. Formerly they nested as far north as the salt meadows near Atlantic City, New Jersey.

In the extensive marshes of the Bear River delta, stilts seem to have constituted themselves sentries and guardians for all the curlews, plovers, and other shore birds nesting in the district, which is a paradise for waders.

These birds show a strong tendency to nest in small colonies, here and elsewhere throughout their summer range. Sometimes high water invades the nest site, forcing the birds to shove fresh material under their precious eggs to lift them high enough to keep them dry. This is an extraordinary example of avian adaptability, since most birds can think of no means of coping with such calamities. Clapper Rails, for example, build high in some dangerous spot, but apparently do not change the nest once it is completed, no matter what.

Himantopus mexicanus (Muller). Described in 1776, based on a Mexican bird.
    SPANISH: Tero real.
LOCAL NAMES: Lawyer, Long-shanks, and Daddy-long-legs.
FIELD CHARACTERS: A tall, slim, black-mantled wader, pure white below, and with very long red legs. The long slender black bill is also distinctive. In flight, the long black wings are unpatterned, but the rump and tail are pale gray. A dainty walker in shallow waters, seldom going in as deep as avocets. Strident calls include a tern-like *kark,* and *yep, yep* that become high *kyips* as the bird's excitement mounts. l. 14–16″, b. 2–2¾″, female larger.
RANGE: Our race breeds about shallow sloughs, salt lakes and salt marshes, from s. Saskatchewan and s. Oregon to s. Colorado and n. Utah; Texas and Louisiana coast; South Carolina to central and e. Florida; thence south through Caribbean region to n. South America. Winters from San Francisco Bay region and western Gulf coast south to southern limits of breeding range. Overreaches breeding range during migration, occurring casually or accidentally, to Newfoundland and Bermuda.

Many students today consider the Stilts one world-wide species. In this view the South American Stilt which breeds throughout that continent except for the northeast corner occupied by the North American race, is lumped with our race in a common species. So is the indigenous Hawaiian Stilt, now reduced to a few score birds, and the equally scarce and shorter-legged Galápagos race.

CHAPTER 8

THE PHALAROPES

T̲HIS SMALL FAMILY of sea-snipe, or swimming sand-pipers, comprises the only truly oceanic shore birds. They are masters of the three elements—the air, the earth and the water. William C. Beebe[33] characterized them perhaps better than anyone else after encountering them on the open sea:

"Sea-ducks haunt the shallower banks of the coast, gulls trust the air of the widest sea, gannets dive deep into the waves for their prey, while skimmers plough their tiny furrows through the ocean, but phalaropes actually live on the surface of the open sea. With their long legs for wading, with narrow lobes instead of broad webbing between their toes, without the slender, narrow wings upon which albatrosses hang through days of storm and stress of weather, phalaropes seem little adapted for pelagic life, and yet here and on the Pacific, hundreds of miles from land, I have seen them in enormous flocks—daring wind and water, spending the whole winter out of sight of land, trusting to the floating bounty of the sea for food, and to the buoyancy of their dense plumage and air-filled bodies for safety. I have never seen them in a full storm, but in a half gale, with spray blowing, and every watery hilltop fountaining into ugly lashing foam, I have watched their marvelous seamanship, paddling steadily up wind, able, by some perfected knowledge, to keep in the sliding, shifting valleys and free of the choking spume-drift."

As breeding birds, phalaropes, like loons and auks, are among the few bird families restricted to the northern hemisphere. Dainty and attractively colored, they are peculiar in many ways. Their toes are lobed with a scalloped flap of skin. Their tendency to ride high on the waves, and the near-vertical position of their long necks are both good field identification points. The females are larger and more brightly colored than the males, and in keeping with this reversal of "masculinity," they take the lead in courting and then let the male build the well-lined nest and incubate the eggs. In feeding, also, they have the curious habit of spinning on the water, perhaps as a means of drawing up small organisms from depths beyond the reach of their bills, whether in a tundra or prairie pool, or in the wake of a whale (but see under Northern Phalarope). Finally, though there are but three species, each is individualistic enough to merit being classified as a separate genus.

Female in breeding plumage

54

RED PHALAROPE
(*Grey Phalarope*)

Phalaropus fulicarius

THIS colorful species breeds farther north, migrates farther south, is more gregarious, and is more truly pelagic than either of the other phalaropes.

Breeding far up on top of the world amid icy solitudes, from Alaska way round to Kamchatka, always close to the arctic circle, the beautiful spring-plumaged Red Phalarope is inaccessible to most of us while it is most attractive. And though numerous off our Atlantic and Pacific coasts during its migrations, it normally stays so well offshore that only storm-driven strays come to our attention. I recall a sizeable flock seen from the deck of a liner headed southwestward, and then about three hundred miles east of Grand Manan. As we bore down on them the birds did not seem in the least afraid of the ship, but paddled here and there in little fleets, showing brightly when the sunlight caught them. Many were still in the gray winter dress, but here and there a red female shone like a jewel of the sea. That was during the second week in May. A few weeks later those phalaropes were probably paddling ashore on some island in Hudson Bay or the arctic archipelago. Ludlow Griscom once saw a thousand north-bound migrants at Monomoy Point, Cape Cod, and pointed out that the main migration of this species is both earlier in spring (April) and much later in fall (early November) than that of the Northern Phalarope off the New England coast.

No matter where seen, these little mariners seem to elicit admiration. W. Leon Dawson [15] had this to say about their antics among the Farallon Islands of California, where, also, they often congregate in numbers.

Oh! but these are agile surfmen! Never, save in the case of the Wandering Tatler and the American Dipper, have I seen such absolute disregard of danger and such instant adjustment to watery circumstance. Here are 30 of these phalaropes "fine mixed", threading a narrow passage in the reefs where danger threatens in the minutest fraction of a second. Crash! comes a comber. Our little world is obliterated in foam. Sea anemones and rock oysters sputter and choke, and there is a fury of readjustment. But the phalaropes rise automatically, clear the crest of the crasher, and are down again, preening their feathers or snatching dainties with the utmost unconcern. Now a bird is left stranded on a reef, or now he is whisked and whirled a dozen feet away. All right, if he likes it; but if not, he is back again, automatically, at the old rendezvous. Life goes on right merrily in spite of these shocking interruptions. Food getting is the main business, and this is pursued with extraordinary ardor.

The arctic summer is brief indeed, and it must be a help to the little male phalarope, who has administered to all the needs of the young, that he does not have to feed them, too, once they free themselves of their shells. A few hours after hatching they can find their own provender; they learn to paddle and plunge on secluded tundra pools, and are adept at the art of survival by the time the various families are ready to start their 2500-mile southern trek. But Sutton,[53] who has observed them closely on the grass tundra of Southampton Island, where they are common breeding birds, warns us that

"our idea of the home-life of the Red Phalarope is on the whole somewhat erroneous. While the male certainly does all, or the greater part, of incubating, certainly the female frequently assists in caring for the brood. Upon occasion she lingers near the nest, much as the male in most species lingers near his mate while she broods. The young are cared for as often by both parents as by the male alone. In fact, as a rule, both male and female brood the young and lead them about. Both parents show about equal concern for their progeny, though the males are apparently bolder in defending them in the face of danger."

The Russian ornithologist Birula[40] has given us a glimpse of the
last weeks these birds spend in the Siberian arctic. Camping on the
Island of New Siberia, well above the arctic circle, he wrote:

During the ebb tide, hundreds of Red Phalaropes frequented the sand flat
up till 2 August. They ran about over the mud picking up food in the shape of
minute invertebrate animals, or busied themselves in fishing for minute crustaceans in the muddy water at the mouth of the river. During flood tide they sought
the pools of the tundra or the muddy shores of streamlets. For a week after 2
August, I saw not a single phalarope on the sand flat, but . . . on 10 August the
flat was once more peopled with flocks of Red Phalaropes consisting chiefly of
immature birds which no longer bore down on their heads, although this was still
present on the heads of the young Sanderlings and Knots. About 14 August the
weather grew cold, with a temperature throughout the day below 10° centigrade,
and the tundra was covered with snow. From time to time a gale arose and the
tundra took on an altogether wintry aspect. On 17 August the temperature during
the night fell to −3.6° centigrade and the seashore as well as the sand flat at ebb
tide was edged with thin ice. Occasionally flocks of shorebirds visited the flat, but
after circling about a few times, went back to the tundra. At the end of a week,
the weather moderated for a short while, the snow melted and the shores no
longer were edged with ice. After 25 August the sand flat was again frequented by
small flocks of Red Phalaropes, which, in dwindling numbers of individuals, remained until 11 September and stayed on the flat only a short while. At this time
I could see that these flocks were going out to sea in a southwesterly direction.
After 5 September I saw no more shorebirds on the sand flat, so that the Phalarope
was the last shorebird to leave the island. The last individual Red Phalarope was
seen on 14 September, going northward. There now came a definite change in the
weather, winter set in and by 8 September the air temperature fell to −9.0°
centigrade.

Having abandoned its northern nesting ground, the Red Phalarope
becomes truly cosmopolitan and is seen on all the seven seas as it makes
its way southward. To American whalers this bird was always a good
omen. Flocks of them followed Right and Bowhead whales, spotting
them under water long before the masthead man bellowed, "Thar she
BLOOWS! BLOOWS! BLOOWS!" This association gave the Red
Phalarope such names as "whale-bird" and "bowhead bird."

Phalaropus fulicarius (L.) Described in 1758. (ref. to *Fulica,* the coot; coot-footed.)
LOCAL NAMES: Gray phalarope, Gray bank-bird, Whale-bird, etc. SPANISH: Chorlo
    palmado castaño.
FIELD CHARACTERS: Almost exclusively maritime. Other sandpipers may swim, but
    none so buoyantly; spinning and dabbling diagnostic once known. Migrant

Reds in spring are easy because of their red breasts, yellowish bills. Gray fall birds much more difficult. Then much like Sanderling or Nothern Phalarope; best told by thick bill with yellow base. l. 7½–9″, b. ¾–1″, female larger.

RANGE: Breeds in high arctic around the pole, south to northern Iceland, perhaps the only place one may see it from the comfort of an automobile. (*Vide*–O. S. Pettingill). Migrates south along all coasts, mostly well offshore. Winters at sea in South Atlantic (perhaps from Gulf of Mexico southward), off West African coast (especially between the Canary and Cape Verde Islands); off the Chilean and Peruvian coasts, about the Galápagos; between Panamá and the Marquesas Islands; in the Arabian Sea and farther south in the East Indies. Many of these are areas of upwelling, where ocean currents bring the deeper, colder and richer waters to the surface and nurture high plankton populations.

55

WILSON'S PHALAROPE

Steganopus tricolor

THIS largest of the phalaropes is the only species that is restricted to the New World, where it is a bird of the northern half of the great grassland region of North America, with outliers east to Indiana and west to the Klamath region of Oregon.

It is thus, by preference or the happenstances of distribution, a fresh water bird and is seldom seen at sea except during migratory passages. In keeping with its habitat, it swims less than the two more boreal species, has longer legs with narrower toe lobes, and behaves more like a typical shore bird than a phalarope much of the time.

A. C. Bent,[7] in his biography of this species, obviously enjoyed recalling the impression of gentleness these pale but attractive shore birds made in contrast with the bustling and noisy birds of several species that occupied the teeming prairie sloughs he visited in southwestern Saskatchewan fifty years ago. Female Wilson's Phalaropes are true to their sex here and several may be seen chasing a single male during the active courtship period. It is then not uncommon for a female to have two mates and two separate families which are cared for by the humble males. The nest, of course built by the male, is exceptionally well hidden, and once the birds are sitting tightly on the four typically pyriform eggs, it is possible to walk across a nesting slough without stirring up any of the several brooding males.

Insects (in the loose sense)—aquatic bugs and beetles, and flies and mosquitos, especially in the larval stage—form a large part of the diet of these grassland birds. Those which feed in the salt flats of the Great Basin region sometimes gorge on alkali flies and brine shrimp, as studies by Alexander Wetmore showed years ago.

Little is known as yet of the migration of these birds once they leave this continent. They move up the Great Plains from Texas in spring, spreading out as they go farther north, in a fairly restricted movement. In autumn, however, they not only retrace this course but overflow onto the Pacific coast and are also of casual occurrence as far east as New England. They reappear on winter quarters on the pampas of Argentina.

Steganopus tricolor (*Vieillot*). Described in 1819, from a Paraguay specimen.
LOCAL NAME: Chorlo palmado tricolor.
FIELD CHARACTERS: Largest and palest phalarope, with especially long needle-like black bill. The female's chestnut neck stripe is distinctive in spring; the males are then much paler and longer-billed than Northern Phalarope males they resemble. In fall, a very pale bird much like Stilt Sandpiper or smallish Yellowlegs (but legs dark). A nervous bird on the beach. Voice an "unmistakable" nasal grunt or honk. l. $8\frac{1}{4}$–10″, b. 1–$1\frac{1}{2}$″, female larger.
RANGE: A fresh water form (or sometimes alkaline flats) on the northern Great Plains and adjacent short-grass slough areas, from central Kansas to central Alberta, and from northern Indiana across to central Oregon, though range now much disrupted by agricultural changes. Migrates up and down the interior prairie, coastwise in California in fall, casual elsewhere. Rare at sea, so presumably overland to winter home on Argentine pampas.

Breeding plumage
(*l*) Female (*r*) Male

56

NORTHERN PHALAROPE
(*Red-necked Phalarope*)

Lobipes lobatus

SITTING on the ocean beach at Eastham, Cape Cod, one October day when the surf ran high, Henry David Thoreau and a companion enjoyed a remarkably close-up view of a phalarope. "One little bird," he writes, "not larger than a sparrow—it may have been a phalarope—would alight on the turbulent surf where the breakers were five or six feet high, and float buoyantly there like a duck, cunningly taking to its wings and lifting itself a few feet through the air over the foaming crest of each breaker, but sometimes outriding safely a considerable billow which hid it some seconds, when its instinct told it that it would not break. It was a little creature thus to sport with the ocean, but it was as perfect a success in its way as the breakers in theirs."

Except for the late date, this may have been a Northern Phalarope but Thoreau doesn't tell us, not being quite sure that the bird whose characteristic antics he describes so well was indeed a phalarope. Occupying the vast realm of the subarctic on all sides of the pole, this species is by all odds the most abundant of the phalaropes. It is also the smallest and the best known species.

The Bay of Fundy, at the northern end of the Gulf of Maine, is re-

ported to harbor upwards of a quarter million of these oceanic sprites
in early August, and great numbers also assemble in the Straits of Belle
Isle in the St. Lawrence at this time. No wonder, then, that flocks of a
thousand or so are seen at various points off the New England coast.

(H.M.H.)

The Dutch behaviorist, Niko Tinbergen,[58] who carefully studied
the breeding behavior of this Red-necked Phalarope on the southeast
coast of Greenland emphasizes the slow maturing of the full complement
of events that make up courtship and breeding. Each step is rehearsed, as
it were, in a ceremonial way; reinforced by mutual stimulation, and becomes effective only in due time. Even a bird which may be renesting,
and who has thus experienced the whole cycle but a few days before,
must repeat each step in the usual ceremonious way, as though it did not
"know" it. And it does not know—it is involved in a mutual "drawing-
out" of instinctive reactions that will insure synchrony in the mating
cycle, and success in perpetuating the species.

During the early stages of courtship the female will pause in her
foraging, jump from the water, rattle her wings and utter a harsh series
of *wit-wit-wit-wit* notes, then fly over the water slowly for 10 to 20
meters. Alighting shortly, she swims stiff-necked, her head held high,
and calls *wedu-wedu-wedu* to attract any attentive male. If another female is nearby after such a ceremonial flight, she will attack it; if a male
is nearby she will court him. Once a male responds to her court and they
mate, she goes ashore and begins mock nest-building, the "scrape ceremony," in which she lowers her breast to the ground while bending
forward steeply, scraping with her legs, and turning around to form a
depression.

The female initiates actual mating by swimming toward the male,
rising on the water before him, beating her wings excitedly, and inviting
copulation by turning away and stretching low on the water. The responsive male will then rattle his wings, rise and settle on her. Males are
at first diffident, but soon become promiscuous and attempt to mate
with any females who entice them, as they will. But they succeed only
with their own mates because both birds must be perfectly synchronized,
emotionally and biologically. The male then joins his mate in performing ceremonial scrapes, and they visit her several scrapes together, giving no indication of which is to serve as the nest later on.

Copulation may be performed four times a day for four days. Twice or perhaps three times daily during this period, they join in mutual scraping ceremonies. Before laying the first egg, the female performs the ceremonial flight she used during courtship but abandoned during the mating period, this to attract her mate's attention to the scrape finally chosen as the nest site. He joins her and performs a nest-building ceremony, picking up scraps of grass or sedge and throwing these over his shoulder. When she tires of this and leaves, he sets about nest-building in earnest. The four eggs are laid one each day, and he begins brooding regularly the second day, leaving the eggs every twenty minutes or so for a brief food foray. All this time the two birds have been very solicitous of each other's presence, calling to one another the moment a mate is lost sight of among the sedge tussocks that dot the tundra pools they feed in. But as incubation progresses, the female gradually grows less attentive; she does not return to help brood the precocial chicks when they hatch twenty days later.

Concerning the purpose of the pirouette in this species, Tinbergen, in one of those original observations it is a joy to read, wrote: ". . . in the pool, where I often observed the action, the Phalaropes could easily reach the bottom, (hence) there was no need for stirring up animals to the surface. I noticed that they only behaved in that way during the first hours in a morning after a cold night, and only when the water was quite calm. Then, seeing that in cold nights the mosquito-larvae did not move at all, but hung motionless in the water at different levels, I all at once understood the value of the Phalarope's behaviour: by the whirling movements in the water the larvae start swimming, as we could observe by imitating the Phalarope's movements, and then they became clearly visible." Motionless larvae, Tinbergen found, were almost invisible. When the water warmed a bit, or the wind rose, the phalaropes abandoned the spinning motions and swam in irregular curves, pecking at the surface here and there.

In North America the migration, north or south, is along a broader front and not so strictly maritime as it is with the Red Phalarope, and flocks may then be seen on western sloughs and lakes, mostly in May and again in August in our latitudes. The wintering grounds were a mystery until a few years ago, when Robert Cushman Murphy[33] completed his remarkable surveys of all the oceanic bounds of South America. Now we know that the vast legions of the Northern Phalarope spend the winter at sea off the Peruvian coast, and elsewhere in all the oceans of the southern hemisphere. (R.C.C.)

Lobipes lobatus (L.) Described in 1758.

LOCAL NAMES: Red-necked Phalarope. SPANISH: Chorlo palmado chico.

FIELD CHARACTERS: Spring patterns easy. In "fall" dress, much like its congeners, and Sanderling. Very fine black bill, with "phalarope-patch" through eye (a vestige of summer stripe), and generally darker coloration are all aids. l. 6½–8", b. ¾–1", female larger.

RANGE: Circumboreal in summer, breeding in arctic and subarctic bogs. Migrates along all coasts, mostly well offshore, but also through western U.S. interior. Similarly in Eurasia. Winters at sea in southern hemisphere.

CHAPTER 9

57

*TWO-STRIPED
THICK-KNEE*

Burhinus bistriatus

BECAUSE our contacts with Europe are closer than with Latin America, most of us are already somewhat familiar with the Stone Curlew, by name if nothing more, but are much less likely to know of the Thick-knee of Central and South America. Yet these birds are generically alike.

The Thick-knees or stone curlews (*Burhinidae*) are sombre-hued, 14–20 inch, curlew-like birds which occur in savannah and similarly open country almost around the world, including Australia, being, however, restricted to tropical America, but occurring in temperate regions in southern Europe.

Though mostly birds of dry, stony or sandy areas in semi-open country, a few of the world's nine recognized species have races which remain (or have become?) littoral in habit. The northern forms are migratory and abandon their summer range each winter.

Alfred Newton objected to calling them thick-knees or bustards, insisting that their voices and general appearance entitled them to being called curlews as much as any of the commoner members of that tribe. But the big golden eyes, large head, and the remarkable habit of depending upon their protective coloration even to the point of allowing a man to pick them up as they lie prostrate among the pebbles, are all distinctive traits.

Night feeders by preference, they subsist on a wide variety of small animals, including occasional predation on the nestlings of other ground nesting birds.

The two or three, long, oval and brown-speckled buffy eggs are laid right on the ground, and these birds are among the very few which are known to move their eggs when disturbed.

Though not much has been written about the American species, they are bustard-like birds of arid areas, with the large pale eyes and powerful running legs of all stone curlews. They tend to be crepuscular and retiring, more likely to trip or run out of sight when approached than to fly, though they can fly strongly, usually low to the ground, with intermittent gliding, but sometimes engaging in showy maneuvers. They are apparently strictly cursorial, never perching in trees. The standing posture is unusually heron- like for a shore bird, with the head drawn in and the back sloping steeply, but when running the body is held horizontal. A peculiar bobbing motion called "head lagging" is sometimes performed, the body being moved independently of the head. When frightened, these big birds flatten themselves out on the ground with head and neck extended.

An interesting nest exchange ceremony has been described for the European stone curlew, as follows [4]: "During the last four or five days of incubation the birds take turns of duty on the eggs. After sitting for a time the cock calls softly and his mate comes running to him over the heath. He rises slowly, and, picking up a small pebble, offers it to her with a bow; then walks off in a slow, dignified way to his observation-post some yards from the nest. After the hen has been sitting for over an hour the cock calls and she answers. When he returns the stone-presentation ceremony is re-enacted, the female picking up the pebble as the male draws near. If he does not take it in his bill she lays it down between the two eggs, rises, bows and hurries in a crouching posture from the nest." (R.C.C.)

Burhinus bistriatus.

FIELD CHARACTERS: A large (17″) plain, soft grayish-brown bird with very faint streaking, white chin, and white eye line bordered in black that joins behind the head. Strong legs, heavy plover-like bill, large pale eye, and hunched-up posture.

RANGE: Occurs from southern Mexico, the Greater Antilles, the Guianas, and northern Brazil, south on the northwest coast to Arica, Chile. On December 5, 1961 one was collected on the King Ranch, Texas.

PART 2

THE SOUTH AMERICAN SHORE BIRDS

Although some southern hemisphere shore birds engage in considerable migratory movements from summer ranges in extreme southern Patagonia and the Andean plateau to milder, northern or lowland winter quarters, none of them cross the tropics to reach Central or North America. Only a few widespread species—jacana, oystercatcher, stilt, the sand and collared plovers, and the thick-knee—can be considered pan-American. The following list includes only the American breeding shore birds not covered in the North American accounts.

PAINTED SNIPE

South American Painted Snipe (*Nycticryphes semicollaris*): A small brown snipe with decurved bill and wedge-shaped tail. Black and white crown stripes, round white spots on dark wing coverts, and black and white "collar," on sides only, are conspicuous. Snipe-like in habits, less erratic in flight, more crepuscular. Occurs from Rio Negro River, southern Argentina, north to Paraguay and central Chile.

OYSTERCATCHERS

Magellan (Fuegian) Oystercatcher (*Haematopus leucopodus*): A strikingly black-and-white bird which replaces the American Oystercatcher in extreme southern South America, from Chiloe Island, Chile, and the Chubut valley of Patagonia, south to Cape Horn, and the Falkland Islands to the east. Unlike the American Oystercatcher, but like the European bird, it is frequently found far inland.

Black Oystercatcher (*Haematopus ater*): A sooty-black species distinguished by its very thin, deep bill reminiscent of the Black Skimmer's. Occurs from the region of Buenos Aires south around Cape Horn and north along the length of the coasts of Chile and Peru.

PLOVERS

Cayenne Lapwing (*Vanellus [Hoploxypterus] cayanus*): With brown back, white margin thereto, black scapulars, and breast band. Mostly north central South America (Amazonia and Mato Grosso).

Chilean Lapwing (*Vanellus [Belonopterus] chilensis*): Much like European Lapwing, i.e., large, spurred, black-breasted, crested, and with greenish back, occurring almost throughout South America east of Andes.

Andean Lapwing (*Vanellus [Ptiloscelys] resplendens*): Much like Chilean Lapwing but without crest and breast band. A bird of mountain streams in puna and temperate zones of northwestern South America.

Patagonian Sandplover (*Charadrius falklandicus*): A small, gray-backed, white-bellied plover with two distinct black bands on the breast. Nests from Chiloe Island in Chile and the Rio Negro in Argentina, south to Tierra del Fuego and the Falkland Islands. Northward in winter to Uruguay.

Puna Plover (*Charadrius alticola*): A small gray plover with a buffy-brown breast band, black bill and legs. A consort of the flamingo and the avocet in the puna zone of southern Peru, western Bolivia, and northwestern Argentina.

Collared Plover (*Charadrius collaris*): A miniature of the Wilson's Plover, though white of throat does not form a collar. Wide-ranging, coastwise and inland, from southern Mexico, southward along west coast of South America to Peru, thence inland to Buenos Aires region.

Falkland Islands Plover (*Charadrius [Zonibyx] modestus*): A "mountain plover," Killdeer-size, with chestnut breast above a single black breast band; brown above and white-bellied. In winter it is gray-breasted. Breeds in extreme southern Patagonia, Tierra del Fuego, and the Falkland Islands. North to Uruguay in winter.

Slender-billed Dotterel (*Eudromias [Oreopholus] ruficollis*): This handsome buffy plover (much like Upland Plover) has a rufous throat, blackish patch on the belly, white axillars, black subterminal band on the tail, and yellow legs. It occupies the Andean plateau from southern Peru to the Straits of Magellan (breeding mostly in far south), and moves down to the plains (east to Buenos Aires) and the lowlands of Ecuador in winter.

Magellanic Plover (*Pluvianellus sociabilis*): An attractive, pearl-gray back and bib, with slightly darker wings, and short pink legs, mark this bird which is resident in the Tierra del Fuego region, occurring north to Chubut in eastern Patagonia in some years only.

SANDPIPERS

Short-winged (Mitchell's) Sandpiper (*Phegornis mitchellii*): Although this bird has been called a sandpiper since 1846, it has recently been listed among the plovers, though few authorities agree on its relationship. To avoid the confusion of calling a plover a sandpiper (or vice versa?) it is here listed among the latter until a critical study assigns it anew.

Its chief plover trait seems to be the conspicuously marked head, with black face and throat, brown cap, and a broad white line encircling the crown, thus forming a superciliary line. The back is dark brown. Sandpiper characters are a rufous hind neck, a banded tail (Solitary Sandpiper-like), a barred breast (somewhat like the Stilt Sandpiper), and a thin bill. Its wings are short, and it is non-migratory. If a true sandpiper, it and two relatives in Oceania are the only southern hemisphere sandpipers. It is a bird of mountain streams in the puna zone of southern Peru and western Bolivia, south to Colchaqua, Chile.

South American Snipe (*Capella paraguaiae*): Typical snipe, considered conspecific with the Common Snipe (*C. gallinago*) by some, whose four races extend across the width and length of South America, except for Ecuador.

Noble Snipe (*Capella nobilis*): Occurs in the paramo zone of the north-central Andes and the temperate zone of Ecuador.

Giant Snipe (*Capella undulata*): Northeastern South America, from Venezuela to Paraguay.

Imperial Snipe (*Chubbia imperialis*): Known only from one specimen taken near Bogota, Columbia.

Jameson's Snipe (*Chubbia jamesoni*): Larger than snipe of the genus *Capella*, the longer-billed, shorter-legged birds of the genus *Chubbia* are often called semi-woodcock. They also occupy woodcock habitat. A bird of the paramo zone of the north-central Andes.

Strickland's Snipe (*Chubbia stricklandii*): Occurs from southern Chile to Cape Horn, and the Falkland Islands.

STILTS AND AVOCETS

South American Stilt (*Himantopus himantopus*): This white-collared stilt is often considered to be conspecific with the Black-necked Stilt of the United States.

Andean Avocet (*Recurvirostra andina*): The bird of saline lagoons on the high puna zone, where it associates with the flamingo and the Puna Plover. The whole wing and tail are black, the head and neck white, the bill more strongly recurved than in the American Avocet.

THICK-KNEES

Two-striped Thick-knee (*Burhinus bistriatus*): Treated in text.
Peruvian Thick-knee (*Burhinus superciliaris*): This species has a dark ear patch and its back is barred. It occurs in the uplands of western Peru.

SEED SNIPE

Gay's Seed Snipe (*Attagis gayi*): These strange, short-legged, protectively colored, almost dove-like birds occupy the barren country of the mountains and the west of South America. The sexes are different in plumage. This species is subdivided into three races occupying (a) the paramo zone of Ecuador, (b) that of adjacent Peru and Bolivia, (c) the puna zone from northern Chile to the Straits of Magellan.
White-bellied Seed Snipe (*Attagis malouinus*): A rare species of the extreme south only, from Cape Horn north to Chubut in Patagonia.
D'Orbigny's Seed Snipe (*Thinocorus orbignyianus*): A white-throated, black-collared bird with a distinctive *Puco-puco-puco* call. Two races occupy (a) the puna zone of Peru and adjacent Bolivia, Chile and Argentina, and (b) the puna south of (a) down to Tierra del Fuego.
Lesser Seed Snipe (*Thinocorus rumicivorus*): Three subspecies occupy (a) the coast of s.w. Ecuador, Peru and n. Chile; (b) the puna of s.w. Bolivia; (c) the southern tip of South America, north to the Rio Negro, and wintering north to Uruguay.

SHEATHBILLS

Snowy Sheathbill (*Chionis alba*): A white, strong-flying, pigeon-like shore bird of the Scotia Sea region, with thick yellowish bill brown at tip, and flesh-colored caruncles at base of bill and beneath eye; legs and feet grayish. Occurs from southern Patagonia (Chubut) and Falkland Islands, South Georgia, Sandwich Islands, and the islands of Antarctica. 16".

PART 3

THE WANDERERS

European
Woodcock

White-rumped Sandpiper (Fall)

Upland Plover on nest

AMERICAN SHORE BIRDS IN EUROPE

I. C. T. Nisbet[36] has recently summarized the factors probably responsible for a higher incidence of American waders in Britain than is true of the reverse. He points out that many species which are abundant in fall on our Atlantic coast are actually very rare in Britain, but that our long-distance migrants are more likely to occur there than the less migratory types, and that species from the western arctic are more likely to cross the Atlantic than those breeding in the eastern arctic, though this may be nearer! Transatlantic crossings, then, are made most often by those American species whose breeding range includes the northwestern tundra—of Alaska and Mackenzie—and whose populations engage in an extensive west-east movement within our continent. These birds "over-shoot" the mark in a very real sense, ending up in Britain instead of the northeastern United States or the Maritime Provinces of Canada.

Semipalmated Plover: accidental in Greenland and Britain.
Killdeer: accidental in Greenland, Iceland, the Faeroes, Britain, the Azores, and Madeira.
American Golden Plover: casual in Greenland, accidental in Britain and Helgoland.

Wilson's Common Snipe: accidental in Britain.

Eskimo Curlew: was accidental in Iceland and Britain.

Hudsonian Whimbrel: accidental in Britain.

Upland Plover: accidental in Greenland, British Isles, and the continent east to Malta.

Spotted Sandpiper: accidental in Greenland, British Isles, and the continent east to Turkey. Probably often overlooked, being so much like the Common Sandpiper in fall.

Solitary Sandpiper: accidental in Greenland, Iceland, Great Britain.

Willet: accidental on the continent (France, Sweden, Yugoslavia).

Greater Yellowlegs: accidental in Greenland, British Isles.

Lesser Yellowlegs: casual in Greenland, Britain, Netherlands, Denmark, the Azores.

Pectoral Sandpiper: casual in Greenland, Iceland, Norway, Britain, France.

White-rumped Sandpiper: casual in Greenland and Britain.

Baird's Sandpiper: casual in Outer Hebrides and England; accidental in s.w. Africa.

Least Sandpiper: accidental in Britain, France, Finland.

Dowitcher: casual in Greenland, Britain, France, Sweden. Though both Short-billed and Long-billed Dowitchers have made the crossing, Nisbet feels confident that a close study of the specimens will reveal that the Long-billed Dowitcher has been the dominant vagrant.

Stilt Sandpiper: accidental in Britain (1954–1955 sight record).

Semipalmated Sandpiper: accidental in England, France.

Western Sandpiper: accidental in Britain.

Buff-breasted Sandpiper: casual in England, Ireland, France, Switzerland, Helgoland, and Egypt. Nisbet suggests that this bird is as likely to occur in Britain as in New England!

Wilson's Phalarope: accidental in England.

Lapwing—winter

EUROPEAN SHORE BIRDS IN AMERICA

European Oystercatcher (*Haematopus ostralegus*): casual in Greenland.

Lapwing (*Vanellus vanellus*): casual in Greenland; accidental in eastern Canada and U.S., south to South Carolina. In 1927 a large winter flight, in the hundreds, reached Newfoundland.

Ringed Plover (*Charadrius hiaticula*): established as a nester in Greenland and the eastern Arctic (Ellesmere and Baffin Islands).

Eurasian Golden Plover (*Pluvialis apricaria*): regular migrant in s. Greenland.

European Woodcock (*Scolopax rusticola*): accidental in eastern Canada and e. U.S. (south to Alabama, west to Ohio).

European Jacksnipe (*Lymnocryptes minimus*): accidental in Labrador (see western occurrences in Siberian visitor list).

Eurasian Curlew (*Numenius arquata*): casual in Greenland; accidental on Long Island.

Redshank (*Totanus totanus*): accidental in eastern Greenland.

* Spotted Redshank (*Totanus erythropus*): accidental on U.S. east coast?

Bar-tailed Godwit (*Limosa lapponica lapponica*): accidental in fall in Mass., Long Island, New Jersey.

Black-tailed Godwit (*Limosa limosa islandica*): accidental in w. Greenland and Newfoundland.

Ruff: (*Philomachus pugnax*): casual in Greenland and eastern U.S. and Canada.

* This species is not given even hypothetical status in the *A.O.U. Check-List*, but the following observations are worth introducing as an illustration of the problem of confirming chance sight records of rare birds.

On May 23, 1955, at Pea Island, N.C., Erard Matthiessen, then secretary of the National Audubon Society, and a well-traveled amateur birder, saw a dark sandpiper among willets, yellowlegs, dowitchers, Black-bellied Plovers, and other species. He sketched it in a notebook and made careful notes thereon. I have this sketch before me now. Mr. Matthiessen's annotations on this tall, black-bellied wader include the following comments: bill straight, reddish orange, dark-tipped (*not* plover bill); head, breast solid black (*no* white); back mottled reddish brown (grouse color); conspicuous white tail patch visible in flight; no apparent wing stripes; under parts [crissum in sketch. *R.C.C.*] lighter (gray); legs dark (possibly reddish).

Mr. Matthiessen sent this sketch to the late Ludlow Griscom, whom Roger T. Peterson had called "the court of last recourse," and early in June it was relayed by Griscom to Richard Bowen of Swansea, Mass., with the simple inscription, "Good luck!"

I was at that time working for the Audubon Society of Rhode Island, and as such, the principal ganglion in the telephone "grapevine" that communicated bird observations in that State. On the afternoon of May 31, Donald Burger of Bristol, a recent but obviously critical devotee of bird watching who had seen a bird decidedly "different" enough to send him to Peterson's newly issued *Field Guide to the Birds of Britain and Europe,* called me to suggest that he had almost surely observed a Spotted Redshank in Tiverton, R.I., the previous afternoon. I was sufficiently impressed with his descriptions to telephone Richard Bowen, a thoroughly competent field man, and suggest that this one seemed worth checking. This Mr. Bowen did in late afternoon. He found the bird almost immediately among yellowlegs and Black-bellied Plovers, and wrote me later that it agreed in every detail with Mr. Matthiessen's sketch, and that the legs were definitely reddish. He was satisfied that this was indeed a Spotted Redshank. The next morning a large group of alerted Massachusetts birders combed "every inch" of the marsh, but the bird had gone. Mr. Bowen almost immediately became a devotee of telescope photography (in color).   (*R.C.C.*)

Sharp-tailed Sandpipers

SIBERIAN SHORE BIRDS IN AMERICA

Mongolian Plover (*Charadrius mongolus*): Breeds in the boreal alpine and low arctic zones of eastern Siberia, and is a casual visitor to Alaska with one report of nesting at Goodnews Bay. Briefly treated in text.

Dotterel (*Eudromias morinellus*): Breeds mostly in alpine and low arctic zone of Eurasia, and is a casual visitor to Alaska, a breeding pair having been taken near Point Barrow. Accidental in Washington. Briefly treated in text.

Jacksnipe (*Lymnocryptes minimus*): Breeds in northern Eurasia. Accidental in Alaska, California, and Labrador.

Wood Sandpiper (*Tringa glareola*): Breeds across northern Eurasia. Accidental in Alaska.

Polynesian Tattler (*Heteroscelus brevipes*): Breeds in alpine zone and low arctic tundra of Chukchee Peninsula. Accidental on the Bering Sea islands. Much like our Wandering Tattler, but slightly smaller, shorter-legged, and almost unbarred in spring. The Russians consider it conspecific with the Wandering Tattler.

Great Knot (*Calidris tenuirostris*): Breeds in arctic-alpine zone of northeast Siberia. Accidental in Alaska. A slightly larger bird than our knot, with no red in the under plumage during breeding season, when, however, it is heavily and darkly streaked on the breast.

Sharp-tailed Sandpiper (*Erolia acuminata*): Breeds on tundra of northeast Siberia. Casual autumn migrant from Alaska to California; accidental in Hawaii. Rufous-capped in spring, but perhaps best told from very similar Pectoral Sandpiper by olive-green or gray-green, rather than yellowish, legs.

Long-toed Stint (*Erolia subminuta*): Breeds in northeast Siberia, especially along Bering Sea coast. Accidental in Alaska. Easily overlooked.

Rufous-necked Sandpiper (*Erolia ruficollis*): Breeds in subarctic and low arctic of northeast Siberia and adjacent northwest coast of Alaska. Treated in text.

Curlew Sandpiper (*Erolia ferruginea*): Breeds on Siberian tundra. Regular visitor (in small numbers) to U.S. east coast may come via Greenland (over the pole) because there is only one record from Alaska, the only undoubted western American occurrence. Treated in text.

Bar-tailed Godwit (*Limosa lapponica*): Breeds in subarctic and low arctic of Eurasia, the eastern race (*L. l. baueri*) now established as a nester in northern Alaska (from the Yukon to the Colville River). These birds apparently migrate down the Asiatic coast, however, because Bar-tailed Godwits which have occurred on the U.S. east coast (only) are of the European race (*L. l. lapponica*). Treated in text.

Ruff (*Philomachus pugnax*): Breeds in temperate, boreal, and low arctic zones of Eurasia. Casual on the Bering Sea islands. Whether these birds come from the west or the east is not known. Treated in text because of eastern America occurrences.

Spoon-billed Sandpiper (*Eurynorhynchus pygmeus*): Breeds in northeast Siberia. Accidental in Alaska.

Spoon-bill Sandpiper—fall

BIBLIOGRAPHY

1. Allen, Arthur A. 1948. "The Curlew's Secret," *Nat. Geogr. Mag.*, 94:751–770. Popular account of the discovery of the nest of the Bristle-thighed Curlew.

2. Allen, Elsa Guerdrum. 1951. The History of Amercian Ornithology before Audubon. *Trans. Am. Philos. Soc.*, New Series, 41:3:385–591.

3. American Ornithologists' Union. 1957. *Check-List of North American Birds*. 5th Edition, Baltimore, Md.

4. Armstrong, Edward A. 1947. *Bird Display and Behavior*. London.

5. Audubon, John James. 1870. *The Birds of America*. New York.

6. Bailey, Alfred M. 1943. The Birds of Cape Prince of Wales, Alaska. *Proc. Colorado Mus. Nat. Hist.*, XVIII:1:1–113.

Beebe, W. C. (see Murphy, R. C.)

7. Bent, Arthur Cleveland. 1927. Life Histories of North American Shore Birds. Order Limicolae (Part 1). *U.S. Nat. Mus. Bull. 142*. Washington.

———— 1929. Life Histories of North American Shore Birds. Order Limicolae (Part 2). *U.S. Nat. Mus. Bull. 146*. Washington.

Birula, A. B. (see Pleske, T.)

8. Brandt, H. 1951. *Alaska Bird Trails*. Cleveland.

9. Bray, Reynold. 1943. "Notes on the Birds of Southampton Island, Baffin Island and Melville Peninsula," *Auk,* 60:504–536.

10. Cook, Faxon W. 1946. "Occurrence of the Hudsonian Curlew on National Wildlife Refuges along the Atlantic Coast," *Auk,* 63:90–92.

11. Cooke, Wells W. 1911. "Our greatest travellers," *Nat. Geogr. Mag.,* vol. 22: 346–365.

12. Coues, Elliott. 1871. *Birds of the Northwest.*

13. Cruickshank, Allan D. 1942. Birds Around New York City. *Am. Mus. Nat. Hist. Hdbk. Series, No. 13.* New York.

14. Dawson, William Leon. 1903. *The Birds of Ohio.*

15. ———— 1923. *The Birds of California.*

16. Deane, C. Douglas. 1944. "The broken-wing behavior of the Killdeer," *Auk,* 61:243–247.

17. Dixon, Joseph. 1917. "The home life of the Baird Sandpiper," *Condor,* 19: 77–84.
    1927. "The Surf-bird's Secret," *Condor,* 29:3–16.
    1933. "Nesting of the Wandering Tatler," *Condor,* 35:173–179.

17a. Elliott, John J., 1956. "Sanderling feeds with Hudsonian Godwit," *Linnaean News-letter,* 10:7 (Dec.)

18. ———— 1956. "An old report of Eskimo Curlew on Long Island," *The Kingbird,* 6:86–87.

19. Forbush, Edward Howe. 1912. *A History of the Game Birds, Wild Fowl, and Shore Birds of Massachusetts and Adjacent States.* Boston.

20. ———— 1925. *Birds of Massachusetts and Other New England States.* Boston.

21. Gabrielson, Ira N., and Frederick C. Lincoln. 1959. *Birds of Alaska.* The Stackpole Co., Harrisburg, Pa.

22. Gavin, Angus. 1947. "Birds of Perry River District, Northwest Territories," *Wilson Bull.,* 59:195–203.

22a. Gilliard, E. T. 1958. *Living Birds of the World.* New York.

23. Grinnell, Joseph. 1900. Birds of the Kotzebue Sound Region. *Pac. Coast Avifauna,* No. 1.

24. Hamilton, Wm. J. III. 1959. "Aggressive behavior in migrant Pectoral Sandpipers," *Condor,* 61:161–179.

25. Hoffman, Ralph. 1927. *Birds of the Pacific States.* Houghton Mifflin Co., Boston.

26. Hope, C. E., and T. M. Shortt. 1944. "Southward migration of adult shorebirds on the west coast of James Bay, Ontario," *Auk,* 61:572–576.

27. Hudson, William Henry. 1920. Birds of La Plata.

28. ———— 1922. A Hind in Richmond Park.

29. Hubbs, Carl L. 1960. "The Rock Sandpiper, another northern bird recorded from the cool coast of northwestern Baja California," *Condor,* 62:68–69.

30. Mackay, George Henry. 1891. "The habits of the Golden Plover (*Charadrius dominicus*) in Massachusetts," *Auk,* 8:17–24.

31. McCabe, T. T. 1942. "Types of shorebird flight," *Auk,* 59:110–111.

32. Murie, Olaus Johan. 1924. "Nesting records of the Wandering Tatler and Surf-bird in Alaska," *Auk,* 41:231–237.

33. Murphy, Robert Cushman. 1936. *Oceanic Birds of South America.* Am. Mus. Nat. Hist., New York.

34. Nelson, E. W. 1884. "The breeding habits of the Pectoral Sandpiper (*Actodromas maculata*)," *Auk,* 1:218–221.

35. ——— 1887. Report upon Natural History collections made in Alaska, 1877–81. Washington.

36. Nisbet, I. C. T. 1949. "Wader migration in North America and its relation to transatlantic crossings," *British Birds,* 52:205–215.

37. Peterson, Roger Tory. 1947. *A Field Guide to the Birds.* Houghton Mifflin Co., Boston.

37a. ———, Guy Mountfort, and P. A. D. Hollom. 1954. *A Field Guide to the Birds of Britain and Europe.* Houghton Mifflin.
Guide to the Birds of Britain and Europe. Houghton Mifflin.

38. Pitelka, Frank A. 1950. "Geographic variation and the species problem in the shore-bird genus *Limnodromus,*" *Univ. Calif. Publ. Zool.,* 50:1:1–108.

39. ——— 1959. "Number, breeding schedule and territoriality in Pectoral Sandpipers of northern Alaska," *Condor,* 61:233–264.

40. Pleske, Theodore. 1928. "Birds of the Eurasian Tundra," *Mem. Boston Soc. Nat. Hist.,* 6:3:111–485.

41. Pough, Richard H. 1951. *Audubon Water Bird Guide.* Doubleday & Co., Inc., Garden City, N.Y.

42. Preston, F. W. 1949. "The Pacific flyway of the golden plover," *Auk,* 66:87–88.

43. Roberts, Thomas S. 1932. *The Birds of Minnesota.* Vol. I. Univ. Minn. Press, Minneapolis.

44. Rowan, William. 1926–27. "Notes on Alberta waders included in the British List," *British Birds,* 20:2–10, 34–42, 82–90, 138–145, 186–192.

45. Simmons, K. E. L. 1955. "The nature of the predator-reactions of waders toward humans; with special reference to the role of the aggressive-, escape- and brooding-drives," *Behaviour,* 8:130–173.

46. Smith, S. Bayliss. 1950. *British Waders in Their Haunts.* London.

47. Snyder, L. L. *Arctic Birds of Canada.* Univ. Toronto Press.

48. Soper, J. Dewey. 1940. "Local distribution of eastern Canadian arctic birds," *Auk,* 57:13–21.

49. ——— 1946. "Ornithological results of the Baffin Island expeditions of 1928–1929 and 1930–1931, together with more recent records," *Auk,* 63:223–239.

50. Stone, Witmer. *Bird Studies at Old Cape May.* Vol. I. Delaware Valley Ornith. Club, Philadelphia.

51. Storer, Robert W. 1951. "The seasonal occurrence of shorebirds on Bay Farm Island, Alameda County, California," *Condor,* 53:186–193.

52. Sutton, George Miksch. 1925. "Swimming and diving activities of the Spotted Sandpiper (*Actitis macularia*)," *Auk,* 42:580–581.

53. —— 1932. The Birds of Southampton Island. *Mem. Carnegie Mus.,* vol. XII, Pt. 2, Sec. 2.

54. Sutton, George M., and David F. Parmelee. 1956. "On certain Charadriiform birds of Baffin Island," *Wilson Bull.,* 68:210–223.

55. Taverner, P. A. 1942. "The distribution and migration of the Hudsonian Curlew," *Wilson Bull.,* 54:3–11.

56. Taverner, P. A., and G. M. Sutton. 1934. "The Birds of Churchill, Manitoba," *Ann. Carnegie Mus.,* 23:49–50.

57. Thayer, Gerald H. 1909. *Concealing Coloration in the Animal Kingdom.* McMillan Co., New York.

58. Tinbergen, Dr. N. 1935. "Field observations of east Greenland birds/1. The behaviour of the Red-necked Phalarope (*Phalaropus lobatus* L.) in spring," *Ardea,* 24:1–42.

59. Tomkins, Ivan R. 1944. "Wilson's Plover in its summer home," *Auk,* 61:259–269.

60. —— 1947. "The oyster-catcher of the Atlantic coast of North America and its relation to oysters," *Wilson Bull.,* 59:204–208.

61. Tuck, Leslie M., and Louis Lemieux. 1959. "The avifauna of Bylot Island," *Dansk Ornith. Forenings Tidsskrift,* 53:137–154.

62. Urner, Charles A. 1935. "Shore-birds and closed seasons," *Bird-Lore,* 37:265–267.

63. Urner, C. A., and R. W. Storer. 1949. "The distribution and abundance of shorebirds on the north and central New Jersey coast, 1928–1938," *Auk,* 66:177–194.

64. Van Tyne, Josselyn, and Andrew J. Berger. 1959. *Fundamentals of Ornithology.* John Wiley & Sons, Inc., New York.

65. Van Tyne, Josselyn, and William H. Drury, Jr. 1959. "Birds of southern Bylot Island, 1954," *Occ. Papers Mus. Zool.,* Univ. Michigan, No. 615, 1–37.

66. Vogt, William. 1938. "Will and Kate," *The Yale Review,* 27:733–743.

67. Webster, J. Dan. 1941. "The breeding of the Black Oystercatcher," *Wilson Bull.,* 53:141–156.

68. Wetmore, Alexander. 1926. Observations on the Birds of Argentina, Paraguay, Uruguay, and Chile. *U.S. Nat. Mus. Bull. 133.*

69. Williamson, Kenneth. 1950. "Interpretation of 'Rodent-run' Display," *Ibis,* 92:28–33.

70. Witherby, H. F., F. C. R. Jourdain, Norman F. Ticehurst, and Bernard W. Tucker. 1940. *The Handbook of British Birds,* vol. IV. London.

71. Wynne-Edwards, V. C. 1952. "Zoology of the Baird expedition (1950). I. The birds observed in central and south-east Baffin Island," *Auk,* 69: 353–391.

INDEX

Actitis, macularia, 112
Aphriza, virgata, 74
Arenaria, interpres, 75
    "   *melanocephala,* 79
Attagis, gayi, 226
    "   *malouinus,* 226
Avocets, The, 201
Avocet, (American), 202, 230
    "   Andean, 225

Bartramia, longicauda, 108
Belonopterus (see *Vanellus*)
Burhinidae, 20
Burhinus, bistriatus, 221
    "   *superciliaris,* 226

Calidris, canutus, 133
    "   *tenuirostris,* 233

Capella, gallinago, 87
    "   *nobilis,* 225
    "   *paraguaiae,* 225
    "   *undulata,* 225
Catoptrophorus, semipalmatus, 121
Charadriidae, 20
Charadrius, alexandrinus, 46
    "   *alticola,* 224
    "   *collaris,* 224
    "   *falklandicus,* 224
    "   *hiaticula,* 38, 231
    "   *melodus,* 42
    "   *modestus,* 224
    "   *mongolus,* 49, 233
    "   *montana* (see *Eupoda*)
    "   *semipalmatus,* 39
    "   *vociferus,* 52

"　　　*wilsonia,* 50
Chionididae, 20
Chionis, alba, 226
Chubbia, imperialis, 225
　　"　　*jamesoni,* 225
　　"　　*stricklandii,* 225
Crabplover, 19
Crocethia, alba, 198
Curlew, Bristle-thighed, 100
　　"　　Eskimo, 103, 230
　　"　　Eurasian, 231
　　"　　Hudsonian, 96
　　"　　Least, 107
　　"　　Long-billed, 92
　　"　　Stone, 221, 226

Dotterel,
　　"　　Eurasian, 59, 233
　　"　　Falkland Island (see under
　　"　　Plover)
　　"　　Slender-billed, 224
Dowitcher, Long-billed, 170, 230
　　"　　Short-billed, 166
Dromadidae, 20
Dunlin, 162

Ereunetes, mauri, 179
　　"　　*pusillus,* 176
Erolia, acuminata, 233
　　"　　*alpina,* 162
　　"　　*bairdii,* 150
　　"　　*ferruginea,* 159, 234
　　"　　*fuscicollis,* 147
　　"　　*maritima,* 136
　　"　　*melanotos,* 143
　　"　　*minutilla,* 154
　　"　　*ptilocnemis,* 140
　　"　　*ruficollis,* 157, 234
　　"　　*subminuta,* 234
Eudromias, morinellus, 59, 233
　　"　　*ruficollis,* 224
Eurynorhynchus, pygmeus, 234
Eupoda, montana, 56

Glareolidae, 20
Godwit, Black-tailed, 231
　　"　　Bar-tailed, 189, 231, 234
　　"　　Hudsonian, 191
　　"　　Marbled, 187

Haematopodidae, 20
Haematopus, ater, 224
　　"　　*bachmani,* 32
　　"　　*leucopodis,* 223
　　"　　*ostralegus,* 231
　　"　　*palliatus,* 28
Heteroscelus, brevipes, 233
　　"　　*incanus,* 117
Himantopus, himantopus, 225
　　"　　*mexicanus,* 205
Hoploxypterus, (see *Vanellus*)

Jacanas, The, 20, 23
Jacana, spinosa, 24

Killdeer, 52, 229
Knot, Red, 133
　　"　　Great, 233

Lapwing, Andean, 224
　　"　　Cayenne, 224
　　"　　Chilean, 224
　　"　　European, 231
Limnodromus, griseus, 166
　　"　　*scolopaceus,* 170
Limosa, fedoa, 187
　　"　　*haemastica,* 191
　　"　　*limosa islandica,* 231
　　"　　*lapponica,* 189, 231, 234
Lobipes, lobatus, 217
Lymnocryptes, minimus, 231, 233

Micropalama, himantopus, 174

Numenius, americana, 92
　　"　　*arquata,* 231
　　"　　*borealis,* 103
　　"　　*minuta,* 107

"   *phaeopus*, 96
"   *tahitiensis*, 101
Nycticryphes, semicollaris, 223

Oreopholus (see *Eudromias*)
Oystercatchers, The, 27
Oystercatcher, American, 28
"   Black, 32, 224
"   European, 231
"   Magellan, 223

Painted Snipe, 18
Phalaropes, The, 209
Phalarope, Grey, 211
"   Northern, 217
"   Red, 211
"   Red-necked, 216
"   Wilson's, 215, 230
Phalaropodidae, 20
Phalaropus, fulicarius, 211
Phegornis, mitchellii, 224
Philohela, minor, 83
Philomachus, pugnax, 195, 231
Plovers, The, 36
Plover, American Golden, 60, 229
"   Black-bellied, 66
"   Collared, 224
"   Falkland Islands, 224
"   Eurasian Golden, 231
"   Kentish, 46
"   Magellanic, 224
"   Mongolian, 49, 233
"   Mountain, 56
"   Patagonian Sand, 224
"   Piping, 42
"   Puna, 224
"   Ringed, 38, 230
"   Semipalmated, 39, 229
"   Snowy, 46
"   Thick-billed, 50
"   Upland, 108, 229
"   Wilson's, 50
Pluvialis, apricaria, 231
"   *dominica*, 60

Pluvianellus, sociabilis, 224
Pratincole, 19
Ptiloscelys, (see *Vanellus*)

Recurvirostridae, 20
Recurvirostra, americana, 202
"   *andina*, 225
Redshank, 231
"   Spotted, 231, 232
Reeve, 195
Rostratulidae, 20
Ruff, 195, 231, 234

Sanderling, 198
Sandpipers, The, 81
Sandpiper, Bairds, 150, 230
"   Bartramian, 108
"   Buff-breasted, 182, 230
"   Curlew, 159
"   Least, 154, 230
"   Mitchell's, 224
"   Pectoral, 143, 230
"   Purple, 136
"   Red-backed, 162
"   Red-necked, 157, 234
"   Rock, 140
"   Rufous-necked, 157, 234
"   Semipalmated, 176, 230
"   Sharp-tailed, 233
"   Short-winged, 225
"   Solitary, 116, 230
"   Spoon-billed, 234
"   Spotted, 112, 230
"   Stilt, 174, 230
"   Upland, 108
"   Western, 179, 230
"   White-rumped, 147, 230
"   Wood, 233
Sandplover, (see Plovers)
Scolopacidae, 20
Scolopax, rusticola, 231
Seed Snipe, D'Orbigny's, 226
"   Gay's, 226
"   Lesser, 226
"   White-bellied, 226

Sheathbill, Snowy, 226
Snipe, Common, 87
"   Giant, 225
"   Imperial, 225
"   Jack, 233, 231
"   Jameson's, 225
"   Noble, 225
"   Painted, 223
"   Paraguian, 225
"   Seed, 226
"   South American, 225
"   Strickland's, 225
"   Wilson's, 12, 87, 230
Squatarola, squatarola, 66
Steganopus, tricolor, 215
Stilt, Black-necked, 205
"   South American, 225
Stint, Long-toed, 234
Surfbird, 72

Tattler, Polynesian, 233
"   Wandering, 119
Thinocoridae, 20
Thinocorus, orbignyanus, 226
"   *rumicivorus*, 226
Thick-knee, Peruvian, 226
"   Two-striped, 221

Totanus, erythnopus, 231
"   *flavipes*, 130
"   *melanoleuca*, 126
"   *totanus*, 231
Tringa, glareola, 233
"   *solitaria*, 116
"   *totanus*, 231
Tryngites, subruficollis, 182
Turnstone, Black, 79
"   Ruddy, 75

Vanellus, cayanus, 224
"   *chilensis*, 224
"   *resplendens*, 224
"   *vanellus*, 231
Whimbrel, Eurasian, 99, 231
"   Hudsonian, 96, 230
Willet, Eastern, 121, 230
"   Western, 125
Woodcock, American, 83
"   European, 231

Yellowlegs, Greater, 126, 230
"   Lesser, 130, 230

Zonibyx, modestus (see *Charadrius*)

Ringed Plover Chick

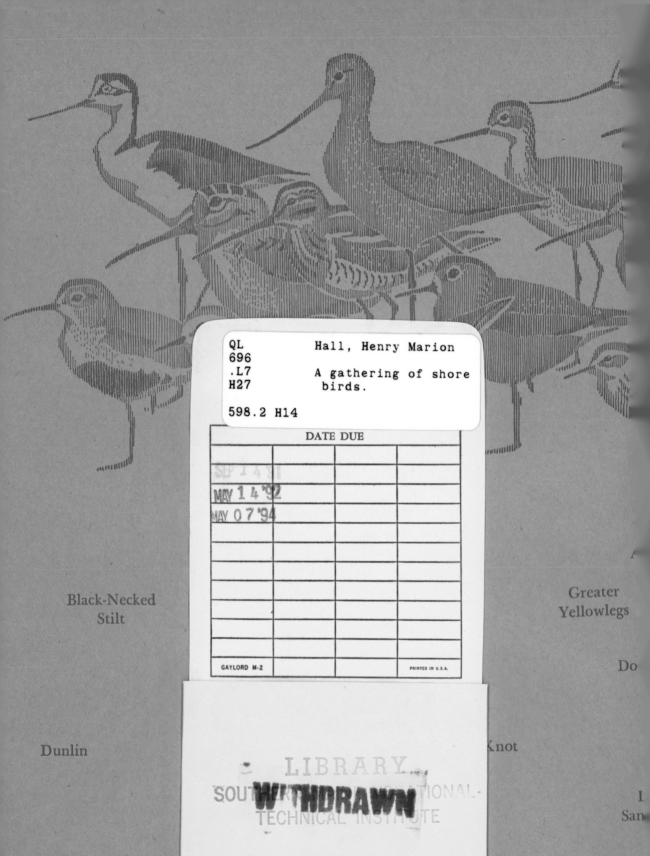

Black-Necked
Stilt

Greater
Yellowlegs

Do

Dunlin

Knot

I
San

E SIZES O